THE MEANING OF IS

This book is dedicated

to my wife Jeri

and sons Adrian and Derek,

whose strength, love and insights sustained me

during the turbulent times covered in the book,

and whose sacrifices were

much greater than mine.

The Meaning of IS

The Squandered Impeachment

and Wasted Legacy of

William Jefferson Clinton

BOB BARR

STROUD & HALL PUBLISHERS

STROUD&HALL
PUBLISHERS

Stroud & Hall Publishers
225 Central Avenue
Suite 1608
Atlanta, Ga 30303
www.stroudhall.com

The paper used in this publication meets the minimum requirements
of American National Standard for Information Sciences—
Permanence of Paper for Printed Library Materials.
ANSI Z39.48–1984. (alk. paper)

Library of Congress Cataloging-in-Publication Data

Barr, Bob, 1948-

The meaning of Is:
the squandered impeachment and wasted legacy of William Jefferson Clinton
by Bob Barr.

p. cm.

ISBN 0-9745376-2-4
(case bound : alk. paper)
1. Clinton, Bill, 1946—Political and social views.
2. Clinton, Bill, 1946—Impeachment.
3. Clinton, Bill, 1946—Influence.
4. United States–Politics and government–1993-2001.
I. Title.

E886.2B38 2004   973.929'092–dc22

2004013118

Photo credits: **Bob Barr**; **Win McNamee** © Reuters/Corbis; **Patrick Durand** © Corbis Sygma; **San Gabriel Valley Tribune** © San Gabriel Valley Tribune/Corbis Sygma; **Alan Diaz** © Reuters/Corbis; **Richard Ellis** © Corbis Sygma; **Wally McNamee** © Wally McNamee/Corbis; **Mike Stewart** © Arkansas Democrat/Mike Stwart/Corbis Sygma

Contents

| 106TH CONGRESS 1st Session | SENATE | DOCUMENT 106–2 |

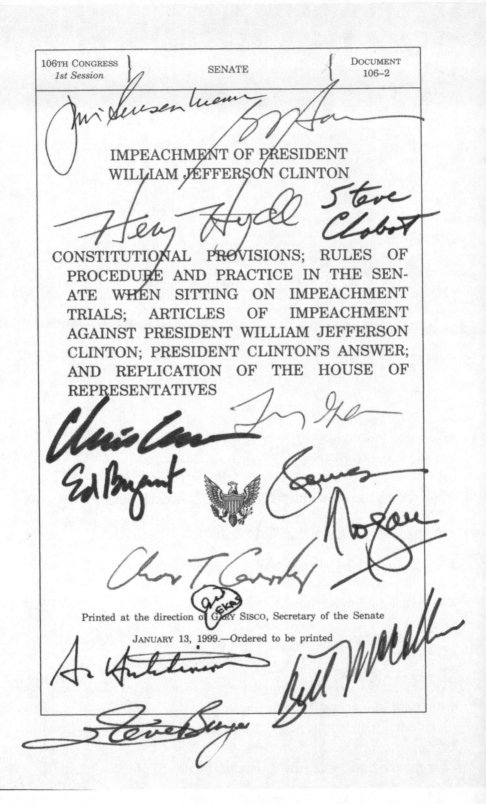

IMPEACHMENT OF PRESIDENT WILLIAM JEFFERSON CLINTON

CONSTITUTIONAL PROVISIONS; RULES OF PROCEDURE AND PRACTICE IN THE SENATE WHEN SITTING ON IMPEACHMENT TRIALS; ARTICLES OF IMPEACHMENT AGAINST PRESIDENT WILLIAM JEFFERSON CLINTON; PRESIDENT CLINTON'S ANSWER; AND REPLICATION OF THE HOUSE OF REPRESENTATIVES

Printed at the direction of GARY SISCO, Secretary of the Senate

JANUARY 13, 1999.—Ordered to be printed

Foreword

One day in the mid-1990s, I interviewed a man who had witnessed puzzling events that he claimed took place at Fort Marcy Park on July 20, 1993. His name was Patrick Knowlton, and he thought he had seen evidence near the parking lot where Vince Foster's body was found. Even after interviewing him, the government did not report his evidence. Ambrose Evans-Pritchard, the indefatigable British reporter from London's *Sunday Telegraph*, came across Knowlton's name in an FBI 302 report while covering the Foster case. He discovered that thugs had threatened Knowlton. He also learned that Knowlton's testimony to the police about what he saw in Fort Marcy Park on July 20 while stopping to urinate by a tree had been badly misreported. Ambrose started spending time with Knowlton, and eventually both were harassed by thugs who looked "Mexican or Cuban."

That day in the mid-1990s, Ambrose had introduced Knowlton to me over lunch. Knowlton's experiences, after his testimony to the FBI, were not what I would expect in the Land of the Free. After the interview as we walked down the steps from Washington's Occidental restaurant, my British friend lamented, "If the greatest democracy on earth abandons the rule of law and becomes as corrupt as a banana republic, what is the future of democracy?"

Ambrose's lament could have come from Bob Barr. Former Congressman Barr's first commitment is to the rule of law and to democratic practice. A former federal prosecutor, he takes the law seriously, not as a law-and-order zealot but as a public official who treasures personal liberty. He believes that in the United States of America the rule of law exists to protect our freedoms. Had he lunched with Ambrose, Knowlton, and I that afternoon, I think he would have shared my suspicion that lawlessness may have threatened those men's well-being and might have attended the investigation of Foster's death. Knowlton seemed to me a perfectly normal American. He was a Democrat, a working-class guy. He had stopped by the park to relieve himself on his way out to the country, and suddenly he was threatened by a couple of tough guys who were not there to protect the environment or public decency.

Only after Ambrose showed him the irregularities in his testimony regarding Fort Marcy Park did Knowlton become part of the Clinton saga, possibly even a "Clinton-hater" or a member of the vast right-wing conspiracy. He is not the first ordinary American to have an accidental brush with the Clintons—in this case with a deceased associate of the Clintons—and see his life go haywire. I have no idea where Knowlton is today, but I can tell you that when I first met him, he seemed perfectly normal and without animus against anyone in government. I can also tell you that I think Foster's death was pretty much what the Starr report finally concluded, a suicide. Yet the death, the filching of Foster's papers in the White House, the Clintons' obstruction of a pro-forma suicide investigation, and the irregularities in the government reports on his death all reeked of scandal. One wonders why. When Secretary of Defense James V. Forrestal committed suicide, there was no such scandal, and kooks back in the Truman Administration insisted he was the victim of Communists or worse.

The Clinton gang has had a way of turning normal life into a carnival of lurid claims and apparently irresolvable scandal. In *The Meaning of Is: The Squandered Impeachment and Wasted Legacy of William Jefferson Clinton*, Barr lucidly catalogues the Clintons' misbehavior. He is particularly enlightening on the Clinton scandals that we now know imperiled national security. He has fresh things to say about the diminished presidency Clinton left after battling so mightily to avoid admitting that, yes, he had fallen for a fat little intern while Osama bin Laden was brewing terror in the Middle East. One of the things I admire most in this book is its cool application of reason to stories that got unreasonably heated during the Clinton years of journalistic investigation, prosecution, and all-out defense by the Clintons. In presiding over my investigative team at *The American Spectator*, where we broke so many stories with so few resources, I learned a lot about the press. I learned how herd-oriented it is. I also learned about the susceptibility of many of its members to unreason and to misuse of the rules of evidence. From claims of dark plots surrounding Fort Marcy Park to Hillary Clinton's excogitation of a vast right-wing conspiracy, there were always journalists who, at the first hint of conspiracy or subterfuge, tingled with delight and swallowed the delusion hook, line, and sinker. The excitement of being made privy to something few others know or believe anesthetizes their powers of discernment, assuming they ever had such powers. Soon they swell with the conceit that they have a special arcane knowledge of events unknown to normal minds.

That is what happened during the Clinton Saga. Journalists with certain intellectual weaknesses for excitement and politicians with an ax to grind all came to the conclusion that something darker was going on than plain facts adumbrated. Clinton was being martyred by Richard Mellon Scaife! Clinton was covering up a murder or secretly dealing drugs from the White House. The martyrdom was the belief of the consensus journalists. Those on the fringes believed the murder and drug charges. All were absurd and unsupported by fact.

Through it all Barr stuck with the facts, as this book makes clear. He proceeded in the best tradition of the incorruptible congressman with his constituents' rights foremost in mind. He was the first responsible public figure to call for Clinton's impeachment.

He nary made a misstep. He challenged his party when it failed to do its duty and convict a perjurer and obstructer of justice, and he challenged the country to understand that when great corruption festers in government, it is a sickness that threatens the Constitution.

The Clintons have been an especial threat to the First Amendment. It astounds me that even this far into the Clinton Saga no awareness of the threat has surfaced in the media. In his embarrassing memoir of service to the Clintons, *All Too Human*, George Stephanopoulos admits how he harassed the press and deceived it from his White House office. That ABC raised him to an exalted seat in its news department shows the low opinion even elite news organizations have for the First Amendment. Such journalists as the *Washington Post*'s Sue Schmidt, *Vanity Fair*'s Christopher Hitchens, and *Newsweek*'s Michael Isikoff were all subject to the Clintons' authoritarian ministrations. Doubtless there were more. *The American Spectator* saw employees dragged before a grand jury. And surely you remember the Clintons' chart, the "media food chain." Supposedly it demonstrated how much of the American press was a willing "food chain" supplying unkind stories against the Clintons. No such chart had ever been taken seriously in American politics outside of the purlieus of the John Birch Society.

Bob Bartley, editor of the *Wall Street Journal*, was dismayed when no journalists rose to the defense of writers the Clintons harassed. I too was somewhat surprised. So was Bob Barr. It is because of the threat to freedom and to American security that Bob has written this book. He has done it with his characteristic high intelligence and grit. It is not good news for the Clintons that they will have Barr around looking over their shoulders for years to come.

R. Emmett Tyrrell, Jr.
Editor in Chief
The American Spectator
Arlington, Virginia
June 14, 2004

Introduction

The day of my first conversation with Bill Clinton is etched in my memory. I was invited to the White House for a special ceremony in the famed Rose Garden, a beautiful patch of horticultural artistry that traces its ancestry back over a century. It was a beautiful day in April 1996, and Clinton made a point of coming over to me after he signed a bill on a portable raised platform perched on the First Lawn.

"Bob," he said, "I know you had some concerns about this bill. I want you to know I understand them and want to work with you to address your concerns." Then he shook my hand and gave me his look that meant "you're the most important person in the world to me for this moment in time"—a look we would all come either to loathe or love in the years ahead.

Many observers have noted a magnetic, hypnotizing quality in Clinton's personality. It was certainly present that spring day, and it was present on every other occasion I met him. If he had decided to lead a religious cult instead of a political campaign, I am sure he would have been one of the most successful cult leaders in history.

He never did address my concerns about the terrorism bill, of course, but I was impressed, as a freshman congressman, that the president knew my name. I was even more impressed that he knew I had led the opposition to many provisions in the anti-terrorism bill, a major piece of federal legislation drafted in the wake of the 1995 Oklahoma City bombing. (We were successful in rebuffing several of the more expansive provisions, and our success lasted until the "USA PATRIOT Act" five years later.) I did not care if the reason for Clinton's interest was genuine concern or simply that he had outstanding staff that whispered the appropriate background remarks in his ear before he spoke to me. Either way, he was an impressive president who possessed a great memory for faces and fine detail, or else he was one who recognized that the key to success in Washington was a good staff. Only later did I realize he was both.

As you begin this book, it is important that you know I am not a Clinton hater. To say I do not like this former president would be a gross understatement, but I do not hate him. In fact, if he lived on my street, I have no doubt he would be the kind of guy who would be a real hoot at neighborhood parties. My problem with Bill Clinton is that he chose to seek an office that every facet of his

Bob Barr, his wife Jeri, and the Clintons at a White House Christmas party.

personality enabled him to win, yet one that those same facets rendered him incapable of filling competently. I deeply and utterly despise—down to the very core of my being—what Bill Clinton did to the office of the presidency, to our national security, and to the social fabric of this great country.

I have never thought of the presidency as being defined by the person who occupies the office. The president is more than a person. The president is an institution. He is the custodian of a unique national treasure that countless men and women have given their blood, sweat, and lives to protect. In his eloquent 1998 essay, "Statesmanship and Its Betrayal," which appeared in the Hillsdale College publication *Imprimis*, Mark Helprin notes that throughout our nation's history, statesmanship is "the courage to tell the truth and thus discern what is ahead." In this most fundamental of roles, that of a statesman, Bill Clinton failed as miserably as any president in our nation's history has failed to meet the challenges posed them.

Bill Clinton is, at heart, a flatterer. He has an unfailing instinct, a sixth sense, for discerning exactly what his audience—whether it is one person or an entire nation—wants to hear. Many successful political figures over the course of our nation's history have enjoyed such a gift. What set Clinton apart was the fact that his sixth sense was coupled with a spectacular ability to tell us precisely what we most want to hear—coupled with a phenomenal gift for convincing us that whatever that may be is a good idea—even when we sense it is not or even if we *know* it may not be in our long term interests.

This is exactly how a sleazy but successful used car salesman might function. Say you're driving by a car lot, and you see a nice-looking late-model sedan sitting on the lot corner, advertised at an impossibly low price. You realize no one in his right mind would sell a car that nice for a price that low, but you figure you'll at least stop in and take a look. As you're standing by the car for sale, a salesman walks up to you with a concocted story. It does not matter what the story is, but let's say the conversation goes something like this:

"A beauty, isn't she?" says the salesman. "Yep," you say, "but how can this car possibly be on sale for the price you have posted? There must be something wrong with it." Now the salesman knows you're not stupid. But he also realizes you would be mighty pleased with yourself if you believed you were the one person driving by that day who realized what a great deal this was and took advantage of it. He says, "I know this price looks low, and it is. You see, this car is owned by a friend of the dealer who needs to liquidate it right away for tax purposes. The only way this guy will avoid bankruptcy is if this car sells today at any price. It's a real gem, though . . . had the oil changed every five hundred miles, kept it in a garage, and only drove it every other Sunday."

About this time, a voice in your head reminds you that when something sounds too good to be true, it probably is. Still, you like the car and the salesman has a certain something—call it personality, cachet, gravitas, the vision thing, or whatever—that makes you *want* to believe him. He seems like a nice, trustworthy, competent person; surely there's no way he could lead you astray. That rational voice in the corner of your brain starts to fade into the distance, along with other painful truisms like "there's a sucker born every minute" and "neither a borrower nor a lender be." As you listen to the salesman talk, the image of yourself perched behind the wheel of this late-model beauty on a sunny coastal road zipping around curves looms larger and larger. You banish your voice of reason to one of the many prison cells in your mind, buy the car, and drive it home, where you discover that the engine is completely destroyed and the car will only run for a couple hundred more miles. By that time, though, it's too late, and embarrassment at being conned has bought your silence.

If need arises for a patron saint of sleazy car salesmen, Bill Clinton will be a shoe-in for the job. The great evil of Bill Clinton's presidency is that he always told us what he knew—or sometimes only *thought* he knew—we wanted to hear. Thus, he always found himself appealing to the base, cowardly, weak elements of the American people and almost never brought out the higher, nobler traits that have made us great over the course of our history. Our greater presidents have always succeeded because they were able to bring to life our best qualities, rather than stir our less noble instincts.

There is a reason I use the word *evil* to describe the way Clinton conducted himself in the presidency. The president—including every one of the forty-three men who have occupied that vital post—has an important job that may often conflict with his political instincts and his short-term popularity. That job (the job of *being* the president) requires telling us what we *should* do, regardless of whether it is what 50.1 percent of us want to do at a given moment.

Is the best president merely one who gets elected twice by solid margins and maintains high approval ratings during his term, or do we expect something more when we define presidential greatness? The answer is simple. A great president is not one who always gives us what we want right when we want it, regardless of the consequences—like a parent yearning for a child's approval. This is true for a parent who chooses not to give a child a second dessert, and it is no less true for the president of the United States of America. The United States president has at his disposal more information than any other person on earth, fueled by a vast fact-gathering apparatus unequaled anywhere in the world. He is capable of predicting the probability of certain occurrences several moves ahead on the national or global chessboard. Somewhere between 50.1 percent and 99.9 percent of public opinion respondents often (a) do not have the same level of information, (b) are too busy with their daily lives to analyze it, or (c) simply don't give a damn. Therefore, using public opinion as one's only guide for leading is nothing more than intentional pandering that will not benefit the country or its people over the long term.

It is the president's job to lead us in the right direction by helping us determine our long-term interests. Whether we are talking about Moses leading the Israelites through the desert, Winston Churchill leading Britain during World War II, or Ronald

Reagan orchestrating the demise of the Soviet Empire, a defining element of leadership is being able or willing to see several moves ahead of the average Joe. Great presidents are the ones who understand this fact and *lead* accordingly. Weak presidents are the ones who do not grasp this fact, fail to use the information they have, run from hard choices, or let themselves be manipulated by their advisors. Evil presidents are the ones who understand what they are supposed to do but choose instead to do what is in their personal short-term interests.

Bill Clinton was neither great nor weak. He fully possessed the capacity to lead, and he certainly had the resources to do so, yet he did not. Not only did he fail to lead in the right direction, he failed to lead at all. In so doing, he repeatedly and knowingly damaged the long-term prospects of our nation. He sacrificed our future national security and depleted our reservoir of past greatness for his immediate political success. He politicized the presidency in a way that ensured its future occupants would hold diminished influence. He permanently took personal freedoms away from American citizens whenever he thought it would generate positive headlines. In this sense, then, Bill Clinton was an evil president.

Not surprisingly, this is not the story Clinton and his supporters want America to believe. Their story is different. Their history books begin with a man who held a governor's seat in a small southern state, who had big ideas that he developed as a young man while hiding from the draft and philosophizing over coffee and uninhaled marijuana in various academic ivory towers in the United States and Great Britain. Our young friend Bill had a sweet wife named Hillary who fed and cared for these ideas, nurturing her young Adonis. Soon, these ideas began swelling and growing inside young Bill until he thought his heart would burst with desire to bring hope to all Americans. Sitting on all this promise, Bill knew deep inside that the only way he could help all Americans was if he ran for president. So he did, and much of America sensed his virility, heard his siren song, and saw his alluring vision. The "just do it" generation, bored with the old-fashioned "vision thing" of

George H. W. Bush, wanted young Bill Clinton's self-proclaimed dream as its own. That is, all except the Clinton haters, who wanted only to destroy Bill and take over the presidency for themselves.

In this Clintonian version of history, the Clinton haters joined into a vast right-wing conspiracy, took over several parts of the United States government, and used them in an attempt to destroy Bill and take hope away from America. These people did not care what happened to America. They only wanted to take back the good parking spaces in front of the White House and the Old Executive Office Building. They could not offer the people more hope than Bill. No one could, of course. He was limited only by his chutzpah—and his chutzpah, like his libido, was boundless. For a time, he enjoyed a near monopoly on this most precious commodity—*hope*. So the Clinton-hating, vast right-wing conspiracy told a bunch of lies about Bill and got him impeached. Despite this, Bill made huge successes for all of us—"growing" our economy, keeping us "safe," and giving us all a better quality of life. It was—or at least appeared to be—a wonderful life. But he and his many shills lament that he could have done so much more to help us, if only the vast right-wing conspiracy had seen the value of hope and wanted to share in it instead of trying to destroy Bill.

While the above description is more sarcastic than serious, it is a valid representation of the challenge we face. Bill and Hillary Clinton and their coterie of defenders have told this story so many times in so many different venues to so many receptive audiences that in much of America—and indeed the world—it is still accepted as gospel. Like the ex-con who harbors illusions of innocence to his deathbed, Bill and his defenders will continue to tell this story as long as they are able to breathe.

This book, then, is an attempt to set the record straight. At heart, it is the story of one man who finally decided enough was enough and resolved to take on the White House. At least from that perspective, it is a positive story. Bill Clinton had to be held accountable, a core group of constitutionalists decided to do it, and they succeeded, but only partially. Clinton was impeached by the House but not removed by the Senate, which is like taking a biopsy of a sore but failing to remove the underlying cancer that caused it. He should have been removed, and for that matter, he should have been impeached earlier. Every day he spent in office caused further damage to our nation, and there is no getting around the reality that the continuation of his presidency for a full eight years was a national disaster of enormous proportions, the extent of which remains unknown to this day.

This is also the story of a Republican Party that, I believe, wanted to keep Bill Clinton in office. There were numerous reasons many Republicans wanted Clinton to stay where he was, and I have no doubt that this party's leaders conspired to get Clinton off the hook before, during, and after the impeachment trial. This is a difficult story to tell, but it is one that also needs to be told.

Some would argue this is all about history and that only academics care about Bill Clinton at this point in time. Those who make this argument are wrong. Make no mistake about it; people *are* paying attention. The vast majority of the American public may not care how the Clinton presidency is defined by history, but I can guarantee you that at least two groups of people are not missing a beat.

The first group is the ambitious men and women who would one day like to sit behind the big desk in the Oval Office. Every four years, one of these people will get the chance to do so. If history ultimately reveals to them that Clinton's manipulations resulted in a presidency judged as a great success, then they will engage in the same behavior and we will all pay the price. We will pay it again and again, each time from further behind the eight ball.

The second group carefully watching how history defines the Clinton presidency is America's enemies. They may be a group of Islamic terrorists sitting around a radio and drinking coffee in a European cyber-café. They might be wondering whether the American people will again elect and support a president who refuses to act with resolve and sacrifice to execute them mercilessly if they attack America again. Or they may be a group of Chinese military and economic leaders seated around an ornately carved teak conference table planning a strategy to take over a key segment of the American economy. These plotters might wonder whether they will again be permitted to brazenly purchase the cooperation—or at least the silence—of American leaders with campaign contributions, or whether that is failed strategy best left in the policy junk heap.

Let there be no doubt. America has real enemies who want to take away our jobs, our freedoms, and our lives. Whether we like it or not, our adversaries will base their decisions on our resolve to stand up to them. They always have and they always will; it's called power politics. A key signal on that front is whether we approve or disapprove of the actions Clinton took as president. What will make us more vulnerable?

In other words, this book is about telling the whole truth about Bill Clinton's legacy. However, it is not enough for you to read this book and know the truth. It is essential that you tell it to others as loudly and as often as it takes to be heard. We cannot allow the liberal news media or Clinton's tangled web of allies to define his legacy without our voices being heard. This is a battle for the kind of country in which we want our children and grandchildren to live, and it is one we cannot afford to lose.

Before we begin our story, I would like to mention two additional things. First, I write this book not as a Republican or Democrat. Thanks largely to the Clinton legacy, these old party labels are in many respects the pale shadows of a time when they actually represented a real choice. I consider myself an independent; at heart, I am a constitutionalist, someone who believes the Founders got it right, a citizen who wants to live in a nation governed by the rules they laid out. I am willing to support candidates who share this belief and this perspective. More often than not, these candidates are Republicans, but that is not always the case. When it comes to protecting lives and freedoms, I care far less about party labels than I do about real principles.

Secondly, on a less important subject, I will not mangle normally simple phrases for the sake of political correctness. I am not going to write "he or she" when I mean "he," call a short person "vertically challenged," or say I think someone has "limited analytical capabilities" when I mean they are the biggest idiot that ever walked the earth. In short, if you are easily offended, then you either should put this book down and consider the price you paid a donation to the publisher, or you should steel yourself to be jolted, if not offended. This story is too important (and I am too dedicated to telling the truth) to let it be crippled or undermined with an excessive concern for political correctness or hurt feelings. This story offends me, as well it should. It offends me because it is a chronology of a systematic assault on practically every value I hold dear. I hope it will offend you too. If so, you're a constitutionalist and I am proud to have you on the team.

1

Preface to 9/11:
Clinton and National Security

When it comes to the Clinton presidency, one issue stands head and shoulders above the rest in terms of the damage his actions did to the nation he swore to protect. That issue is national security, and it remains the foremost reason Bill Clinton should have been impeached and removed.

My first inkling that something was deeply amiss in the Clinton White House occurred late in 1996. At that time, Bill Clinton was on his way to defeating Bob Dole in a blowout election. By the end of the election, Dole would finish with more than 50 percent of the vote in only six states: Alabama, Alaska, Idaho, Kansas, Nebraska, and Utah. Ironically, despite this runaway victory, many of the worst abuses of the Clinton administration first came to light in the final days of the 1996 election.

Like Richard Nixon, Bill Clinton was on his way to a one-sided victory, and like his similarly disgraced predecessor, he insisted on breaking the law anyway. The tip of what turned out to be a large iceberg emerged in the closing days of the 1996 presidential campaign. To make a long story short, the 1996 Clinton-Gore campaign incorporated the most vast and effective scheme to circumvent the law ever conceived and executed by an American presidential campaign. It was becoming readily and disgustingly apparent that the campaign operated under the same principle Richard Nixon articulated in a 1977 interview with David Frost. Nixon said, "When the president does it, that means it is not illegal." That was dead wrong in 1977, of course, and it was just as wrong in 1996. Like Nixon, Clinton believed that he *was* the law and was therefore not subject to its constraints.

Much of the evidence pertaining to these issues was contained in reports prepared by then-FBI director Louis Freeh and federal prosecutor Charles LaBella. The Freeh and LaBella reports made a case that the charges constituted sufficient evidence of illegal behavior to require the appointment of an independent counsel. Attorney General Janet Reno—who had the final say on this question—refused to appoint. Not only did she refuse to appoint an independent counsel, but she also made certain she would not be bothered with listening to contrary advice by freezing the FBI out of the process early on. I have no doubt that she did so because she knew these charges had the potential to bring the Clinton administration crashing down in flames. Above all, she wanted to protect her boss, Bill Clinton, who had installed her in a position for which she was dramatically under-qualified. Consequently, she was willing to do absolutely anything to prevent the contents of Freeh and LaBella's memo from becoming public.

How did the attorney general work toward this goal? First, Reno gave Lee Radek, the lawyer who headed the Justice Department's "public integrity section," a top role in the process. This made good sense from Reno's perspective because Radek was susceptible to political pressure. In fact, two senior FBI officials reported that he told them he was "under a lot of pressure not to go forward with the investigation" because the attorney general's job might "hang in the balance."[1] Reno knew she could control Radek not because he was a particularly partisan figure, but because he was a career DOJ official who was part of that clubby group of lawyers in Washington who do not like to make waves and who seek, more than anything else, the approval of the establishment. Consequently, Radek was weak-kneed, easy to pressure, and not eager to upset his buddies by aggressively investigating anyone, much less the president. Radek was so lackadaisical at investigating corruption that the Bush administration removed him from his former post and reassigned him to an obscure corner of the Justice Department to work on asset forfeiture matters. In short, he was the perfect candidate for Janet Reno to name as the top lawyer in the campaign finance investigation.

Reno faced two problems inside the Justice Department in her scheme to cover up the illegal activity that surrounded Bill Clinton's 1996 reelection campaign. The first was FBI director Louis Freeh and the second was Charles LaBella, a San Diego prosecutor appointed to lead a task force investigating the charges. Both Freeh and LaBella have stared down their share of criminals. LaBella had several notable successes in prosecuting top public officials for breaking the law, and Freeh was something of a law enforcement legend for his prosecutions of everyone from Sicilian organized crime bosses to terrorists. Both men independently concluded that substantial criminal conduct had taken place in connection with the 1996 Clinton campaign. Furthermore, the attorney general herself hardly kept her distance from the fund-raising scheme. In just one example, she received a personal memo updating her on the Democratic National Committee's plans to raise $100 million prior to the 1996 elections. The memo included a hand-scrawled note to "Janet" from a top party fund-raiser. Needless to say, this put Reno in an awkward position.[2]

How did Reno deal with this dilemma? She certainly did not want LaBella or Freeh voicing their opinions in any kind of public forum. Washington uses two time-honored methods to cover up embarrassing facts. The first is to appoint a blue-ribbon commission to investigate secretly for two or three years and then issue a long report after the underlying issue has long since gone stale. Even this option, however, was too aggressive for the Janet Reno cover-up.

Instead, she used the second method, letting Freeh and LaBella express their opinions in confidential memos. Freeh and LaBella both took her up on the offer, and being straight shooters, they told her exactly what they thought about the cover-up she was orchestrating, which was not much. Both memos were blistering, and LaBella was ultimately drummed out of the Justice Department for daring to speak the truth.

There is a good reason Attorney General Janet Reno kept those documents hidden from public view for so long, despite the enormous pressure she faced to turn them over. If the Freeh and LaBella memos had become public in 1997, they would have galvanized our efforts to focus the investigation of Clinton's abuse of power on the national security matters that *should have* formed the heart of our inquiry. In fact, Director Freeh's memo to the attorney general is dated November 24, 1997, less than three weeks after the day I shocked official Washington by filing impeachment inquiry papers in the House. If these memos had become public at this time, the entire course of events that followed would have changed, quite possibly bringing Bill Clinton and his small army of corrupt henchmen to account in an immediate and public fashion.

These memos have now belatedly been made public. Most media outlets systematically ignored the contents of both memos, but they contain extremely damning conclusions reached by some of the most respected law enforcement officials in America. Director Freeh's memo outlines an FBI investigation focused on three categories of illegal activity: conspiring to violate campaign finance laws, selling access to the White House to a range of opportunists, and "efforts by the People's Republic of China and other countries to gain foreign policy influence by illegally contributing to U.S. political campaigns and to the DNC through domestic conduits."[3] According to Freeh, all of these separate courses of criminal conduct connected with a "core group" including "the President, the Vice President, and a number of top White House advisors." The FBI wanted to focus on this "core group," while the Justice Department's

President Clinton passes behind U.S. Attorney General Janet Reno shortly before he commended her for her actions in the Elian Gonzalez case.

Radek investigation was working from the "bottom up," building cases only against the smallest and least significant members of the conspiracy. In other words, Freeh outlines a clear case that the criminal conduct orchestrated by the "core group" was being covered up and permanently delayed by a carefully crafted plan to painstakingly investigate smaller figures.

Chuck LaBella's independently drafted memo makes exactly the same points as Freeh's, although in a more detailed fashion. As he puts it, the White House used "access to the White House and high level officials" as "leverage to extract contributions from individuals who were themselves using access as a means to enhance their business opportunities."[4] Maybe I am an old-fashioned prosecutor who is not up to date with current legal lingo, but two words describe this conduct in my mind—*bribery* and *extortion*. When you strip away all of the complexities of the scheme, you are left with something no different from the behavior of a state legislator who accepts an envelope of unmarked bills in return for a highway contract or a bureaucrat who quashes an investigation in return for two weeks at a sunny resort.

Not only did Bill Clinton take campaign contributions from agents of foreign governments, but he also gave at least one of them a top job at the Department of Commerce. The now-infamous name of this particular individual is John Huang. Huang got his job because he raised massive amounts of cash—more than $1 million—for Bill Clinton. As was later discovered, much of this money was illegally laundered foreign cash funneled into the Clinton campaign. During his time at Commerce, Huang participated in more than a hundred top-secret intelligence briefings and applied for and received a security clearance that further expanded his access to national secrets. He also had what can only be described as an extremely high level of access to the White House, with Secret Service entry logs listing approximately eighty visits (that we know of). Across the same period of time when Huang was working for the government, he continued to maintain close contacts with the Lippo Group, an Indonesian corporate giant with close ties to the military and government of Communist China and believed to play a significant role in Chinese military and political espionage. The bottom line in this case is that Huang was clearly working for someone other than the United States taxpayers when he infiltrated our government. For example, legendary Watergate reporter Bob Woodward of the *Washington Post* uncovered information indicating the FBI had reports that "Huang, while serving as a senior Commerce Department official in the Clinton administration, passed a classified document to the Chinese government."[5] Unfortunately, the full extent of the damage he did in that capacity is still unknown.

John Huang was far from the only agent of a foreign power to be welcomed into the highest levels of government in return for making campaign donations to Bill Clinton. Charlie Trie operated a Chinese restaurant in Little Rock, where he first met Clinton. After Clinton was elected, he followed his patron to Washington and became a self-styled "consultant," which apparently meant he was responsible for laundering contributions from foreign nationals who wanted to contribute illegally to Clinton's campaign and for passing information back to his controllers, whoever they might be. Trie was good at this task, raising massive sums for Clinton and receiving an appointment to the Presidential Commission on Asian Trade Policy in return. All told, the operative laundered and funneled hundreds of thousands of dollars in illegal foreign cash to the campaigns of Clinton and other prominent Democrats. Trie's cash also bought access. Often, he would visit the White House to pal around with top officials, and many times he brought his buddies, including arms smuggler Wang Jung, along. A search of Trie's office later revealed evidence that he was involved in espionage activities. One note, written on stationery from a Hong Kong hotel, contains references to bribery, technology export licensing, and Hughes Electronics, a company that figured prominently in China's efforts to steal U.S. military technology.[6]

The Clintons also welcomed domestic criminals into the White House. One of the worst such cases was that of Jorge "Gordito" Cabrera of Miami. Cabrera was a top cocaine trafficker for Colombian drug cartels. In 1995, the Clintons invited him to attend the White House Christmas party and get his picture taken with the president, following his large donation of campaign cash. This may give Clinton the distinction of being the first U.S. president ever to fund part of his reelection campaign with illicit drug profits. As one top investigator put it in a conversation, "some of that money literally had Pablo Escobar's fingerprints on it."[7] There is little doubt that the Clinton campaign and the president were aware of Cabrera's illegal activities, since he had already been indicted for drug trafficking twice and was convicted of lesser charges under plea bargains in both cases. A month after attending the fund-raiser, local detectives arrested Cabrera. He is now serving a long prison sentence in Florida on a conviction for bringing more than 6,000 pounds of cocaine into America.

Interestingly, Cabrera managed to extend his hands back into another of Clinton's political campaigns from inside his jail cell. A close associate of Cabrera would later become the top soft money donor to Hillary Clinton's campaign, though she was forced to return the more than $20,000 after being caught with her hand in the drug money jar. In classic Clinton fashion, Hillary attempted to distract attention from the contribution by accusing her then-opponent Rudy Giuliani of taking contributions from a company the EPA had once listed as a polluter. There you have it. Hillary Clinton took drug money and Rudy Giuliani took money from a company that once showed up on a list of polluters. "Everybody does it," or so the Clinton logic went.

In the twisted world of Bill Clinton, inviting drug traffickers to the White House may have made perfect sense. But in reality, Bill Clinton's cavalier attitude toward mind-altering drugs is one of the worst aspects of his legacy. The war on illegal, mind-altering drugs is our longest war. It has ravaged our communities, killed our youth, caused terrible violence in our neighborhoods, schools, and workplaces, and funded international terrorism. It has also cost us greatly in blood and treasure. I know, because as a U.S. attorney I faced the most hardened criminals who poisoned our country with narcotics. They, like the 9/11 terrorists, are murderers.

In February 2002, President George W. Bush told the American people that more than 20,000 of their fellow citizens had died the year before as a result of illegal drugs. When Bill Clinton took over as president in 1993, only 12,000 Americans had died of illegal drug use. Think about it: that is a massive and unacceptable escalation in the number of deaths. And it has been going on for decades.

When Bill Clinton took over the White House in 1993, the first thing he did was gut the Office of National Drug Control Policy, the so-called drug czar. The staff was slashed from 155 down to 24 people. Clinton decided that interdiction of drugs coming into the United States and assistance to our anti-drug allies in Latin America were wastes of effort and resources. He could not have been more wrong. The war on drugs was over. We did not lose . . . Clinton surrendered.

By 1996, he realized his folly and started to gin-up the war on drugs (after all, he wanted to get reelected and he knew the public had a different opinion of illegal drugs than he did). Clinton made impassioned speeches, threw more money at the problem, and hired a new drug czar, retired Army General Barry McCaffrey, but it was all cheap theatre. Clinton's dedication to winning the war on drugs was no more serious than his protestations that he was being unfairly accused of having affairs with White House underlings. His new approach to the issue lasted exactly as long as the election cycle, and then he went back to his old policy of undermining efforts to stop the flow of drugs whenever possible. By the time Clinton left office, Gen. McCaffrey's reputation had become another casualty of the White House. The fact was—all talk aside—that the general reportedly had never even met one-on-one with Clinton on the drug issue. He had been ignored, and so had the war on drugs.

When I first came to Capitol Hill, I made it a point to be assigned to the House Speaker's Task Force on Drugs. My experiences in prosecuting drug cases and having lived and worked in Latin America made me sensitive to this multifaceted issue, and I felt qualified to make a meaningful contribution. Evidently, Speaker Gingrich, Dan Burton, and Dennis Hastert felt the same way, because they packed me off on overseas fact-finding trips on the drug issue. From the cocaine trafficking centers of South America to the needle-exchange dens in Switzerland, I got a firsthand education on the worldwide epidemic of drug abuse and its links to funding terrorism. In fact, it is difficult to look behind a terrorist and not find a connection to mind-altering drugs. The opium poppy fields of Afghanistan have kept Osama bin Laden's Al Queda organization going.

Bob Barr with House Speaker Dennis Hastert at a cocaine lab in the South American jungles.

It was in South America, where I had lived as a youth, that the full tragedy of the drug problem hit me. In Colombia I saw the full extent of how the Clinton administration had neglected the war on drugs and ignored its links to terrorism. When I arrived in the capital city of Bogota, it seemed as if a white flag of surrender was flying over the U.S. Embassy. It was a terribly deflating experience. I was blessed by having long-standing Colombian friends who I made a point of visiting on my trips to that beautiful Andean country in conflict. They always told me what they thought and, of course, it did not always jibe with what I was hearing from the U.S. Embassy.

We had courageous allies like Gen. Rosso Jose Serrano, the legendary Colombian cop who broke the backs of the Medellin and Cali drug cartels. Five thousand of his policemen were killed in the line of duty, and he needed our help but was not getting it, at least not until a Republican-led Congress finally forced the Clinton administration to get him the assistance he deserved. As every DEA agent has told me, and as I know from personal experience, Serrano is a true hero in the war on drugs. Today, because of what he did, he cannot even live in his own country because the remaining drug lords will kill him.

Consider that in the United States today, at least 85 percent of the cocaine on our streets comes from South America, and 95 percent of that comes from Colombia. Heroin, 60 percent of which originates in Colombia, is taking an increasing toll due to the rising purity and strength now available on the street. DEA veterans tell me that emergency room admissions for heroin overdoses have doubled in Chicago, New York, and Atlanta.

Sadly, the damage Bill Clinton did to our drug interdiction programs did not end with his presidency. The system became so broken during his tenure that it remains a shadow of where it stood during the Reagan administration. Paradoxically, our drug detection capabilities have increased while our will and ability to destroy drugs has dropped. DEA agents go up to a map and point out where the opium poppies are grown in Colombia. We know where the plots are, but due to poor management, weak leadership, and a poorly executed plan—administered by desk-bound State Department bureaucrats—we do not eradicate them. It frustrates me, and then I think of what it does to the DEA agents in Bogota, Lima, Quito, and La Paz who put their lives on the line every day to fight drug trafficking. They must be going nuts, and the fact that this is yet another piece of Bill Clinton's failed legacy is undoubtedly cold comfort to them. Most Americans do not realize that since 1990, ten DEA special agents have been killed in the line of duty fighting the war on drugs in South America and we lose more aircraft fighting the narco-terrorists in Columbia than we have in fighting terrorists in Iraq and Afghanistan combined.

The DEA agents know the real cost; however, the liberal-minded State Department policies in effect today remain a hangover from Bill Clinton's drug war charade. In a sad postscript to this issue, the Clinton administration added insult to injury. While DEA agents were dying in Colombia, a marquee project of former drug czar McCaffrey was the taxpayer funded anti-drug ad campaign. That program—like many in the Clinton White House—was a poster child for corruption. Companies favored by Democrat fund-raisers were bilking the U.S. taxpayers for millions of dollars, all the while saying the work was done to protect American children from drugs. In August 2000, after congressional investigator Gil Macklin alerted me to the scam, I contacted the U.S. Justice Department concerning over-billing by the New York city-based Ogilvy & Mather public relations firm. Despite the typical lethargy by congressional and administration leaders in Washington, eventually—after four years—criminal indictments were handed down.

The list of foreign nationals, criminals, and deeply corrupted individuals Bill Clinton welcomed onto the most exclusive piece of real estate in America goes on and on. In fact, I could easily fill the remainder of this book listing their names and the reasons why they never should have been allowed on the White House grounds, much less invited inside the Oval Office. In the final analysis, what matters most is that Bill Clinton allowed anyone willing to put up a large admission fee access to the top levels of the U.S. government.

Bill Clinton damaged American national security through his *actions* vis-à-vis agents of hostile nations and criminals in the White House, but he also extracted a toll through *inaction* in other cases. Clinton deeply wanted Americans to believe that history had ended, democracy reigned supreme across the globe, and there was nothing left for America to fear. Consequently, there was no reason to continue developing expensive weapons systems designed to deter massive conventional military action or a nuclear first strike because "the Cold War was over." In his worldview, those of us who felt otherwise were unenlightened foreign policy Neanderthals living in the 1950s. Similarly, there was no reason not to wear down America's most elite military forces in countless "police actions" in small strife-torn countries around the world. If there were no more threats against American interests, then why not send our troops on "humanitarian," "nation-building," and "peacekeeping" boondoggles around the globe? Real competition between nations in the future would occur only on the economic front, with militaries withering away to glorified police forces.

Like so much of what passed for public policy in the Clinton administration, this logic was predicated upon a lie—that America faced no threats to global hegemony on either the nuclear or conventional military fronts. In order for Clinton to use the military as he wanted, the American people had to believe this lie. Getting us to believe the lie meant covering up hard evidence that the world was still a dangerous place.

Some of the most troubling such incidents are outlined through a series of classified documents and interviews obtained by investigative journalist Bill Gertz.[8] In one such incident Gertz recounts, a Norwegian missile test triggered a false alarm in Russia that sent the nation closer to the brink of nuclear war than it had ever been. When this missile which turned out to be a scientific investigation of atmospheric phenomena—was launched, Russian President Boris Yeltsin activated a device known as a *Cheget*. The *Cheget* is a small device with three buttons. One button orders no nuclear strike, another button attempts to cancel a nuclear strike, and the third orders Armageddon. No Russian leader—even during the Cuban Missile Crisis—had ever activated the *Cheget*. If anything that occurred during the Clinton presidency merited screaming front-page headlines, it was this incident. In a time of supposed peace and prosperity, the two greatest nuclear powers in the world had come perilously close to nuclear war. Yet, it was virtually ignored. *Cheget,* what *Cheget?* We haven't seen one. Don't worry, be happy.

Even worse, controls over nuclear weapons in Russia and other parts of the former Soviet Union were so lax that the possibility of terrorist groups or rogue states obtaining nuclear weapons— including "suitcase bombs" developed by the KGB—was quite high. After the disintegration of the Soviet Union, the previously rigid central controls over a massive nuclear arsenal were shattered. A 1998 audit conducted by the left-of-center Brookings Institution put the total number of active Russian nuclear weapons at more than 10,000. This included 70 nuclear bombers, 751 ICBMS, and 384 submarine-launched ballistic missiles. The morale of the troops guarding these weapons was low, their pay was insufficient, and command and control facilities were in a state of woeful disrepair. Yet the Clinton administration went all out to keep this information buried and out of the public spotlight. Top administration officials repeatedly assured the public that we had nothing to fear from the Russian nuclear arsenal, with Pentagon Spokesman Kenneth Bacon continually assuring us that Russia's Strategic Rocket Forces were "well disciplined" and "well commanded." If it took lies to maintain *Pax Americana,* then lies were what the American public was served by the Clinton administration.

The Clinton tendency blithely to ignore the potential threat of hostile foreign nuclear powers was also evident in the amount of attention it devoted to protecting our nation's most closely held nuclear secrets. The most notable offender in this area is the People's Republic of China, which conducted a remarkably focused espionage effort throughout the Clinton administration. The number one goal of this effort was to put the Chinese strategic nuclear arsenal on a par with the American arsenal by stealing our most closely held nuclear secrets. The Clinton administration failed to meet this challenge, and its negligent security policies were the largest single reason behind the frightening success of the Chinese effort.

To document exactly how many military secrets the Chinese had compromised, Congress formed a bipartisan commission headed by California congressman Chris Cox. The unanimous findings of the commission were released in a detailed report. The report essentially found that there were few elements of American missile technology not penetrated by Communist Chinese agents. Chinese agents, who easily infiltrated national laboratories run by the Clinton Department of Energy, stole our most advanced nuclear warhead designs. These designs are now being employed to develop ICBMs capable of hitting the mainland United States with a first strike. The PRC also obtained computer models, guidance system designs, and virtually every cutting-edge technology needed to construct world-class nuclear weapons and delivery vehicles. Even though top officials became aware of the scope of this penetration as early as 1995, President Clinton did not bother to receive a briefing on it until 1998, according to the bipartisan Cox report. The administration also failed to brief Congress on the problem or ask for additional resources to effectively tighten security. In short, the Clinton policy toward Chinese espionage was the equivalent of coming home from work, finding burglars at your house, making them cookies, and then helping them load the rest of your stuff into their van, all the while waving to neighbors and telling them everything is okay.

Even worse, Bill Clinton personally acted to shift American nuclear policy in ways that benefited his campaign supporters. One of Clinton's major donors was Bernie Schwartz, the CEO of Loral, a company specializing in building and launching satellites. Another was Mike Armstrong of Hughes, a company with similar interests. Both companies, in return for hefty checks from the PRC, sent top experts to China to improve the functionality of its fleet of missiles. They did this illegally, without obtaining the appropriate licenses. According to the Cox report, Hughes chose not to bother applying for a license because the Department of State would be "unlikely to grant the license."[9] Undoubtedly, Hughes and Loral decided their close ties to Bill Clinton were all the companies needed to move forward with a deliberate scheme to compromise the security of the United States. Furthermore, both companies benefited from a 1996 Clinton policy that shifted control over satellite export policies from the tighter grasp of the Department of State over to the Department of Commerce, where national security is considered little more than a nuisance. Like companies doing business in banana republics around the world, Hughes and Loral simply concluded that with Bill Clinton in office, it was cheaper and easier to pay off top officials than follow the law. Similar relaxations of export restrictions allowed Communist China to improve its military technology in areas ranging from high-speed computing to jet fighter engines.

These policies did not merely make China more dangerous. As we have now learned—and as Bill Clinton clearly knew when he was president—the Chinese military is operated much like a national corporate conglomerate. Powerful insiders use the military for commercial activity, and that commercial activity includes selling advanced weaponry to nations that cannot obtain it elsewhere. Those nations include Pakistan, which is now a nuclear state constantly teetering on the edge of takeover by Islamic extremists. In short, China is an advanced weaponry superstore where dictators, authoritarian regimes, or terrorists are always welcome to browse and purchase lethal weaponry.

Bill Clinton's disregard for the threat posed by hostile *foreign* powers to U.S. interests is now legendary, but his respect for domestic law enforcement was not much better. Prior to being elected to Congress, I served as a federal prosecutor in Atlanta, appointed by President Reagan. After leaving, I stayed in touch with many of the law enforcement professionals with whom I worked during my days at the Department of Justice. In 1995 and 1996, I and others in Washington began hearing rumors that the Immigration and Naturalization Service had basically stopped doing much criminal enforcement and was spending most of its time—under orders from the White House—naturalizing as many new citizens as possible prior to the 1996 election. It seems the Clinton-Gore campaign operatives figured that citizenship was yet another doggie biscuit to be handed out to potential electoral supporters.

Under the direct command of Vice President Al Gore through his "Reinventing Government" initiative, the INS began a forced march toward creating more than one million new citizens prior to the 1996 elections under the "Citizenship USA Program." Unfortunately, the program moved forward so quickly—in order to meet the election deadline—that about one in five individuals it made citizens was not subject to legally mandated FBI background checks. Sadly, almost one in ten of those foreign nationals who were awarded the most priceless gift America can grant turned out to have felony records in their native countries. Ironically, many U.S. states still do not allow convicted felons to vote, but here was the Clinton White House turning *foreign* felons into citizens with the full rights and privileges thereof, including voting. In fact, a congressional examination of the cases revealed that rapists and child molesters were being granted citizenships—even one inmate was actually granted citizenship while sitting in jail. Needless to say, the agents and officers I knew at INS during this period were livid that the Clinton administration was putting criminal aliens on the street at a rate far faster than they could pick them up. In fact, as a practical matter, most of these ex-cons and security risks blended into communities across America once they received their citizenship papers and would never be "found," at least until they committed their next crime.

There is little doubt that this conspiracy to violate the immigration laws reached all the way to Bill Clinton's desk. As early as 1994, when individuals interested in speeding up the naturalization process met with the president and other White House officials, they won an eagerly receptive audience. As Hillary Clinton herself said, Citizenship USA was intended to "provide the Democrats with a strategic advantage." When the program did not move quickly enough, one of Gore's top aides wrote that the "president is sick of this and wants action."[10] Accounts in the *Washington Post* and elsewhere indicate that Bill Clinton requested and received personal briefings on this initiative, and was well aware of the controversy it might provoke.[11] In the end, Clinton got his million new potential

Democrat voters and the rest of us got more than 10,000 felons as fellow citizens. At the same time, even though Congress had significantly increased the INS budget, enforcement funds never seemed to make their way to the field. Agents reported being ordered to curtail official travel and stop using cell phones for investigative purposes in order to cut costs, even as record INS budgets were being passed by Congress.

I was not the only one deeply concerned about what Bill Clinton had done to the INS. The Judiciary Committee's lead impeachment investigator, David Schippers, was a tough Democrat lawyer from Chicago who had not really been exposed to Washington politics prior to being hired by Henry Hyde to conduct the impeachment inquiry. However, one of the first things he zeroed in on as an investigative target was the Citizenship USA scandal. As he put it, the INS was "running out of control."[12] The Government Reform and Oversight Committee—through the work of a subcommittee led by Dennis Hastert—also did an exceptional job of developing evidence related to this scandal. Despite the evidence, in typical Clinton administration fashion, INS Commissioner Doris Meissner was trotted out on Capitol Hill, where she lied under oath, saying that the INS was not being influenced by political pressure from the White House. This behavior should not have surprised us, since Meissner had already shown the bad judgment to attend at least one fund-raiser to help the DNC raise illegal foreign cash, where individuals undoubtedly lobbied her with specific and personal interests in seeing immigration enforcement further loosened. Amazingly, her judgment was *so* bad that she even allowed herself to be video-taped trolling for campaign cash on one of the famous "White House videos."

To understand the seriousness of this abuse of the immigration process, think back to the September 11 terrorist attacks that occurred a few years later. The attacks were made possible largely because the hijackers were able to manipulate U.S. immigration laws to do basically whatever they wanted in our country, even though they were foreign nationals engaging in highly suspicious behavior.

The seriousness of the problem was underscored when—six months *after* the attacks—the INS sent letters granting two of the dead hijackers student visas. If this is not the behavior of an agency completely destroyed by years of consistent mismanagement, I don't know what is.

The Citizenship USA initiative was discontinued when its abuses came to light and its political usefulness ended after the 1996 election, but its legacy remained long after its official presence ended. By forcing INS—an already troubled agency dealing with a huge social problem—to ignore its criminal enforcement responsibilities and turn felons into voters at a breakneck pace, Clinton personally enlarged one of the holes in America's national security armor that the September 11 hijackers exploited to their maximum advantage, resulting in the deaths of thousands of American citizens. If just one of the hijackers had been caught in the INS net, the resulting information might well have resulted in an unraveling of the plot.

Domestic criminal laws were not the only element of American national security Bill Clinton manipulated to suit his political ends. It is my belief that he also used our military forces—and the lives of individuals in other nations—as pawns in a game to enhance his own public status. This is a strong thing to say about anyone, so I'll explain why I feel this way.

Throughout his administration, Bill Clinton was anything but eager to act against terrorists and rogue states that threatened American interests. Though deeply anti-military, Clinton was eager to use our armed forces, but he most often did so in the context of multilateral "policing" actions in states such as the former Yugoslavia, Somalia, and Haiti. The idea of striking potential terrorists with overwhelming firepower in an effort to wipe them off the face of the earth was completely out of character for Clinton. Yet, on two occasions, this is exactly the kind of action he took. In fact, if you closed your eyes, you would have thought that Ronald Reagan had reappeared in the Oval Office to manage security policy for a few hours in each case.

The first case involved missile strikes against sites that were purportedly a chemical weapons factory in Sudan and terrorist training camps in Afghanistan. There is now serious doubt that the alleged chemical weapons factory made anything other than legitimate pharmaceuticals. As for the "terrorist training camps," it appears the cruise missiles destroyed nothing of significance. In short, the attacks made American counter-terrorism policy appear random, ineffectual, poorly planned, haphazard, and lacking in good intelligence; in fact, all of these characterizations were accurate and painfully apparent. Appearing on NBC a few days after the attacks, Clinton's secretary of defense told America that "this is not a one-time event, as President Clinton and Secretary Albright have indicated. This is a long-term engagement."[13] Of course, we all know how tragically empty those words turned out to be.

In the second case, Bill Clinton ordered a massive bombing of Iraq in retaliation for Iraq's failure to allow U.N. weapons inspectors to visit sites where the administration believed nuclear, chemical, and biological weapons were being manufactured. Here again, the attacks were a temporary blip in an otherwise empty patter of vacillation and inaction in the face of Saddam Hussein's obvious attempts to acquire powerful new weapons to take American lives or enable others to do so. The net effect of this particular bombing is that it further enforced Hussein's view that we did not have good intelligence on his activities and that he could do whatever he wanted without fear of a strong or consistent military response from the United States. This perception, of course, turned out to be wrong, but the actions Bill Clinton took to reinforce it contributed to the conclusion reached by the Bush administration that only resolute ground action would end the menace this dictator posed to American interests.

These two cases are alike primarily because they represented deviations from standard Clinton foreign policy. Unfortunately, they were quickly followed by a return to negotiations and a misguided reliance on the criminal justice process to handle terrorism alone. However, these events are united by the fact that both occurred on the two days when Bill Clinton's presidency faced what were perhaps its greatest threats. When Clinton bombed Sudan and Afghanistan, he had just finished testifying before Ken Starr's grand jury on his decision to lie and obstruct justice in the wake of a sordid affair in the White House. When Clinton bombed Iraq, the House of Representatives was voting on whether or not to impeach him. When the House passed the articles of impeachment, the bombing abruptly stopped.

This is simply too much coincidence for me and many other observers to believe. There is no way any honest observer can look at this confluence of events and conclude that Bill Clinton was acting only in the national security interests of the United States. These strikes were calculated and cynical moves carefully timed to give the appearance that Clinton's accusers were focused on an insignificant sexual affair while the nation's security was in grave danger. Morally, this is perhaps the lowest depth to which Bill Clinton sunk during his presidency. In these cases, his actions were those of a narcissistic sociopath who was willing to kill others to protect his hold on the presidency. I can only imagine how the soldiers who participated in these strikes feel about being ordered to risk their lives so that Bill Clinton could appear presidential. It is also a virtual certainty that these military actions sent a clear message to many in the Arab street that the lives of Muslims were worth less than a few points on Bill Clinton's public approval ratings. Using military power effectively and decisively with suffi- cient justification engenders respect and peace. Using it capriciously and weakly only ensures further conflict. In this particular case, Clinton's actions clearly fell into the latter category.

In many areas, Clinton's national security policy failed from incompetence as much as corruption. Perhaps the most egregious failure was his decision to repeatedly pass up opportunities to elim- inate Osama bin Laden prior to the attacks of September 11, 2001. As former defense secretary William Cohen testified, three opportunities to assassinate bin Laden were passed up because Clinton was not "sure." A similar offer from the Sudanese government to hand over bin Laden was also spurned. One particularly spectacular failure is outlined by the Air Force officer assigned to follow Clinton with the nuclear launch codes for several years (which Clinton actually managed to misplace in at least one instance). In his book *Dereliction of Duty*, decorated Air Force Lt. Colonel Buzz Patterson explains that Clinton passed up a chance to attack and kill Osama bin Laden because he was playing golf for several hours and did not want to be bothered.

The Clinton administration failed to act against terrorism largely because it had a fixation with applying the American criminal justice process abroad in such a way that terrorists could be captured, brought to trial, and put in jail if convicted. This line of reasoning is absurd, and most Americans with a high school education realize how absurd it is. Simply put, how could Bill Clinton possibly think international terrorists could be dissuaded by the threat of prosecution in the U.S. courts?

I can just see him walking into a mud hut in Islamabad and saying, "Now guys, you listen up. If you keep doing bad things, we're going to send some FBI agents with tazers to stun you and bring you back to the United States. We're going to give you a trial, and if the jury finds you guilty, we're going to put you in a place with climate control, workout facilities, a bed of your own, three meals a day, access to religious services, and free health care. So, you shape up now, stop it with the suicide bombings, and go get jobs, maybe in Americorps or something."

You can guess what the response would be. The howls of laughter would be heard halfway around the world in Washington, D.C. By consistently failing to apply a realistic and consistent anti-terrorism policy, the Clinton administration painted a large bull's-eye on America. By waiting around to be victimized, we ensured we ultimately would be.

Clinton also mismanaged the U.S. intelligence community so badly that it may take decades to repair the damage. I worked for the Central Intelligence Agency for a significant portion of my adult life. When I served with the CIA, the agency enjoyed a reputation as one of the most effective intelligence-gathering tools in the world, able to penetrate virtually any target and gather information. Although I cannot talk about much of what I did there, I learned a fundamental lesson of gathering intelligence of which I am frequently reminded. In short, there are two kinds of intelligence commonly used in the policy documents the Intelligence Community delivers to top decision makers. The first kind, dubbed ELINT and SIGINT (electronic intelligence and signals intelligence), results primarily from the activities of the technical divisions of the CIA and the separate National Security Agency, which manage a vast and phenomenally expensive electronic data and voice interception apparatus around the world. The second type of intelligence, referred to as HUMINT (human intelligence), comes from individual operatives placed undercover in every dark corner of the world where America's enemies huddle to plot evil.

As I learned at the CIA, SIGINT and ELINT information is useless unless it is backed by assessments from field operatives on the ground. Electronic intercepts can tell us, for example, that a group in Indonesia wired funds to suspected terrorist operatives in Iran and that those operatives were heard discussing where to purchase plastic explosives on an open phone line. This is useful information, but it does not tell us a thing about the intentions or plans of these individuals. Most importantly, electronic intelligence only tells us fragmentary pieces of information, usually about events that have already taken place. It rarely allows us to learn what will happen, where a target will be sleeping on a given night, or what is going on in that target's mind. Without this kind of information, we end up with a large collection of fragmentary bits of intelligence and no understanding of the full picture they paint. As the September 11 Commission has amply outlined, this kind of information alone is useful primarily in hindsight, helping us understand why we should have suspected an attack but didn't.

Under the Clinton administration, the CIA, NSA, and the other agencies that are part of the U.S. intelligence community were continually directed to focus their resources on investing in expensive technology to intercept communications. As former CIA director James Woolsey publicly admitted, this technology was not used only for military purposes but was also put to the benefit of private American companies conducting business overseas. Simply put, the policy of the Clinton administration on intelligence gathering was that if an operation involved inserting a human operative into a hostile environment, often under deep cover for years at a time, it simply was not going to happen. This illustrates the Clinton doctrine of "immediate gratification," evident in many areas of the administration's policies. Furthermore, we were not going to invest the resources it would take to maintain even a small force of undercover operatives with covert skills and deep understandings of particular countries, cultures, and languages around the world. This is a decision that would culminate in disaster soon after Clinton left office.

In terms of fighting terrorism, one of the worst things Bill Clinton did to the nation he was entrusted to protect occurred in the final days of his administration. Even though George W. Bush had legally won the presidential election (an outcome that would soon be upheld by the United States Supreme Court), President Clinton was so eager to help his vice president wrest the election from Bush that he allowed the president-elect virtually no time for an orderly transition. By refusing to give President-elect Bush the keys to the transition office or access to the transition budget, the Clinton administration ensured that the already tight time frame for a transition was cut dramatically. This meant that the new president would have far less time to screen qualified individuals for top posts and set policies on national security issues than any of his modern predecessors (including, of course, Clinton himself). This occurred in the context of a new president taking the helm after

Clinton had already done serious damage to American national security capabilities. When he chose to obstruct an orderly transition of power, Bill Clinton ensured that there would be a critical period during the early part of the Bush presidency when the national security apparatus functioned at far less than optimal level. Just how crucial that gap would be would become apparent less than eight months into the Bush presidency.

Although Clinton's unwillingness to exercise self-control over his personal desires was not often discussed as a national security risk, it clearly was. Think about the degree to which the president was willing to obstruct justice, perjure himself, and abuse his office to hide evidence of just one of his affairs when the people who knew about it were American lawyers. Imagine what would happen if he were trying to prevent that knowledge from coming to light if it were possessed by agents of a foreign power. There is no telling how many economic or national security interests he might have been blackmailed into neglecting in a desperate attempt to cover up his misdeeds.

Whether a president likes it or not, his personal conduct while in office relates directly to the national security of the United States. Unlike the misbehavior of most private citizens, when the U.S. president exposes himself to risk, he is exposing all of us to risk. This means the president—and other officials in key national security roles—must be willing to conduct themselves in a way that does not make them a threat to themselves and all American citizens. This is a heavy burden to carry, and many people are simply not up to the task. They might have an addiction to drugs or alcohol, a gambling problem, or an inability to control their spending or sexual impulses that they do not want exposed. When I served with the CIA, these are the kinds of issues that would disqualify someone from obtaining or retaining a security clearance. Despite arguments by many liberals to the contrary, these kinds of people were not rejected for national security posts because the government wanted to pass judgment on whether their personal conduct was right or wrong. It was simply the case that serious personal shortcomings or problems might give a third party an easy pressure point, constituting a liability that would endanger the entire system.

The process of electing a president is strikingly similar. The media and the opposition relentlessly probe the backgrounds of candidates. During that process, personal problems that would under any normal circumstance be irrelevant or unimportant become national liabilities and properly influence the voters to reject candidates who might pose a threat. In most cases, such people are rejected early in the election process. By virtue of his unusually effective persuasive skills, Bill Clinton was able to dodge this bullet. As a result, America suffered a hit, the severity of which remains to be seen.

Our system has many legal, ethical, and procedural standards that are used to ensure national security is never sacrificed to short-term political needs or even less significant policy goals. Protecting our nation should always be the *sine qua non* of government action. No matter what benefit a policy shift or official action offers, it cannot be taken at a cost to national security. This is a rigid standard, as it should be. Some rules are made with "wiggle room" and flexibility, but not national security standards. They are ironclad and not open to exception.

One thing you can say about Bill Clinton is that he always viewed rules as obstacles to be overcome, as problems to be solved or evaded. It was a game—a "challenge"—to this risk-taker from Hope. Restrictions of any kind were to be applied to other people. Clinton was so confident in his own judgment that he arrogantly assumed the country would always be better off if he made up his own rules as he went along. Administrations always make mistakes, and they sometimes make bad mistakes (as President Nixon did). However, something different and far more sinister was at work in the Clinton case. In congressional hearings, press accounts, and numerous other venues, it quickly became apparent that if Clinton and his top staff did not like a law, they simply ignored it.

Clinton's defenders sometimes argue that his failings in office were purely personal and that the only real victims of his shortcomings were his wife and child. Did Bill Clinton have any direct personal role in the tragedy of September 11? Of course not. But he is clearly culpable for systematically failing to take decisive action during his presidency to defend America against the clear and present danger of terrorism. During the eight years of his presidency, Clinton and his cronies systematically neglected American national security in some cases and actively undermined it in others. It should therefore come as no surprise that a group of Islamic radicals concluded they could bring America to its knees by taking several thousand lives and striking at our economic and political heart on that September day in 2001.

Disturbingly, the idea that Bill Clinton was some kind of national defense genius is still being aggressively peddled at the top levels of the Democratic Party. Just this year, presidential candidate John Kerry told the *Associated Press* that "[w]hen Bill Clinton left office, not one young American was dying anywhere in this world."[14] This is a nonsensical statement, of course, but what Kerry is willfully ignoring is the fact that Americans *were* giving their lives abroad to protect our freedom. A few of the examples of the threat we faced from terrorism even then include the bombing of the *USS Cole* in 2000, the Khobar Towers attack, and the 1993 World Trade Center bombing. Whether Clinton realized it or not, America was indeed at war then, with the same terrorists who would go on to take thousands of American lives. This is a fact John Kerry might wish to ignore or gloss over, but that makes it no less true.

2

Pimping Out the Presidency:
Clinton and the White House

As with any institution, the White House has a culture that presidents inherit when they take over from their predecessors. Whether one agrees with their politics or not, there is no denying that the immediate prior occupants of 1600 Pennsylvania Avenue had an enormous respect for the presidency. Ronald Reagan and George H. W. Bush knew the presidency was a truly "sacred institution"—not just a "job," an "adventure," or an "opportunity"—and they treated it as the most precious thing they would ever guard in their lives. President Reagan, for example, refused to remove his suit jacket in the Oval Office due to his respect for the institution.

My friend Gary Aldrich is the first person to have revealed to the world that things inside the White House changed completely the day Bill Clinton and his campaign operatives moved into 1600 Pennsylvania Avenue. Gary, a highly-decorated FBI agent with more than thirty years of experience, was assigned to work inside the White House on national security issues in the Bush and Clinton administrations, so it is difficult to call him anything other than an extremely credible source. As he puts it, the idea that the White

Bob Barr and his wife Jeri with Gary Aldrich and his wife Nina at Inauguration.

House was one of the most tempting targets for America's enemies—who might seek to attack it or conduct espionage inside it—simply did not seem to carry any importance with the Clinton administration.

When we think about top-notch law enforcement agencies, the U.S. Secret Service invariably comes to mind. The Secret Service has a reputation for employing the best of the best special agents, brave men and women who willingly would lay down their lives to protect the officials they are assigned to guard. Simply put, no one takes security more seriously than a Secret Service agent. For this reason, the Secret Service is particular about who is allowed into the White House. If someone is likely to be an agent of a foreign power or is involved in criminal activity in the United States, they are or should be—with good reason—not allowed inside the White House and certainly not when the president himself is in.

During the entire history of the modern U.S. presidency, the Secret Service has always had *carte blanche* to protect the White House and its occupants. This system has worked well, particularly when you consider the number of people both in and outside the United States who would trade their lives to kill the president or conduct espionage inside the most important governmental building in the world's most powerful nation. Without revealing information that might be useful to America's enemies, the way this system basically works is that the Secret Service reviews each potential visitor to the White House and determines whether or not they pose a risk based on a variety of information. The Secret Service then decides whether or not to issue a pass for each proposed visitor.

The president and top White House staff, of course, can object to those decisions and overrule them if they wish. But most presidents and their top personnel wisely respect the Secret Service and follow its recommendations. As Gary Aldrich has explained, this process was—to say the least—ignored, if not actively ridiculed, during the Clinton years. Bill and Hillary were not about to let some government employee with a badge and gun tell them who they could and could not have in the White House. These are the kinds of people the young Clintons would have called "the fuzz" or "pigs" during their years in and around the radical anti-war movement, and it does not appear their opinion of law enforcement changed much in the intervening years. By God, if they wanted criminals and agents of hostile foreign powers to hang out in the White House, no one was going to tell them no, particularly if "friends of Bill" were showing up with campaign cash. In short, not only did the Clintons ignore the recommendations of the brave men and women who were willing to give their lives to save the president's, but they also actively reprimanded agents who dared to raise questions about security risks inside the White House. Consequently, the agents who were responsible for keeping bad people out of the White House eventually threw up their hands and decided they were not going to be able to keep these people out. Soon, as Aldrich reported, campaign donors and friends of donors—some of them with distinctly unsavory backgrounds—were wandering around the White House unchecked and unchallenged, at the direct behest of

Bill and Hillary Clinton.[1] This laxity was, of course, duplicated in other executive branch agencies during the Clinton administration—Energy, Commerce, and our secret nuclear weapons labs. We may never know the full extent of the damage this policy caused to America's security.

Over the course of his presidency, the American people would see Bill Clinton turn the most respected institution in America into a cesspool of small-time corruption reminiscent of a small state capitol. One of the most outrageous things the Clinton team did was convert the White House into a mechanism for dispensing goodies to major donors and other political cronies, on a scale not seen since the Ulysses S. Grant presidency. The defining characteristic of the Clinton White House during 1996 was greed. The most publicly visible sign of that greed was the Clintons' decision to turn the Lincoln Bedroom into the world's most expensive hotel room, available to any donor willing to pay the entrance fee. However, this is only a small bit of evidence pointing to a much larger scheme.

First, a bit of background. There is deeply-held, almost fanatical belief among Democrat campaign operatives that the ideas of their party are absolutely superior to those of any other party. Not only are their ideas better, but they are also supported by many more Americans than would support Republican principles. The problem, as they see it, is that the playing field is not level. As many Democrats see the world, the Republicans raise more money, so they are able to hide the truth about their evil ideas and distort the facts about the Democrat agenda. Bill Clinton and his political handlers left little doubt that they bought this argument hook, line, and sinker. They were fanatically devoted to the goal of proving this perceived wisdom wrong by raising more money than the Republicans, even though they were running far ahead in the polls and had already raised large sums of money. However, Bill Clinton—and Al Gore, his chief fund-raiser—faced a problem. The business community and financially successful individuals tended to be Republicans or supportive of the GOP, meaning that the only way Bill, Al, and Hillary could raise more money would be to systematically pimp out the presidency and its attributes to the highest bidder.

We already know about the most serious result of this behavior, which was the damage done to our national security by Bill Clinton's greed. But this desire to raise money no matter the cost impacted the presidency as an institution as well. From large legal violations to small ones, Bill and Hillary Clinton, Al Gore, and their top operatives systematically ignored federal law in their quest for campaign cash.

Under federal law, for example, it is illegal for "any person to solicit or receive any contribution" from "any room or building occupied in the discharge of official duties" by "an officer or employee of the United States or any department or agency thereof." This law is well-known and rigidly followed on Capitol Hill. Both political parties maintain offices on private property away from but near the House office buildings, which members religiously visit to dial for dollars. Considering the numbers of dollars you have to dial for to run a competitive campaign these days—speaking from personal experience—you end up spending far more hours in these cramped cubicles than you would like. This was a pain in the neck, and it would have been much more convenient and efficient to call donors from our taxpayer-funded offices on Capitol Hill or back home in our districts. However, this would have been illegal and also wrong. After all, no taxpayer should be forced to pay for any elected official—president, congressman, or senator—who they may or may not support, to spend their time at taxpayer expense and in taxpayer-funded offices raising campaign cash. Even worse, no citizen should ever feel that they have to give a campaign contribution to a government official in order to get the attention they deserve. The seriousness of this offense is underscored by the fact that you can get up to three years in jail for committing it.

Members of Congress and thousands of other elected officials followed this law, but not Bill Clinton and Al Gore. They were a law

unto themselves, and like so many other rules—large and small—
they did not believe this one applied to them, and they violated it
repeatedly. The vice president demonstrably broke the law more
than eighty-six times, and there are numerous documents—such as
memoranda and notes—indicating the president was also a repeat
offender. This occurred despite the fact that everyone in the administration was well aware of the law. White House Counsels Bernie
Nussbaum and Abner Mikva had both circulated written memos
warning that making fund-raising phone calls from the White
House offices would constitute a violation of federal law.

When faced with evidence clearly showing he had improperly
made fund-raising calls from his office in the White House
complex, Gore made his famous argument that "there is no controlling legal authority" that would render unlawful his dozens of
personal fund-raising calls from his plush office next to the White
House, in the ornate Old Executive Office Building. I still do not
think anyone—including Gore—is sure exactly what he intended
this statement to mean, but it does not change the fact that both the
president and the vice president intentionally violated a specific
federal law numerous times in their mad scramble for cash. The
Clinton administration then went on to argue that the law was old
and that it was not often enforced, so they should not have to follow
it. These arguments are both ridiculous. Murder has been illegal for
a long time as well, but that does not mean anyone can kill and get
away with it simply because our homicide statutes are "so old."
Furthermore, the mere fact that the vast majority of elected officials
had followed this law—meaning there was no need to enforce it in
past cases—certainly did not provide an excuse for Bill Clinton and
Al Gore to ignore it at will. Once again, scratching the surface
revealed the basic Clinton-Gore mentality that "laws apply to
everyone but us."

Illegal fund-raising activity in the Clinton administration was
by no means limited to the grounds of the White House. In fact, the
fund-raising adventures of Bill and Al took them to some interesting places. One of those places was the Hsi Lai Buddhist Temple

outside of Los Angeles. As a religious institution, the temple had tax-exempt status and hence could not legally be the site of a partisan political fund-raiser. This is commonly known, as evidenced by the fact that candidates of both parties rarely if ever attempt to hold fund-raisers at churches, synagogues, or mosques. As shown by numerous documents uncovered by various investigations, the vice president was aware of the law and the fact that he was attending a fund-raiser at a Buddhist temple staffed by saffron-robed monks, and yet he brazenly chose to break the law.

The Clinton administration did not pay any more attention to election laws than it did to tax laws. Under U.S. law, presidential campaigns have two options for financing their activities. In one scenario, they can accept voluntary spending limits and, in return for doing so, receive millions of taxpayer dollars to conduct their campaigns. Once public funds have been accepted and the spending cap agreed to, it is a violation of federal criminal law to spend past the cap. The other option a presidential candidate has is not to take a dime in public funds, in which case you can spend as much as you want on your campaign. Bill Clinton, however, decided he did not

Vice President Al Gore visits the Hsi Lai Temple on campaign fundraising swing through the San Gabriel Valley.

like feeling hemmed in by either legal scenario. He wanted to have his cake and eat it too, and nothing like the measly U.S. Code was going to stop him. So he concocted an illegal scenario of his own.

In what amounted to a complex money-laundering scheme, the Clinton-Gore campaign first agreed to the statutory spending caps and pocketed a large taxpayer subsidy for its activities. Then it raised millions in so-called "soft money." Soft money is a different political animal than hard money because it cannot be used directly by a campaign. The other kind of money used in campaigns—"hard" money—is subject to a strict legal regime designed to prevent any single donor from gaining too much influence over a campaign, as well as to keep foreign contributions and illegal cash out of the political process. Unlike hard money, soft money can be raised in virtually any amount from a much broader array of sources than hard money. The downside is that soft money cannot legally be spent to advocate the defeat or election of a particular candidate, and the campaigns themselves can have no role in directing how it is spent.[2]

The Clinton-Gore scheme involved raising large amounts of soft money and directing it to the Democrat National Committee and the state Democrat Parties. That money was then funneled back to the Clinton-Gore campaign in the form of checks written by these third parties to the Clinton-Gore media consultants for "independent" advertisements. (This was not a novel scheme; I had prosecuted a similar illegal scheme involving power companies illegally funneling money to candidates back in the 1980s when I served as U.S. Attorney.) However, these ads were anything but independent. Bill Clinton himself directed the content of the ads in close concert with Dick Morris and other close advisors. None of the third parties who were allegedly spending the money independently ever had control over the content of the ads for which they paid. As Morris wrote in his book about the 1996 campaign, Clinton "worked over every script, watched each ad, ordered changes in every visual presentation, and decided which ads would run when and where."[3] Some of the infamous "White House videos" confirm this. In short, Bill Clinton personally raised millions in illegal cash, and those dollars were illegally spent under his close personal supervision.

This may sound like an inside-baseball problem to many Americans. After all, many citizens figure that all campaigns—Democratic and Republican—bend the rules, and when we hear about these kinds of issues, we assume that everyone does it and go on about our business. Both parties do commit violations of campaign laws, to be sure, but in fact *not* everyone does it, and certainly not as brazenly or to the degree practiced by the Clinton-Gore team in the 1996 election year. The vast majority of campaigns follow these laws, and when they are broken, it does matter. It matters because breaking election laws ensures the playing field is unfairly tilted toward the campaign that is willing to break the law. Raising and spending money illegally is no different than voting dead people, throwing away ballots cast for your opponent, closing the polling place in a minority neighborhood, or any of the other tactics that have been used during American history to prevent some citizens from casting a vote for the candidate of their choice and having that vote count equally. When Bill Clinton set up a complex scheme to break the election laws, he took a shot at the heart of American democracy, the system of free and fair elections upon which we depend to ensure the people get the leadership they choose. Like Richard Nixon before him, Bill Clinton stole the 1996 election, even though—also like Nixon—he would probably have won it without breaking the law. Both presidents wanted to be sure they won, and by a wide margin, and they did not care what they had to do in order to achieve that goal.

Bill Clinton was willing to do anything to raise money, including selling to the highest bidder many of the assets he was entrusted to manage on behalf of the public. Some of those assets were seats on official U.S. trade missions to other nations. In an increasingly global economy, such missions play a critical role in the creation of jobs in America because their success or failure helps determine whether the benefits of trade accrue to the United States or other nations.

We first became aware of the abuse to trade missions when media reports surfaced in 1994 that major donors to the Democratic Party and Bill Clinton's campaign were appearing frequently on the official lists of U.S. delegation members. Slowly, litigation directed at the White House started to uncover what was actually going on. In a nutshell, Clinton political operatives decided to attach a specific dollar amount that any donor could pay if they wanted to go on an official U.S. trade mission. That donation amount, according to memos obtained by Judicial Watch from inside the White House, was set at $100,000.[4] This is, of course, both an abuse of power and a violation of the law, not that Bill Clinton cared. In fact, the Democrat National Committee showed such a blatant disregard for legal standards in this case that it went so far as to print brochures announcing the plan to potential donors. According to testimony offered by a close associate of the secretary of commerce, the entire scheme originated with none other than Hillary Clinton.

Trade missions were not the only thing for sale at the Clinton White House. In fact, it would probably take less time to list the national assets that were not for sale than it would to enumerate those on the auction block. According to Department of Justice documents prepared by the LaBella task force, the catalog offered to donors included invitations to White House coffees, opportunities to travel on Air Force One and Two, overnight stays at the White House, complimentary access to DNC events, participation in official U.S. sponsored trade "missions," and many other special perks. President Clinton also auctioned off meetings with himself and Hillary (although I cannot help pitying the poor folks who paid to hang out with Hillary). I truly believe that if he had figured out a way to do it, Clinton would have sold seats on the space shuttle or let developers put condos on Mount Rushmore. While any successful campaign legally rewards supporters with access to the candidate they support, something different in scope and type took place in Bill and Hillary Clinton's borrowed home at 1600 Pennsylvania Avenue. Donors to Clinton got access not only to political rewards, but also to the policymaking apparatus itself, with U.S. taxpayers footing the bill.

Some of the deepest damage done to the office of the presidency during Clinton's term resulted from the tactic of immediately stonewalling any request for information, no matter how small or insignificant it might be. Needless to say, courts, Congress, and prosecutors do not respond favorably to delaying tactics and refusals to grant information, and they almost always take legal action to compel the president to provide the information they are legally authorized to have in the first place. With a few notable exceptions, most presidents realized this fundamental fact and cooperated—albeit sometimes grudgingly—with investigations. During the Clinton presidency, however, legal strategies to avoid compliance were dispensed in a rapid-fire fashion, and noncompliance was as absolute a policy as one could find in this or any other administration.

More often than not, stonewalling strategies revolved around the assertion of specific privileges to withhold information. Some of the privileges Clinton asserted had a vague basis in law, while others were completely made up. All told, Bill Clinton asserted more claims of privilege than all of the presidents going back at least to Richard Nixon combined. If legal delaying tactics were an Olympic sport, Bill Clinton would hold the all-time world record. Every time Clinton raised a privilege as a bulwark against disclosure in the courts and lost, he ensured the next person to occupy the office would begin in a weaker position. In the end, the legal prerogatives of future presidents were damaged, perhaps irrevocably.

The president's ability to obtain frank and confidential advice from White House lawyers was one of the important prerogatives thrown up as a wall to block inquiries by Team Clinton. When Bill Clinton took office, it was unclear whether or not White House lawyers could give advice to presidents without fear of being forced to repeat that advice on the witness stand. Although the law on this point was not clear, the privilege was generally respected as a matter of courtesy by congressional and judicial authorities.

However, Bill Clinton was so eager to use taxpayer-funded lawyers as his personal legal defense team that he was almost immediately forced into court to argue that White House lawyers could treat him as they would any other client charged with committing a crime. Of course, this logic ignores the fact that White House lawyers work for the United States of America, not for William Jefferson Clinton or any other single occupant of the Oval Office at a given time. Predictably, when Clinton made an argument to the opposite effect, the courts did not agree. Consequently, the idea that any president in the future might have a reasonable expectation of getting frank legal advice on a range of issues was severely diminished.

The Clintons did not stop with undermining the constitutional power of the presidency. They also felt the need early in his (or their) presidency to politicize the role of the First Lady. As most Americans remember, Bill Clinton put Hillary Clinton in charge of a task force to develop a new health insurance plan for America. In itself, this was outrageous, since no one at the time had elected Hillary Clinton to the presidency (or to the local dog-catcher's office for that matter). The idea that an unelected spouse could be assigned the role of designing one of the most important new social policies in American history was deeply troubling to many Americans, not just to conservatives. Hillary's gender in this case is irrelevant. If she were elected to the presidency and Bill were the first husband, then it would be just as improper for him to take a significant role on a substantive national policy issue.

Making this bad situation much worse, Hillary insisted on meeting secretly to work on the plan. This resulted in a head-on collision with federal laws requiring government meetings to be open to the public if they involved non-governmental individuals. The only way for Hillary to keep her meetings secret was to make

Hillary Rodham Clinton speaks about health care reform on the south lawn of the White House.

the rather audacious claim that she was, in fact, an official of the United States government, even though she had not been elected or appointed to any official position. Somehow, Hillary's legal team actually managed to sell this bill of goods to the Court of Appeals for the D.C. Circuit.

Like most Americans, I went through life assuming that the first lady was the president's spouse, not an official of the United States government. (Congressional spouses are afforded deference as spouses of members, but they have absolutely no status in or concerning official matters.) By turning this logic upside down, the Clintons ensured that future first ladies (or first husbands) would arrive at 1600 Pennsylvania Avenue unsure of their legal status. I have no doubt this precedent one day will cause significant problems for future presidents. For example, is the first lady also subject to such laws as the Privacy Act? The list of problematic questions goes on, and creative lawyers are clearly going to take advantage of it in the future. Interestingly, it might also be used to prevent White House officials from being compelled to testify about conversations with other private individuals. Such a privilege—if asserted based on this precedent—would certainly encourage all kinds of corrupt conduct currently banned by law. In fact, it is this very argument that Vice President Cheney's legal team made in a bid to keep information about his energy policy task force secret when sued by Judicial Watch.

One of the worst assertions of privilege Clinton made was the so-called "Secret Service protective privilege." With a fanaticism that seemed odd for a president who often seemed contemptuous of the Secret Service, Clinton argued that its agents could be legally blocked from testifying under oath due to a privilege he essentially made up out of thin air. The basic argument of this "Secret Service protective privilege" is that if the president had to worry about whether the Secret Service would testify against him if he broke the law in front of them, then the president might try to evade his protective detail in order to break the law in secret. Needless to say, this laughable argument rested on such a tortured chain of legal reasoning that it is difficult to know which part of it is most disturbing.

First of all, the Secret Service—like all federal law enforcement agencies—owes its first duty to upholding the law of the United States, not to protecting the personal interests of the president. If agents were loyal to the president rather than the nation to which their oath of office is directed, they would more closely resemble the praetorian guard of a Roman emperor or the goons protecting dictators in many Third World countries. Secondly, the idea that the president needs sufficient room to be allowed to break the law without his protective detail spilling the beans is ludicrous. If an individual is not willing to follow the law for four years, then they should not offer themselves as a candidate for the presidency. Fortunately, every court that heard this argument reached a similar conclusion, and it was summarily tossed out of court. However, by attempting to abuse the Secret Service to shield his conduct from prying eyes, Clinton set yet another precedent that would diminish the prestige of the office and possibly the Secret Service in the future.

In addition to undermining the legal system as it involved the office of the president, Clinton's behavior had broader effects as well. No American who viewed his appearance before the grand jury on August 17, 1998, could help being disappointed by the obvious disregard our nation's top law enforcement official had for the law. We all remember how he refused to agree on a common definition of words we all understand, such as "sex" and "is." In this embarrassing video, Clinton even spends fifteen minutes fighting about what it means to tell "the whole truth" when he is put under oath. Aware that the prosecutor is on a clock, the president stalls and prevaricates to the point that the grand jury becomes completely frustrated. He refuses to answer "yes" or "no" even to the simplest of questions. When pinned down, he always blames someone else for his behavior, first Paula Jones's lawyers and then the prosecutors in the case. In sum, the American people—who already knew their president had obstructed justice and perjured himself—were once again forced to watch him thumb his nose at the law. This tape will become required viewing for any prosecutor who wants to see an uncooperative witness performing at the top of his game, as well as by defense attorneys who want to coach a witness on evading honest testimony.

The message here was simple: the law does not apply to Bill Clinton. If you are elected to the highest office in the land, you can do whatever you want and get away with it. It was striking how far we had come in the few decades since Watergate. Say what you want about Richard Nixon, but the man eventually had the decency and moral fiber to resign. To Bill Clinton, the presidency was, like his entire adult life, all one big game, and the only duty he had was to win it. He stayed in office to complete his term; in that sense, he may be seen to have won. But the American people lost. I have no doubt that future defendants and witnesses will evaluate their options differently in trials after having witnessed the spectacle

Clinton put on. After all, if the president is given *carte blanche* to abuse the legal system, it is difficult to see why any ordinary citizen would feel bound by its rules.

Another way in which Clinton permanently changed the White House concerns the role played by White House staffers on a day-to-day basis. In most past administrations, the White House staff did what most Americans would expect them to do. They managed diplomatic relations, monitored threats to American interests, discussed economic policy, planned state dinners, answered mail, and performed the countless other administrative duties a government must do if it is to be truly effective. Under Clinton, things may have started out this way, but they rapidly took a different turn.

At first, Clinton's top staffers seemed concerned about the sorts of things to which they should have been paying attention. Then, quickly, their boss managed to get them involved in scandal after scandal, largely because he did not tell them the truth. As Clinton aide George Stephanopolous wrote, receiving a subpoena had become a "routine matter, another item in the in-box."[5] In some cases, Clinton's staff was made up of fundamentally good people stuck in difficult situations. For example, Charles Ruff, who taught me during law school at Georgetown and served as White House counsel during the impeachment, was an honorable man with a deep respect for the law. I have no doubt he felt he could do more good serving a corrupt president as ably as possible than he could by staying on the sidelines.

There were, of course, some truly bad apples among President Clinton's staff. Take Sidney Blumenthal, for example. If you look up "effeminate intellectual" in the dictionary, you will likely see a picture of this guy beside the entry. Most of his early career was spent at highbrow, left-leaning publications like the *New Yorker* and the *New Republic*. In other words, he was steeped in an inbred culture of intellectual snobbery and padded expense accounts, where only the most pompous, snide, and arrogant writers survive. He probably could have kept on working in the media, but his coverage of the Clintons became so fawning that it even turned the stomachs of his liberal editors. He then went on to become something called a "senior advisor" to the president, which apparently meant his role was to feed Bill and Hillary's paranoia and cater to their delusions that everyone from newspaper editors to members of Congress was singularly obsessed with destroying them. When he wasn't doing that, Sid seems to have spent most of his time calling up his buddies in the media and trashing anyone who dared criticize the president. This conduct earned him the apt nickname "Bill's Dirt Devil" from the *New York Post*, and his fascination with absurd conspiracy theories inspired his fellow staffers to call him "Grassy Knoll," a reference to the conspiracy theories still circulating about the JFK assassination. All in all, Sid would have been a much better fit, say, as assistant copy editor at a left-wing literary journal with a circulation of two hundred readers than as a top White House official.

Craig Livingstone is another example of someone who never should have been allowed anywhere near the government of the United States, much less allowed to serve in close proximity to a president (or a county commissioner for that matter). His most notable prior employment was as a bar bouncer in a Washington nightclub, experience that the Clinton administration apparently believed qualified him to direct the White House Office of Personnel Security. In fact, Livingstone was hired, according to a statement made by a top official, because "Hillary wants him."[6] The person occupying this post is responsible for ensuring that people who are unstable, have criminal pasts, or might be agents of a foreign power are not employed by the White House. To most Americans, this seems like an important job. Clearly, Hillary Clinton understood how important the position was as well, but her goal was most definitely not keeping the White House secure. Her motivation appears far more sinister.

After managing to worm his way into the position, Livingstone immediately used his new power to start obtaining confidential and potentially embarrassing FBI background files on more than 700 prominent Republicans. In what would later become the "Filegate" scandal, these files were casually thrown around the White House, even though they contained raw and unsubstantiated information on numerous aspects of the private lives of individuals who had received government security clearances. This matter would later culminate in the firing of the FBI's Chief Counsel Howard Shapiro for his role in transferring the files. Unfortunately, we may never know the full extent of information obtained by Clinton's dirty tricks operatives. According to information obtained by the public interest law firm Judicial Watch through its investigations and lawsuits, there is a six-month gap in the log tracking the movement of the files through the White House. This is undoubtedly not mere coincidence.

Needless to say, the Clintons were not planning on hiring these Republican folks, so the administration's intent in obtaining the files was clearly malevolent. Furthermore, individuals close to the process observed White House aides putting information from the FBI documents into computerized files, raising the possibility that information obtained from them is still sitting in some political hack's office; a political "sleeper cell" waiting to be used to take out one or more key Republican figures or other enemies of Hillary. They may well have gotten away with the caper if they had not entrusted the task to small-time political hacks like Livingstone or to petty, hyper-imaginative writers like Blumenthal. In one respect, however, perhaps the country was fortunate; imagine the damage these folks could have done had they insisted true professionals man their ramparts instead of political hacks like Livingstone. This was clearly at least one area where Richard Nixon was smarter than his protégé from Arkansas.

Webster "Web" Hubbell was another class act the Clintons brought with them to the White House. Webb worked at the Rose Law Firm with Hillary, and the two of them often commiserated over lunch at a nearby Italian restaurant along with Vince Foster. It turns out that Webb was exactly the kind of sweaty-palmed, former football star turned small-time lawyer one would expect to cheat on his taxes and rip off any client stupid or corrupt enough to hire him. Predictably, he did all of these things and ultimately spent quite a bit of time at the Cumberland Federal Correctional Institution in Maryland paying his resulting debt to society.

Let's say you are Bill—and in this case, most importantly, Hillary—Clinton. What do you do with an old pal like this? Most presidents would send them a nice card every year at Christmas and maybe invite them to a reception once or twice. Not being traditionalists, however, Bill and Hillary figured that was no way to reward an old friend, so they made a rip-off artist from Little Rock the number three official at the United States Department of Justice.

In Hubbell's case, the DOJ job was also likely part of an effort to keep him from telling anyone what he knew about Hillary Clinton's financial dealings at their law firm, and by most accounts this plan—along with several hundred thousand dollars in unearned hush money from Clinton pals—succeeded. The most notable contributor of bribe money to Hubbell was the Lippo group, an Indonesian company with close ties to Communist China that would figure prominently in later foreign cash scandals during the administration. Hubbell could likely have saved himself all or some of the jail time he served by talking, but like other "friends of Bill" he steadfastly refused to do so. Hubbell knew he had been rewarded with cash and a high government job, neither of which an attorney with his mediocre skills would have come close to earning. Consequently, he would have lain in front of a train if Hillary told him to do it. Like many other people with whom the Clintons liked to surround themselves, Webb turned out to be far more loyal than he was competent or honest (which was precisely the point). In this regard, Clinton outshone his predecessor-in-crime, Richard Nixon.

People like Livingstone, Hubbell, and Blumenthal would not have been invited to visit the White House under most administrations, much less hired to work in sensitive posts there. Having a retinue of small-time thugs and political con artists on staff was a hallmark of corruption in the Nixon presidency. Observing the same thing occurring in the Clinton administration provided a clear

Vince and Lisa Foster in company of Bill and Hillary Clinton at a theater premiere.

sign that something was deeply amiss. In fact, it seems undeniably the case that revulsion over events at the Clinton White House may well have played a role in Vince Foster's sad and lonely death at Fort Marcy Park. As deputy White House counsel—and personal lawyer for the Clintons in some instances—Foster often bore the brunt of defending Bill and Hillary's frequently unconscionable and often illegal behavior.

The behavior of White House staff following Foster's apparent suicide—the first case of a suicide by such a high-ranking government official in forty-four years—was odd to say the least. Actually, the words "obstruction of justice" define the White House response to this incident better than any others. Acting in many cases under the direct orders of Hillary Clinton, top White House staffers systematically blocked an open and comprehensive inquiry into Foster's death. First, Hillary's chief of staff led an expedition immediately following news of the death to rummage through Foster's office, unescorted by law enforcement officers (who inexplicably and unprofessionally turned a blind eye to this evidence tampering). It is still unknown exactly what they were seeking and what they removed or destroyed. Later, the officers investigating the death would complain that the White House witnesses they interviewed had been coached. Even White House Counsel Bernie Nussbaum got into the action, removing items from Foster's office and personal effects, making it impossible to have an accurate inventory of this key evidence following Foster's death. In short, a handful of senior White House staff had conspired to obstruct justice at the behest of the First Lady, Hillary Rodham Clinton, and the FBI, and ultimately Attorney General Reno let them do it.

Setting cases like Sid, Webb, and Craig aside, the White House staff was not anywhere near as guilty as their boss. Some were overeager young people that Clinton had the bad judgment to put in positions of responsibility beyond their years and experience. Others were competent Washington professionals who simply could not turn down the contribution White House service would make to their resumes, regardless of who actually held the office. However, they all made one great mistake from which future individuals in their positions should learn. Clinton lied to them again and again and made them go out and lie to other people time after time, and they never actually told him that enough was enough. No matter what Clinton did, they stuck by him. You might think this blind loyalty is a good thing, and in some situations perhaps it is. But in the White House, the staff owes an obligation to their country—*our* country—that transcends their responsibilities to the occupant of the Oval Office. There is a time and place for blind loyalty, but even soldiers are not expected to follow orders if the orders are illegal. (Indeed, they are told not to follow such orders and that they can be court-martialed if they do.)

Things have not always been this way. Think back to the Nixon White House. One of the key events that brought down his presidency was the infamous "Saturday Night Massacre," when Nixon lost both an attorney general and a deputy attorney general in one night because they refused to do his bidding when they believed it was wrong. When respected individuals walk away from powerful positions because their consciences or judgment no longer allow them to participate in wrongdoing, it sends a clear message to the public that something is amiss and that there is value in standing up for what is right.

Interestingly, this approach to public service has surfaced in other situations, some of them involving situations just as sleazy as President Clinton's (such as presidential candidate Gary Hart's illicit liaisons on the yacht *Monkey Business*). In each case, a top aide to an influential leader decided that they could no longer be forced to serve lies to the public all day long. While some Clinton staff, such as Paul Begala, publicly agonized over Clinton's lies, ultimately none of them ever left his side. Others, such as Erskine Bowles, simply stayed away from anything related to scandal politics in an effort to keep doing their jobs and keep their own hands clean in order to preserve their ability to succeed in future political endeavors. In doing so, all of them put personal loyalty and private ambition ahead of their obligations to their nation, doing all Americans a great disservice. This reflected their fundamental perspective on public service: it was all politics and everything was political; you served the person, not the country. For the Clinton team, the campaign never really ended. The enemy was always wrong, charges were always lies, and neither facts nor standards existed in any kind of objective sense. The kind of standards that form the basis of ethical public service never had a chance to grow, much less flourish, in the Clinton White House. They were smothered at birth by an administration that did not get it when it came to honesty, integrity, respect, and patriotism.

What should be a continuing concern to Americans is that many of the partisan hacks appointed to government posts during the Clinton administration engaged in a practice called "burrowing" in its final days. Burrowing basically occurs when political appointees—who would normally submit pro forma resignations when a new president takes office—secure jobs as regular, tenured federal employees. And, as anyone who has ever actually tried to fire a bureaucrat knows, they are protected by so many different laws that years can often elapse between an attempt to fire a federal worker and their actual departure from the workplace. Because Clinton and Gore refused to allow George W. Bush any kind of transition period by insisting for weeks that Gore won the 2000 election, many of these burrowers—as well as some political appointees—were still parked in government jobs when the new president was sworn in. And, as America learned when Clinton terrorism official Richard Clarke stuck a knife in Bush's back, these partisan sleeper-cells are merely waiting for an opportunity to lash out with partisan attacks.

Interestingly, the blind loyalty of Clinton's staff spilled over into all kinds of other venues. For example, Democrats in Congress during the impeachment process exhibited the same kind of loyalty, no matter how many times Clinton made them look like fools for doing so. If some of these Democrats had been members of Jim Jones's cult, I have no doubt they would have been first in line to drink poisonous Kool Aid if their leader asked them to, a leader who had anything but their best interests in mind. Anyone who witnessed the post-impeachment pep rally these folks and their chief cheerleader Al Gore held for Bill Clinton at the White House could only shake their heads in disgust at the utter mindlessness of Clinton's coterie of hard-core confidants. In my view, the lemming had found a new replacement in the lexicon of American similes.

At least one reason accounting for some of the silence of Clinton's staff in the face of repeated lies was due to early adminis-tration efforts to enforce loyalty with the executive branch version of iron discipline. For example, Clinton sent an important signal to anyone who might be an effective critic of his conduct—or who might have harbored subversive (that is, independent) views—when he systematically fired every U.S. attorney in the Department of Justice in the first days of his administration. By selecting the one department in government he knew had the lawful power to truly limit his actions, and crippling it as one of his first major moves in office, he made sure everyone knew it was him—not Janet Reno—

who would be calling the shots, and call the shots he did. It was clear from day one that in the Clinton administration, you either served Clinton and his agenda or you had no job.

Clinton was also not above publicly crushing critics who dared challenge him. One such individual was former Arkansas attorney general Steve Clark, whom I got to know fairly well through the legal fraternity of which we were both members during the 1970s. Steve was an extremely skilled politician, a polished speaker, and one of the only Democrats in Arkansas capable of mounting a serious challenge against Bill Clinton in the 1990 gubernatorial election. As the election shifted into gear, Steve was mysteriously and viciously targeted by an audit of his expense reports. The allegations were trivial, but they were sufficient to end his career and clear the path for Clinton to run for governor and later president.

The same message was heard loud and clear at the Department of Justice when Clinton became president. Truly effective attorneys general rarely last an entire administration; those who do the bidding of their boss in the White House enjoy long tenure. It is no accident that Janet Reno enjoyed one of the longest. If you stuck by Clinton no matter what, you would be rewarded. At the time, we did not know that Clinton would reward a young lady named Monica Lewinsky for filing a false affidavit by offering her basically any job in the country she wanted. However, we did know that Webb Hubbell was handed a massive check on his way to jail in the form of so-called "legal fees." There is no doubt that Clinton himself—or top figures in the administration—orchestrated a series of payments from campaign donors to Hubbell that far exceeded any legitimate services he might possibly have performed.

Persons on Clinton's staff were not the only ones enabling the president. Much of the stonewalling mentality at the White House resulted from Hillary Clinton's involvement in the process. By all accounts, Hillary had a significant problem keeping her delusions of persecution under control. In her mind, someone—the media, Republicans, whomever—was always conspiring to get her and Bill. This resulted in her repeated insistence on meeting any request for legitimate information with a mute wall of noncompliance. Needless to say, trying to hide the truth is quite possibly the worst management approach a president can take. The facts usually come out eventually, and—as many historians have noted—the crime is almost always far less damaging than the cover-up.

Anyone who watched the entire Clinton presidency and still had doubts about how little he cared for the office need only have observed his actions during the last days of his failed presidency. First, he started handing out presidential pardons like candy, embarrassing himself and many of his allies on Capitol Hill. Then his staff systematically vandalized the White House on their way out the door, like a bunch of school kids playing a graduation day prank.

Many in the news media—and many Republican leaders— argued that vandalizing the White House was small potatoes, something that was not worth much time in the national spotlight. Our party's campaign gurus felt that calling attention to the problem would cost us points in the polls because the public would think we were being petty and trying to take one last shot at Bill Clinton as he left office. Well, I will tell you something. People did care. I cared. Their behavior was like the icing on the cake for an administration that had repeatedly disrespected everything our nation held dear. It was like scribbling "Jimmy loves Suzy" on the Declaration of Independence in the National Archives or spray painting a peace sign on the Lincoln Memorial. Sure, it was not going to cause the collapse of our national fabric, but it was a symbolically powerful sign of exactly how the Clinton White House viewed the nation it was elected to represent.

Although I was warned not do so by the GOP leadership and representatives of the incoming Bush administration, I ordered an audit from the General Accounting Office. At a minimum, I wanted a full accounting of everything the Clinton people had done to 1600 Pennsylvania Avenue as they left office. When that report came back, it showed that more than $20,000 in expenses was required to repair the damage. That is not much in terms of the federal budget, but remember that we are talking here about a single building. Imagine how trashed your own house would be if the bill to repair the damage totaled $20,000. The list included the destruction of more than sixty computer keyboards, desks that were glued shut, overturned furniture, and trash piled in the middle of offices. Everything from doorknobs to a presidential seal had been looted.

This was not the first time Clinton staff had shown their contempt toward the physical property they were entrusted to protect. After one flight by Air Force One to Clinton's new home, the presidential aircraft was cleaned out of anything that was not bolted down. Mysteriously, many of these items showed up on Ebay, offered for auction shortly after their disappearance. In 1994, Clinton's team had even ripped off towels from the Navy aircraft carrier *USS George Washington* while on their way to a D-Day commemoration in France.[7] And these are just the instances in which theft was noticed and reported. God only knows what these people got away with otherwise.

This leaves me with two questions. What kind of petty, vindictive, juvenile delinquent would scrawl profanity on the walls of the White House? What kind of president would hire the small army of such individuals it would take to do this much damage to a national treasure? Predictably, the DNC giggled in response, the new Bush administration turned a blind eye, and Bill Clinton certainly was not interested in responding, but I think this particular incident stands as a powerful historical marker to the kind of mentality that pervaded all levels of the Clinton administration during its eight years in office.

As the late Barbara Olson detailed in her analysis of the closing days of the Clinton administration, the Clintons themselves were certainly not shy about loading up as much taxpayer property as they could and carting it off to their new mansion in New York.[8] In what can only be described as looting, Bill and Hillary backed a truck up to the White House and carted off numerous items, many of which they were forced to return after they were later found to be taxpayer property. The night before Clinton left office, as my wife Jeri and I were driving past the White House heading to a reception, she noted a white moving van parked at the portico. She turned to me and said, only half jokingly, "There they are, stealing stuff from the White House right before they leave tomorrow." Only later did I discover how right she was.

For most Americans, it is not difficult to imagine what would happen if we were caught trying to haul more than $20,000 in taxpayer property out of a federal building. We would be convicted and jailed in short order. Somehow, I do not think the excuse that it was all a big accident ("oops, so sorry, you can have the stuff back") would cut it. But that line of reasoning worked out fine for Bill and Hillary.

Additionally, not content to live on their outrageous and unprecedented multimillion-dollar post-White House payments from book deals, speaking fees, and other business, the Clintons felt the need to extort pricey gifts from numerous individuals with personal interests in national policy. As Barbara Olson puts it, Hillary "took the trouble to register with luxury retailers, as though she were about to become an impoverished new bride." The list of gifts the couple ultimately received includes everything from fine china to sculpture to sofas to a $450 pair of cowboy boots. This is precisely the same kind of petty corruption for which Clinton's secretary of agriculture was sent to jail. Other elected officials across America—including former New Jersey senator Bob Toricelli—have learned the hard way that you cannot take bribes, even if it is just a Rolex watch. Not Bill Clinton, though. Once again, he broke the rules and got away with it. The only reason this particular example of corruption seems small is because the other instances in which it occurred during his presidency are so large.

The greatest final abuse of power Bill Clinton achieved was not the largest of his presidency, but it was probably the most difficult to defend. Even his most hardcore defenders, people who would follow him off a cliff, seemed dumbfounded when Clinton gave out last-minute pardons to 177 convicts under extremely questionable circumstances. Here was an abuse of power so naked and obvious that no one with any ability to think independently could defend it with a straight face. It was a system of supply and demand gone completely out of control, and the commodity being sold was the integrity of the U.S. legal system.

The list of pardoned individuals included Susan McDougal, who went to jail rather than testifying about her role in the Whitewater affair. Former HUD Secretary Henry Cisneros was let off the hook for lying to the FBI about payments made to a mistress. How's that for hush money? Perhaps the most notorious case involved that of fugitive financier Marc Rich, whose pardon was successfully lobbied for by his wife Denise and DNC fund-raiser Beth Dozoretz, both major donors (and gift givers) to Bill Clinton. These were not minor gifts. For example, Denise chipped in a tidy $450,000 to help build the Bill Clinton monument—oops, I mean library—in Arkansas. At the time, her husband had not only committed serious federal crimes, but he was also still running from American authorities, hiding out in Switzerland. No other president would have even considered pardoning this guy, but for a sufficient fee Clinton gladly stepped up to the plate.

If Clinton was going to benefit from improper pardons, it was only fair for him to let his entire corrupt extended family have a slice of the pie as well. Hugh Rodham (Hillary's brother), Tony Rodham (another Hillary brother), and Roger Clinton (Bill's brother) were all actively seeking cash payoffs for delivering pardons from their brother and sister. Those payoffs included everything from a Rolex watch to hundreds of thousands in cash. The same kind of low-rent corruption that was a hallmark of Clinton's time in Arkansas had now soiled one of the greatest and heretofore constitutionally respected powers of the presidency—the power to pardon.

Since payoffs to relatives were clearly in order in determining who got pardons, why shouldn't Hillary herself get directly into the act? Why not, indeed. Hillary jumped into the pardon fray, using her considerable leverage with Bill to free any criminal who might boost her Senate run. Four Hasidic men convicted of stealing millions from the federal government in New York got pardons from Bill, and then their area of the state—which generally votes Republican—turned out a statistically unbelievable number of pro-Hillary votes.[9] New York Democratic politics being what they are, one cannot patronize just one ethnic group. So Hillary moved to solidify her Puerto Rican constituency by convincing Bill to offer clemency to sixteen members of a terrorist group known as the FALN, a Puerto Rican separatist group. In 1975, the group bombed a tavern in Manhattan, killing four and wounding fifty-six Americans. It was responsible for numerous other bombings, and there is no indication the pardoned terrorists were remorseful for their actions or that they would not commit similar acts if released. For an administration that professed to be concerned about terrorism, this was a slap in the face of every law enforcement officer who had ever worked to capture a terrorist and every family that was victimized by one.

If nothing else, the pardon scandal was so indefensible that it prompted President Clinton to do something he almost never did: publicly defend his actions. In an op-ed published in the *New York Times*, Clinton trotted out one lame excuse after another to defend the indefensible. The piece is, in a word, laughable. There was no way to explain away this particular abuse. Practically every lawyer who got anywhere near the process—Democrat or Republican, public or private—warned Clinton that he was seriously deviating from prior pardon policy, making poor decisions, and likely violating the law. Blaming someone else in time-honored Clinton fashion would not work either; granting pardons is a purely presidential prerogative. Bill's name was signed on each pardon, and he could not well accuse anyone else of doing it. The trick of blaming Republicans would not work either. It did not take an investigation to uncover this information, but again Republican leadership was characteristically silent. To this day, Clinton has yet to express any remorse or regret for his actions in this area.

One of the most insidious things the Clinton presidency left for America was an almost complete debasement of the idea that the president also has a responsibility to lead in ethics and morals as well as public policy. Our first inklings of this problem in the 1992 campaign came when one sleazy scandal after another seemed to overtake the Clinton campaign. Whether it was draft dodging, marijuana smoking, questionable financial activities, or a parade of allegations of adultery, the one consistent thing was that another scandal always waited on the horizon. Perversely, the thing that seemed to save Clinton during the campaign is that the scandals were so sleazy and disgusting that many people simply did not believe the charges. After all, they reasoned, how could a serious presidential candidate be this out of control in his personal life?

If this problem first surfaced during the campaign, it reached epidemic proportions during the impeachment. The most consistent defense offered by the coterie of hard-core Clinton defenders that fanned out to fashionable watering holes every night and talk shows every Sunday to defend him was that a moral dimension to presidential leadership simply does not exist. In other words, the only responsibility the president has in office is to perform "official" functions—to send legislation to Congress, hold cabinet meetings, manage the economy, and act as commander in chief of the armed forces. So, this logic goes, the president can do anything he wants in his private life, just like "average" citizens. Moreover, they argued, didn't great leaders like Roosevelt and Kennedy govern with a whiff of salacious personal scandals floating in the background?

Like so much of what Clinton and his defenders said, this may not be technically untrue. The Constitution does not expressly proscribe a president's personal conduct, nor should it. That does not mean, however, that the president gets, or was even entitled to receive, a free pass for behaving like a depraved Caligula in the Oval Office. Everything the president says, everything the president does, gets magnified and repeated by thousands of little Bill Clintons in communities around America. And, of course, in 1789 or in 1996, a crime—"high" or otherwise—is a crime. Murder is murder and

Bill Clinton in televised broadcast during Lewinsky case.

perjury is perjury, whether committed while one is sitting at a desk in the Oval Office or at a table in a law firm conference room.

Clinton showed the most blatant disregard for this dimension of the presidency when he stood before the entire nation and made a blanket denial about Monica Lewinsky. In this jaw-jutting, finger-wagging moment, Clinton lied to each and every American. If the top official of our government could do this, why should the fun stop with him? Why should any American care about telling the truth or about any of the other myriad standards of character we try so hard to instill in our children?

We now have public uncertainty over whether using the "F" word on the radio airwaves and network TV should be allowed. Or if allowed, should it be allowed in one context and banned if used in another, as the Federal Communications Commission formally concluded early in 2004? As the ghost of Clinton reminds us, it all depends on what the meaning of "F" is. We have leaders who seem truly confused over whether marriage should be between a man and a woman, a man and a man, a woman and two men, or vice versa. We have middle and high school students caught engaging in oral sex and offering as a defense the memorable phrase "it isn't sex." Guess who these young hedonists cite as the authority for that one? Perhaps most famously, we have Super Bowl halftime shows featuring everything from public nudity to, as Senator Zell Miller so aptly put it, an "ignoramus with his pointed head stuck up through the hole he had cut in the flag of the United States of America, yelling about having a bottle of Scotch and watching lots of crotch."[10] Guess it all depends on what the meaning of "is" is . . . .

Is Bill Clinton personally responsible for all of this? No. It all began happening before he was elected, and it will continue to occur far long after his term of office ended. But repeatedly cheating on his wife and child, abusing the trust of an intern half his age, blatantly violating campaign laws, and being self-centered enough to do things like park Air Force One on the LAX tarmac to enjoy a $400 haircut did not set a good example for anyone. The problem is like trying to charge with arson someone who throws a can of gas into a house already consumed by flames. They did not start the fire, but they also did not help anyone else put it out. When that person is the president of the United States, people notice and, unfortunately, many emulate.

As a member of Congress, one group of people you meet with frequently is schoolchildren. One of the great ironies of American politics is that those who are too young to vote often take a great interest in the operation of government, while many adults are generally quite satisfied to go through life pretending as if Washington does not exist. Before Clinton's personal life took the national stage, visiting schoolchildren with whom I met on the steps of the U.S. Capitol—literally in the shadow of the statue of freedom atop that great cast-iron dome—tended to ask about flags, statues, the Constitution, and the other trappings of government on Capitol Hill. During impeachment, these questions still came up but were frequently replaced by ones of a different character. Kids as young as third grade asked more than once about the "president's girlfriend," innocently assuming this kind of behavior was another perk of office. More than anything else, this experience brought home how far Clinton's actions had lowered the majesty of the office of president and how far into the roots of our society the disease had spread.

3

Ripping Away at Our Rights:
Clinton and the Constitution

If there was one unshakable belief at the core of Bill Clinton's being, it was that Americans were incapable of making the smallest of decisions without his input. Of course, he could not find the time individually to tell all of us how to live our lives, so he resorted to using government—first in Arkansas and then in Washington—to ensure that as many Americans as possible were forced to live according to his rules.

As one might imagine, this belief put Bill Clinton on a collision course with the Constitution, most notably the Bill of Rights. However, as author James Bovard—the best writer covering the federal assault on freedom in America today—succinctly puts it in *Feeling Your Pain*, "[t]he Clinton recipe for public safety was: if politicians frighten enough of the people enough of the time, then everyone will be safe."[1] No area of personal behavior was too small for Clinton to micromanage and there was no provision in the Constitution he would not ignore in order to achieve this goal.

The Second Amendment was initially and predictably one of the first targets of the incoming president. In fact, chipping away at our right to keep and bear arms was one of the few things Bill Clinton seemed to believe in doing consistently throughout his presidency. Early in his administration, Clinton stated his support for moving toward a complete ban of handguns, telling *Rolling Stone* in 1993 that "I don't think the American people are there right now. But with more than 200 million guns in circulation, we've got so much more to do on this issue before we even reach that."[2] In 1994, as negotiations were under way in an attempt to settle Paula Jones's sexual harassment suit, Clinton was personally twisting arms in Congress to ensure passage of his "crime bill" with its infamous gun ban and midnight basketball programs. If nothing else, the sheer creativity of Clinton's assault on our rights was impressive. We had gun buyback programs, mandatory trigger locks, attempts to force cops to carry weapons that would not fire reliably, and repeated attempts to keep "dangerous" antique firearms out of the hands of collectors and museums. This was a man who was singularly fixated with the idea of disarming the American populace in direct violation of the Second Amendment and the right to keep and bear arms that it protects.

The Clinton administration never let the truth stand in the way of its obsession with gutting the Second Amendment either. In the late 1990s, the latest craze in the anti-gun community was the idea of using lawsuits to hold gun manufacturers responsible for the actions of criminals who use guns. This logic is, in a word, preposterous. It makes exactly as much sense as suing Ford Motor Company for drunk driving deaths because that company makes the cars drunk drivers drive, or suing Motorola for drug violence because it makes the cell phones used illegally by drug dealers. Like guns, cars and cell phones are often used in crimes, but stopping crime is a job for law enforcement, not for the companies who make automobiles or communications technology. Judges have agreed with this at an extraordinarily high rate, practically laughing lawsuits against firearms companies out of court. A product is only as good or bad as the person using it.

However, the great weakness of gun companies—a circumstance anti-gun activists quickly identified—is that they do not have deep pockets. They are typically small, family-owned companies without the revenues or cash reserves to defend themselves against a barrage of lawsuits, at least without also filing for bankruptcy. The Clinton administration wanted badly to get a piece of this action, and its lawyers were busily seeking any thread of legal rationale that would allow the federal government to join with ambulance-chasing plaintiff's lawyers and sue gun companies.

Into this vacuum stepped the Department of Housing and Urban Development (or HUD), which prides itself on being the "landlord for three million poor people" in America. HUD concocted the creative—even if not credible—notion that its mission to house all those poor people, some of whom were victims of gun crimes, also gave it jurisdiction to shut down firearms companies. Surprisingly, it turns out that poor people also get shot sometimes. Since HUD had failed miserably in maintaining the safety of the housing projects it owned, what could possibly be a better move than blaming gun companies for those shootings? This is evidently what ran through the minds of HUD's in-house lawyers when they boarded a plane and flew—at government expense—to a posh Manhattan office building where they met with a pack of lawyers who badly wanted to sign those three million poor people up as plaintiffs in a class action suit against gun companies.

First of all, poor people are actually the most likely to be harmed by lawsuits that raise the price of firearms. If you are a criminal, the gun you are buying is most likely stolen or smuggled from a cheap foreign manufacturer. You do not care how much it costs because you cannot engage in your "job" without it. However, if you are a single parent living with your young child in a housing project, the situation is much different. The locks on your door are shoddy, HUD cannot keep the streetlight out front working, and so many criminals lurk around that the police will not even patrol your street. In that situation, many people would want to have a firearm in the home for self-defense, and the Second Amendment guarantees them that right. But if you are poor and the government has jacked up the price of firearms, they are out your price range, so you go defenseless while every criminal outside your door is well-armed. The same thing would happen if the government has banned the sale or possession of firearms in the community in which you live.

Many Republicans in Congress felt the same way I did about these lawsuits, and I convinced the chair of one of the subcommittees on which I served to hold hearings on HUD's trip to New York and on its resulting talks with other announced litigants in these anti-gun company lawsuits. Clearly, the agency was planning a massive lawsuit against gun companies. However, when I asked HUD's top lawyer—Gail Laster—about it, she said HUD "does not plan to bring any action on its own against the gun industry." Yet, just four months later, HUD announced it was moving forward with exactly such a lawsuit. The top lawyer for a cabinet level agency had taken an oath to tell the truth and then blatantly lied to Congress.

If this had happened in any other administration, Laster would have been spending her remaining few hours at work putting the finishing touches on her résumé and hoping like hell she didn't get indicted. Predictably, in the Clinton administration nothing happened to her. In fact, I suspect they ordered her a nice cake at government expense and gave her an "Employee of the Month" plaque to display proudly over her desk. With the prevailing feckless leadership in Congress, no action was recommended against her there either. Here again, breaking the rules was encouraged so long as the policy goal was one the administration supported.

Ironically, the same president who professed such a deep concern for the evils allegedly caused by private gun ownership did not seem to care so much about the issue when it came to raising money for his reelection campaign. A guest invited to the White House to schmooze with Clinton at one of the infamous fund-raising coffees was a stalwart humanitarian named Wang Jung. Jung happened to be head of an arms trading firm owned by the Chinese army. He was also under investigation by the U.S. Department of

Justice for illegally smuggling assault weapons into the United States. While President Clinton was going to great lengths to stop law-abiding American citizens from defending themselves (and simultaneously trying to put firearms companies out of business), he was inviting one of the individuals responsible for putting illegal assault weapons in the hands of criminals to the White House for coffee. Apparently, in Bill Clinton's world, American guns were "bad" but Chinese gun merchants were "good."

The Waco disaster was certainly an early indication that all was not well when it came to respect for individual freedoms among senior Clinton administration officials. In an ill-advised and poorly planned raid on the compound, six sect members and four federal agents lost their lives immediately in a resulting shootout. The initial raid appeared so poorly planned and prematurely executed because officials were eager to get the "considerable media attention" that one top BATF official wrote he expected in a confidential internal memo. Sadly, the media attention the administration ultimately got at Waco resulted from the tragedy it caused, not from the laws it was trying to enforce. At the end of the fifty-one-day siege, only nine members of the Branch Davidian cult would walk out of the fire that burned to death more than seventy Americans, including dozens of young children.

After the tragedy, it became evident that the administration could have captured Koresh without bloodshed, perhaps during one of his many and well-known jogs outside the compound or his visits to businesses in town. Yet federal law enforcement leaders, acting in concert with their Clinton administration political bosses, decided to go in heavy, guns blazing and cameras rolling. They concocted a story about methamphetamine labs at the compound in order to get access to military equipment, personnel, and training prior to the raid. Throughout the crisis, the behavior of federal officials appeared that of individuals who were actively seeking a violent end. Two elderly women who surrendered early were put in chains and charged with murder, sending a message to those inside that they should not follow suit. Despite early evidence that negotiating tactics actually were working in getting individuals out of the compound, the FBI inexplicably took a hard line and ended further departures from sect members. When the final assault on the compound began, the government employed incendiary devices and lethal gases and conducted the assault using modified military tanks and helicopters. The result was one of the most disturbing incidents America had ever witnessed, the use of armored weapons and lethal gas by the U.S. government against our own citizens.

As the compound burned and law enforcement officials congratulated each other, the administration announced that everyone inside had torched themselves to death intentionally. It is still unknown exactly how the fire started. However, officials on the scene were clearly aware that a fire was likely, and yet they made no provisions to have fire engines or other emergency vehicles standing by prior to the raid. In fact, emergency vehicles were deliberately kept back. Much later, the FBI was forced to admit that it did use incendiary munitions after officials—including Janet Reno—testified under oath that they did not do so. Furthermore, Reno ordered the use of massive amounts of CS gas on those inside the compound, despite widespread evidence that it would be deadly—particularly against infants and small children—if used in an enclosed space. Many of the individuals (including the children) may have been killed by federal forces before being exposed to the fire.

There are still numerous questions surrounding the Waco tragedy. At least two things are certain, however. First, top federal law enforcement officials from Janet Reno down behaved as if they wanted everyone in that compound dead, and their actions achieved exactly that result. Secondly, the same top Clinton administration officials participated in an extensive effort to cover up the truth about what really happened at Waco. In fact, the contact number provided to the Texas Rangers captain should he have any questions about what the FBI was authorized to do rang at the desk of none other than White House lawyer Vince Foster. More than seventy Americans lost their lives because of the actions of their government at Waco, and not a single member of the federal government has ever been appropriately punished for what can only be described, at best, as gross negligence.

Ironically, much of the information that ultimately came to public light regarding the Waco tragedy came not from congressional investigators but from outside groups and individuals. This taught me an important lesson, namely that having an outside support structure of citizens and organizations that care about an issue is an invaluable asset. Often, this is the only way to obtain accurate information and make sure new facts see the light of day. I would have the opportunity to apply this lesson in a real way on the road leading to impeachment just a few years later.

The extent to which federal law enforcement agents stuck together to protect their own regardless of right and wrong was also quite disturbing. The most vivid example of this phenomenon occurred one morning before a day of hearings on Waco. We were scheduled to question some of the agents responsible for the events that occurred at Waco. I was convinced—and still am—that some of these federal officials had falsified important evidence.

When the phone rang in my Washington office that morning, the voice at the other end of the line belonged to Bob Mueller, now the director of the FBI under President Bush. I knew Bob from his service in the Department of Justice while I served as the United States attorney in Atlanta. His message was clear.

"Bob," he said, "Don't go too hard on these guys. We know most of them, and they're good people."

That was certainly true. I did know some of them, and they were good people. But many of the men, women, and children who had the bad judgment—or did not get a choice at all—to follow Koresh were good people too. They were dead, and they died because federal law enforcement officers—who were extensively trained to know better—had helped kill them. Just because some of those officers were folks with whom we had worked, and whom I considered friends, did not mean they deserved to get a free pass and not even be asked to explain their role in this unprecedented tragedy. I kept pursuing my hard line of questioning, but as we all know, it was largely in vain. We succeeded in getting important facts on the record, but the official version of the story is still largely one of a fiery mass suicide that the federal government was powerless to prevent. This, like so much of what passes for commonly accepted official stories in Washington, is a lie.

You might think the experience at Waco taught the Clinton administration a thing or two about how respecting the rights of citizens could save lives. Those of us who had such hopes need only look at the Elian Gonzalez case to see how futile they were. As most of us remember, Elian was a six-year-old boy rescued from the Atlantic Ocean by a fisherman, clinging to an inner tube after the boat carrying his family sank and took his mother's life. The same INS that—at Bill Clinton's personal direction—had systematically ignored the immigration laws a few years earlier decided that its number one national priority was returning this child to Fidel Castro in Cuba. In a nation full of illegal aliens, Janet Reno's Department of Justice felt that this single six-year-old child, who barely escaped drowning while trying to flee Cuba, posed the gravest of all threats to American national interests and that no expense should be spared in removing him from American soil.

After endless blundering in litigation and negotiations with Elian's Cuban-American family in Miami, the Clinton administration struck the home where he was living with a ferocity eerily reminiscent of Waco. In a pre-dawn raid, 130 federal agents stormed the small, modest house with automatic weapons drawn, shouting obscenities and spraying tear gas. Numerous individuals—including a TV cameraman—were physically assaulted by the agents, who wore full battle gear and carried enough firepower to stage a military coup in a small country. Fortunately for the cause of truth and justice, they failed to incapacitate a photographer, who snapped a photo that was so dramatic it won him a coveted Pulitzer Prize. The photo itself shows a menacing INS agent pointing an MP-5 submachine gun at the head of the young child, his finger near the trigger and at the ready. As any law enforcement official will tell you, the MP-5 has an extremely high rate of fire, and it is most useful for quickly killing several people grouped together in a close space. This has earned it the nickname "room broom" from many who use it, and the intent of arming agents in such a manner is clear.

Against a house full of people who posed no threat, the Justice Department had fielded a paramilitary force sufficient to eliminate a hardened military target garrisoned by a cadre of trained commandos. The only reason this did not result in tragedy is that its targets took the assault remarkably well. Those of us who witnessed the incident were given a vivid reminder that Waco—and other cases of unjustified force resulting in the deaths of Americans, such as Ruby Ridge—had taught the Clinton Justice Department precisely nothing.

In past years, being a Democrat meant having a certain appreciation for civil liberties that went far beyond mere expediency. To be sure, Democrats did not always protect individual freedom, but they were

Elian Gonzalez is taken by U.S. federal agents from his home in Miami.

far more reliable allies for the American Civil Liberties Union than were Republicans. This assumption of American politics cracked and ultimately shattered during the eight years of the Clinton administration. The first sign that this philosophy was dying occurred when many respected liberals went out of their way to cover up actions by federal law enforcement in the Waco attack. It went completely out the window when the Clinton administration introduced its draft anti-terrorism legislation following the tragic Oklahoma City bombing. To Clinton, the bombing provided a golden opportunity to reassert his own relevance in the political process. To do this, he wanted badly to be perceived as a leader whose response in a crisis would cause the masses to adore and respect him. This tragedy would replenish his cache of political chips with which to exert control over Congress, which at that time—as a consequence of the historic losses Clinton's party suffered in the 1994 elections and the resulting ascendancy of Newt Gingrich to the House Speakership—was threatening to push him into irrelevancy.

Here again, Clinton cared more about political perceptions than policy realities, and the laws he pushed to serve his political ends would have ramifications far beyond the parameters of the vehicle he chose. In this instance, the American criminal justice system paid the price. What is even more ridiculous in retrospect is that the same administration that systematically refused to address foreign terrorism was more than willing to crack down on its own citizens.

The FBI, as far back as I can remember, has always maintained a wish list of new authority it wants to get. One such document was actually leaked to our office as the result of a bureaucratic feud between the Department of Justice and the Bureau of Alcohol, Tobacco, and Firearms (BATF). This "wish list" was one of those truly scary documents that you almost hope you'll go a lifetime without seeing. Although written in confusing bureaucratese, the document essentially proposed a dramatic expansion of the Department of Justice's power in the event of a "terrorist emergency." Among other things, the wish list would have granted the

DOJ new powers to seize assets, conduct wiretaps without court orders, and force companies to cough up private information on their customers.

Most troublesome, according to this wish list, the department would have been able to commandeer and use at will commercial transportation assets and personnel from other agencies, including military agencies. Traditionally, of course, the military has been prevented from any involvement in domestic law enforcement under so-called "posse comitatus" laws. As authoritarian regimes around the world have shown time and again, there is a good reason to keep domestic law enforcement and military action separate. Military forces are simply not trained or equipped to deal with domestic crimes (at least in a society based on the rule of law), and asking them to do so invariably results in tragic consequences. The "wall" thus erected is not a "technicality" but rather a fundamental building block of a free, democratic society. Any effort to break down this wall should be taken as a significant warning sign to vigilant citizens.

At the time, the Justice Department was preparing the new proposal as something to shop around to its allies in Washington in hopes of seeing all or parts of it enacted. Were it not for the fact that it took power away from competing federal agencies, this document would probably never have come to light. A reliable source at BATF gave our office a copy of the proposal (with official blessing), since the BATF—which at the time was controlled by the Treasury Department rather than the Department of Justice—would have been one of the primary losers if the new proposal were enacted. Justice, of course, publicly denied it had been considering the proposal once we publicized it, but many of its provisions have subsequently become enacted bit by bit, often as amendments to unrelated bills and later in the USA PATRIOT Act.

When the Oklahoma City bombing occurred, the House Republicans had just finished meeting our obligations under the Contract with America. In our rush to pass the contract in the first one hundred days, however, our leaders seemed not to have thought about what we would, could, or should do next. In short, there was no phase two. The Contract with America was a brilliant campaign game plan (the original now resides in the Smithsonian Institution) and an excellent initial strategy to seize momentum from the Clinton administration, which until the election of 1994 was riding high. Republican failure to follow up on its success left a major vacuum in the national policy arena. Bill Clinton, unlike Newt Gingrich, correctly remembered that in politics, a vacuum invites filling. The FBI knew it too.

During the Clinton administration, we saw an unholy alliance of convenience between federal law enforcement bureaucracies desperate to expand their power and a president on a desperate quest to recover some of the legitimacy he lost through an almost endless series of scandals. Although the FBI still gets most of what it wants from Congress, at least some of us had learned to ask a few hard questions and stop the most overblown proposals. Up until the Nixon Administration, however, the bureau pretty much got whatever it wanted. But Watergate brought with it an appreciation for how much a malevolent president and his staff could do to abuse unchecked FBI powers. Since then—or at least until September 11—the FBI has been forced to justify its requests for new power, a prospect it generally finds far less than desirable.

It was on this very issue that I won my first significant legislative victory as a freshman member of the House in 1996. In response to a series of incidents, including the TWA airline crash (later ruled to be an accident), the Olympic bombings in Atlanta, and the Oklahoma City tragedy, the Clinton administration—with the generous assistance of the FBI—drafted a massive anti-terror package and sent it to Congress. The presumption of the FBI and the administration at the time was that the bill would quickly be rubber stamped by a Congress eager to appear active on an issue that was clearly a pressing concern. Consequently, they stuffed the measure with everything the Justice Department had wanted to get for years.

I am anything but a supporter of terrorists and criminals. I spent a large portion of my adult life working for the CIA and prosecuting criminals at the Department of Justice, so I am not unsympathetic to law enforcement. However, I have a theory about law enforcement: investigations can be hampered more than benefited by new authority and fancy technology. In my experience—privacy concerns aside—relying too much on sophisticated laboratories and massive wiretapping operations rather than on shoe-leather police work often resulted in cases that took too long to bring to trial and were far too weak and complex once they got there. For example, wiretapping can quickly overwhelm an investigation, particularly if multiple targets are involved or language barriers are present. Merely trying to cope with the resulting information is like trying to drink from an open fire hydrant. Despite the shortcomings, many agents like these methods because they are easier in many ways than old-fashioned investigative work.

In addition to often making law enforcement less effective, new authority always carries with it a loss of freedom. Power, like matter, can neither be created nor destroyed. Enacting new laws is a zero-sum game, where new authority granted to the government must come at the expense of individual freedom. Government obviously needs power to do its work effectively, so the operative question is where to strike this balance. Federal agencies need enough power to ensure security (to the extent security is ever possible in our uncertain world), but we do not want them to have so much power that freedom is lost.

The package the Clinton administration sent to Congress in 1996 did not even try to strike such a balance. However, there were real and serious problems with the bill. One was a proposal to put a substance known as "taggants" into everything from gunpowder to commercial explosives. Unfortunately, there was no evidence that such materials—which were intended to allow law enforcement to trace the source of weapons and explosives used in crime—would achieve their intended result. As one might imagine, the nature of an explosion is such that designing materials that—after the explosion—will identify the device that caused it is exceptionally difficult, if not impossible. Although there was no evidence taggants would achieve their intended result, there was significant reason to believe they would have unintended consequences. Commercial explosives manufacturers told us that adding them to already volatile compounds might result in accidents of significant scope. In other words, we might end up causing dozens of deaths on mining or construction sites without benefiting law enforcement. Moreover, adding taggants to gunpowder can alter the performance characteristics of ammunition, one reason law enforcement officers do not favor their use in ammunition.

Another request in the bill allowed for so-called "roving wiretaps." Under the existing law, if an agent wanted to tap a phone, they had to convince a judge that there was probable cause to believe the target of the tap was using the phone to commit a crime. This quite reasonable standard struck a balance between the privacy of individuals unrelated to the investigation and the authority law enforcement needed to catch criminals. In the world of roving wiretaps, things would be different. Instead of getting an order to tap a phone, law enforcement agents would receive authority to tap any phone that a target might possibly use. Needless to say, this would result in federal agents listening to a great many conversations on numerous different phones involving innocent people discussing all kinds of topics unrelated to the investigation.

These provisions—and many others in the bill—made me feel strongly that there needed to be hearings and an amendment process applied in committee to the president's package before it hit the floor. However, GOP leaders—including Henry Hyde and his counterpart in the Senate, Orrin Hatch—felt that they had the votes to pass the bill and wanted to do so as quickly as possible. So I set out on a campaign to educate my fellow House members. I sent "Dear Colleague" letters to everyone on these issues, held meetings with my colleagues, worked closely with such diverse groups as the ACLU and the NRA, and talked about the issues to any media outlet that would listen. Beyond getting under their skin a bit, I do not think the leaders of the House and Senate felt that my work was having much of an impact because they continually blew me off and brought the bill to the floor.

When the bill arrived on the floor, we had a surprise waiting. By banding together with libertarian-leaning conservatives and civil libertarians in the Democrat ranks, I had secured enough votes to pass an amendment removing many of the problematic provisions from the bill. This resulted in the House and Senate leadership being forced to negotiate with us, incorporate our concerns, and bring a compromise bill that drew wide support to the floor for passage.

I still remember Henry Hyde's remark when my amendment curtailing his bill passed the House. As I walked by he looked at me, chuckled, and said, "Congratulations, Bob, you whipped our ass." Even though I served with Henry as the chair of my key committee (Judiciary) for years after that, he never once used his position of authority in an attempt to even the score, despite the fact that most other chairs kept enemies lists in their heads, if not in writing. This is how I had always hoped the House would work, as a place where honest disagreements could be aired and debated and policies improved for the better. Sadly, there were not many Henry Hydes left in the House of Representatives in the last decade of the twentieth century.

Not only was Clinton not shy about asking for new powers, but his administration was also eager to use them aggressively. As no less an authority than the ACLU put it, Clinton led "the most wiretap-friendly administration in history."[3] While this focus on wiretapping everything in America from cell phones to the Internet did not do much of anything to protect us from terrorism, it cost federal law enforcement a great deal of credibility and represented a real threat to personal privacy.

There are numerous other examples of the Clinton administration casting aside even a pretense of protecting civil liberties and rolling over to give federal agencies any new power they wanted. While federal snooping without sufficient cause is nothing new, the Clinton presidency brought with it significant increases in government invasions of privacy. Bill Clinton believed he could make the world a better place by managing our lives for us, and the only way he could do that was if he knew exactly what we were up to at a given moment. (Of course, his own stonewalling in the face of congressional inquiries, including the impeachment, reminded us that this was not a two-way street).

A classic example of how far Clinton was willing to go in violating personal privacy was posed by the "Know Your Customer" proposal his top financial regulators dreamed up in 1998. One of the administration's favorite tactics for rummaging around in people's private lives was forcing private businesses to do its dirty work and report back to the government. This principle underlay "Know Your Customer," which would have essentially turned every banker in America into a government informant (a fear now realized in the USA PATRIOT Act). Banks and other financial institutions would be charged with tracking each financial transaction we made and reporting back to the government on anything deemed unusual or suspicious. To do this, they would be forced to establish a detailed profile of each customer and report anything that seemed out of character for that customer under a vague standard that would make virtually any transaction reportable. The proposal was so poorly designed that someone receiving a small inheritance or cashing in an old savings bond would likely have been labeled a drug dealer.

Fortunately, Congress had the backbone to stand up to this proposal, passing legislation to end it and forcing the Clinton administration to stand down. The only reason we were this successful is that ordinary Americans were so upset by the proposal that they sent in a record number of comments to the agency responsible for it and kept phones on Capitol Hill ringing off the hook until "Know Your Customer" was withdrawn. Unfortunately, however, this was far from the only example of Bill Clinton trampling across the Bill of Rights in his quest to get as much control as possible over our private lives.

Early in his administration, Bill Clinton declared war on communications privacy. At the time, the Internet was coming into its own as a means for engaging in online financial transactions. However, if citizens were going to truly utilize the potential of this new communications medium, we needed a mechanism for keeping our personal information private. Otherwise, everyone from rogue government agents to unscrupulous high tech criminals would victimize us. Fortunately, private sector innovators had created an effective solution to this problem in the form of encryption technology that prevented anyone but the sender and receiver of a message from reading its contents. At the same time, telecommunications technology—from phone lines to faxes—were developing at a rapid pace, giving individual citizens new opportunities, creating jobs, and making our economy more competitive.

To most Americans, this sounded like a great success story for the free enterprise system. The Clinton administration saw things differently. Having all of this information moving around was a great thing, but only if the government was allowed to sift through it for items of interest. In other words, if Americans were going to communicate with one another, we were obligated to make absolutely certain the government could read our mail. This logic, of course, flies in the face of the Fourth Amendment, which guarantees our right to privacy unless the government can demonstrate it has a legitimate reason—such as probable cause that a crime has been committed—to pry into our affairs. For example, at least until 9/11 the government could not open postal mail and read it unless it had a warrant from a judge to do so. This way, only those reasonably suspected of being criminals could be targeted by investigations, while law-abiding citizens could go unimpeded about their business.

This time-tested balance had worked well for more than a century. When Bill Clinton moved into the White House, he threw it out the window. First, top officials developed a concept called the

"Clipper Chip." In essence, Clipper would have required every American to pay extra for things like telephones so the federal government could force manufacturers to install devices in them to facilitate government monitoring. This would have forced any American who wanted to use the telephone to consent to govern-ment monitoring as a condition of doing so. Predictably, when the public found out about Clipper, the proposal was quietly returned to the dark shelf from whence it came. However, the Communications Assistance to Law Enforcement Act (CALEA) quickly followed it; the Clinton administration convinced Congress to pass this act in 1994. Under CALEA, every phone company in America is legally required to install snooping technology in all its new equipment so that government agents can listen in with ease. Making the slap at the Fourth Amendment even worse, CALEA encourages phone companies to pass along the costs to consumers, further jacking up the costs of telephone services. For ten years now, the federal government has used the powers it obtained in CALEA to push companies to spend their resources making sure law enforcement agents can more easily snoop on our communications.

Bill Clinton certainly did not stop ripping away at the Constitution with attacks on the Bill of Rights. Ignoring the Separation of Powers and attempting to make end runs around Congress was a favorite Clinton strategy, and the use of Executive Orders was his favorite tactic for doing it. In their legitimate form, Executive Orders are simply management tools used by the president to keep federal agencies running in the most efficient manner possible. They reflect the clear intent of laws passed by Congress and merely put a finer point on existing law. Bill Clinton turned this logic upside down, using Executive Orders to legislate—in clear violation of the Constitution—because he though it was too much trouble to be bothered by negotiating with Congress. In typically cavalier fashion, Clinton aide Paul Begala described the strategy thusly: "stroke of the pen, law of the land, kind of cool."[4]

Some of the most insidious sets of Executive Orders were those issued by Clinton on the topic of federalism. A bedrock principle of the Constitution, which is woven throughout the debates over its passage and permanently protected in the Tenth Amendment, is that powers not explicitly delegated to the federal government belong to the state governments and the American people. Although the notion of federalism was being consistently eroded by years of contrary legislation and court decisions, no president had ever directly attacked it. With these two Executive Orders, Clinton changed all that. They essentially set up a system where any conflict between state and federal regulations was automatically decided in favor of the federal law. This meant all an agency that wanted to run roughshod over a state had to do was pick a fight, which it knew it would win because the game was rigged ahead of time by Clinton's Executive Orders. Simply put, this amounted to crippling the Tenth Amendment, and it was done solely by executive action without any involvement from the courts or Congress. Unfortunately, as with most Executive Orders, subsequent administrations, as covetous of power as their predecessors, do not repeal but almost always keep such documents in force.

Clinton also decided that he would use an Executive Order to enact new civil rights provisions without congressional approval. Congress had repeatedly refused to add "sexual orientation" to federal civil rights statutes as a protected characteristic, primarily because we believed that equating the "suffering" of homosexual Americans with the abuses that led to the Civil Rights Movement was ridiculous. Such a change was not needed. Moreover, it would involve private employers and establishments serving the public in discovering someone's "sexual orientation" and then trying to ensure everyone got the same treatment. In short, the policy would have been an unmitigated disaster for American society and our economy.

Bill Clinton, "feeling our pain," predictably felt differently. But instead of taking the time to try to convince the country he was right—which he probably could not do—Clinton simply instituted the new policy unconstitutionally by writing up an Executive Order. These two cases are examples of the kinds of abuses of Executive Orders that occurred during Bill Clinton's presidency. There were many more of them, and their language invariably went far beyond anything offered by previous presidents and justified by the Constitution. For Clinton, the knowledge that any grade-school child has—that there are three branches to the United States government—apparently got cast aside on some playground long ago.

All of Clinton's attacks on the Constitution did not emanate from the White House; many of them were based in lesser federal agencies. One of the most tempting targets for a corrupt president to abuse is the Internal Revenue Service. In terms of the volume of information it has on the personal affairs of every American citizen and its power to arbitrarily ruin an individual's life with its broad investigative authority, there is no more powerful government agency that the IRS. Furthermore, unprofessional and ineffective management and a willingness to do the bidding of its political masters had long characterized the agency. In fact, IRS abuses were one of the factors behind President Nixon's forced resignation. The Clinton administration learned two lessons from its corrupt predecessor in terms of abusing the IRS. The first lesson is the most obvious, namely that no agency was anywhere near as effective at harassing and silencing critics. The second lesson is that it was important to keep one's fingerprints off of IRS abuses in order to avoid the kind of public outcry Nixon faced.

The most notable targets of questionable IRS behavior were numerous non-profit organizations that were perceived as hostile to Bill Clinton. The list of targeted organizations included large conservative public policy research institutions in Washington. The groups were diverse. Some were actively investigating Clinton scandals, while others were doing different things such as trying to stop pork-barrel spending. The only factor uniting them is that they were all targeted by IRS audits, while the Clinton IRS did not investigate a single major liberal non-profit. Although Clinton officials steadfastly maintain they had nothing to do with these audits, this is yet another coincidence followed by protestations of innocence that are not believable.

Why might the IRS be eager to do Bill Clinton's bidding? Think back to the time this was happening. Congress had just conducted a series of high-profile hearings and concluded the IRS was an out-of-control federal agency that ran roughshod over any American citizens who dared criticize its actions. IRS agents, managers, and auditors would target individuals they did not like and ruin their lives with unmerited enforcement actions without anyone in the federal government trying to stop them. Most presidents would not have let this happen in the first place, but Bill Clinton did not lift a finger to stop it. Finally, the Senate had heard so many reports of IRS abuses that it blew the whistle on what the agency was up to. How did Bill Clinton respond? According to the *New York Times*, he proposed the largest increase in the agency's budget in thirteen years and suggested hiring hundreds of new auditors to target even more citizens.[5] Once again, playing the game by Bill Clinton's warped rules resulted in a big payoff.

In addition to eroding the freedoms of large numbers of Americans through his assaults on our constitutional rights, Bill Clinton had virtually no respect for the legal rights of individual citizens. One group of people whom Clinton apparently deemed unworthy of legal protections—or even of being treated with basic human decency—were the women whom he variously seduced, attempted to seduce, harassed, and assaulted.

Paula Jones was perhaps the most notable case. The facts of the Jones case are fairly simple. A relatively junior Arkansas state employee, Jones was working the registration desk at an Arkansas hotel for a conference. There, according to her testimony, she caught Clinton's eye, and he ordered the state trooper who was his armed bodyguard to bring Jones to his hotel room. In the room, he attempted to kiss her, exposed himself to her, and repeatedly requested sexual gratification. Jones refused, and Clinton allowed her to leave with an unmistakable warning: "You are smart. Let's keep this between ourselves."

With these words, Clinton let Jones know there would be negative consequences for her if she reported what had occurred in that room. Clinton may even have recognized through his libido-induced fog that his actions constituted sexual harassment. Throughout the encounter, Governor Clinton made repeated references to his close relationship with the head of Jones's agency and offered to use his influence with her boss. As an employee making slightly more than six dollars an hour, Jones was under enormous pressure to comply with Clinton's demands in order to better her circumstances. Without boring you with a boatload of legalese, this constitutes a likely case of *quid pro quo* sexual harassment under Title VII of the Civil Rights Act. Indeed, based on the downward trajectory Jones's career path took after her refusal to accept Bill Clinton's advances, there is a more than plausible claim that she suffered significant punishment from the state bureaucracy, although given the length of time that has passed since then it is difficult to know for sure. Furthermore, the incident was so dramatically untoward that it could likely sustain a hostile working environment claim by itself. In this particular instance, Clinton had exposed himself not only physically but also legally—to a potentially large civil claim for sexual harassment.

One would think Clinton would have realized he was wrong, apologized, and gone out of his way to make sure Jones was treated fairly as a state employee. This, of course, did not happen. Instead, Jones was forced to file a civil lawsuit in order to seek justice and clear her name.

In response, Team Clinton distinguished itself through such tactics as James Carville's remark that "if you drag a hundred dollar bill through a trailer park, you never know what you'll find."[6]

The label clearly stuck like glue, due largely to what one senior journalist told columnist Stuart Taylor, Jr.—the fact that the allegations were coming from "some sleazy woman with big hair coming out of the trailer parks."[7] True, Paula Jones was not someone that the bureau chief of any Washington media outlet would consider inviting to their Georgetown drawing room for tea and crumpets. She was a low-level state employee from Arkansas and came across exactly as such on television.

But does being a low-level state employee from Arkansas who was victimized by the governor—and now president—grant a citizen anything less than equal protection of law? Of course not. The United States Supreme Court ruled unanimously that Jones was allowed to sue President Clinton for sexual harassment while he was in office. One may certainly disagree with the underlying concept and legal application of sexual harassment laws. In particular, the discovery process associated with such lawsuits can wrongly make deeply personal and private facts public knowledge. However, Bill Clinton was a strong supporter of laws against sexual harassment and other forms of workplace discrimination. Rather than confessing that he had used bad judgment and settling the suit, however, Clinton decided to argue that the law did not apply to him. He repeatedly used this argument in an attempt to force Paula Jones out of court, and he would most likely have succeeded if the Supreme Court had not ruled unanimously that the lawsuit should go forward.

The Jones lawsuit, of course, would lead directly to the Monica Lewinsky matter that resulted in President Clinton's impeachment. In terms of the merits of Jones's case—which was quite convincing to many experienced legal observers—we know the president's defense team took it seriously enough eventually to pay her $850,000 to settle, clearly not the behavior of a man wrongly accused of sexual harassment.

As we know, Paula Jones was by no means the only woman targeted by the Clinton smear machine. Kathleen Willey was the wife of a major Democratic donor who had the bad luck to be an attractive woman stuck in a room alone with Bill Clinton at the White House. In typical fashion, Clinton reportedly used the opportunity to grope her in what can only be described as a sexual assault.

After the incident, Willey's husband committed suicide, leaving the family in dire financial straits and putting Kathleen in a position where she felt forced to be courteous toward the White House, since a government job might be her only means of avoiding bankruptcy.

The incident probably would never have come to light had it not been for the fact that Willey was called as a witness in Paula Jones's civil lawsuit. Almost immediately, she was subjected to enormous pressure to sign documents saying that Clinton had not assaulted her. When she refused, odd things started to happen. Someone used a nail gun to flatten all four tires on her car. Her cat Bullseye mysteriously disappeared. Then a jogger approached her one January morning as she was walking her dogs. The jogger asked about her flat tires, her missing pets, and her kids, leaving the ominous warning that "I hope you're getting the message." Clinton's defenders laughed these charges off, but I and many other observers—such as then-CNN commentator and leading Democrat Bill Press—viewed them as credible and troubling. In a nationally syndicated column written for the *Los Angeles Times*, Press argued that after Willey's interview, it had become inescapably apparent that "this President has a problem dealing with women" and the "daily, almost incoherent denials" were not working anymore.[8]

Willey's story is believable because her account fits prior Clinton responses to accusations of personal misconduct. In this case, the stakes were extremely high for Clinton because she was such a credible witness. Past allegations had involved women that—for various reasons—were easy for the Clinton team to smear and discredit. Kathleen Willey cannot be described in that way. She was a highly credible witness with no incentive to lie, and Clinton knew that if her story came to light, it would stick.

For this reason, it is not surprising that the White House got directly into the act, dredging up letters Willey sent when she was desperately seeking a job following her husband's death, and releasing them to the press. The goal was to portray Willey as yet another stalker obsessed with the president through no fault of his own. Releasing the letters likely violated federal law and clearly constituted an abuse of power. In this case, President Clinton was directly and personally involved in the smear campaign. According to depositions taken by Judicial Watch in its litigation, Bill Clinton personally called James Carville to get his advice about how it would play politically if he released Willey's letters, and he talked to other associates about her as well. This was therefore not a decision made by low-level advisors, but one in which Bill Clinton took an abiding personal interest. Once again, Bill Clinton's sleazy personal conduct had led to criminal acts directed against a U.S. citizen, followed by the use and abuse of his office to cover up the incident. This was a frequent pattern of behavior in the Clinton administration, and it is exactly the kind of abuse of power that qualifies as an impeachable offense.

Kathleen Willey maintained contact with me long after the impeachment, calling periodically to see if there was something—anything—we in the Congress could do to help her get justice or at least a fair hearing. I tried, but the Republican power structure, of course, had washed its hands of the impeachment matter in all its aspects the day the Senate rendered its "not guilty" verdict in February 1999.

The most disturbing case that came to light during the impeachment proceedings was that of Juanita Broaddrick. Broaddrick was a nursing home operator in a small Arkansas town. According to her account, Clinton first met her when visiting her nursing home for a campaign stop. He invited her to stop by his campaign headquarters, which she did on a later trip to Little Rock for a conference—along with a friend—because she wanted to "pick up all that neat stuff, T-shirts, buttons." After calling Clinton to see when he would be at the headquarters, Broaddrick talked to him and he offered to come by her hotel and have coffee instead. Upon arrival, Clinton suggested they have coffee in her room since the hotel lobby was crowded. She agreed, thinking they would discuss the campaign. What actually occurred—as Broaddrick tells the story and as is detailed in extensive law enforcement records I and the twelve other impeachment managers combed through—was nightmarishly different.

Clinton had no interest in discussing the campaign and instead, according to Broaddrick's account, raped her. She suffered visible and painful wounds to her face from the attack. When the attack ended, she told the *Washington Post* that Clinton's words were, "'You better get some ice for that.' And he put on his sunglasses and walked out the door." In the same interview, we can tragically see that Broaddrick still blames herself for the event, saying "Stupid me, I ordered coffee to the room."[9]

As Broaddrick acknowledges, there were only two people in the room when the rape occurred, and one of them was going to have his version of the story believed no matter what. This was in Arkansas more than twenty-five years ago. Bill Clinton was the attorney general, the top law enforcement officer in the state. There was no such thing as DNA evidence; it was Broaddrick's word against his. She decided it would be futile to file charges and would in fact almost certainly subject her to further physical violence. While her failure to seek charges against Clinton was the wrong choice, it is easy to see why she made it, and it is undeniably the case that her odds of prevailing against him through the criminal process in Arkansas at the time would have been exceedingly slim.

Listening to Juanita Broaddrick's story and reading the details in the records available to us, it is difficult not to admire her courage. Several witnesses who talked to her about the incident immediately afterward corroborate her story. When she did tell her story, she was a mother and grandmother recounting events that she knew could never be firmly pinned down and that were extremely embarrassing. The incident was publicized after Clinton's acquittal in the impeachment trial. Broaddrick did not seek celebrity, nor was she after a book deal. She wanted only to tell a deeply painful story so her granddaughters would know she did the right thing. While no one but Bill Clinton and Juanita Broaddrick will ever know for certain exactly what happened in that Little Rock hotel room, the preponderance of the evidence, including that available to but unread by all but a handful of House members and no senators, supports Broaddrick's account. It is also consistent with Clinton's well-documented inability to exercise control over his desire for personal gratification at any cost and risk to others.

During the impeachment, even though the full details of the Broaddrick assault and other incidents were available to any senator or House member who cared to look at them, many of the details that came out did so only after the impeachment trial had ended. The outcome sent a message to the American public similar to that conveyed by the O. J. Simpson verdict. In that case, the American people learned that celebrities can get away with committing brutal murders if they have a sufficient amount of cash to pay for high-profile lawyers and the celebrity status to maintain a wide following. In the Clinton case, the message was that sexual assaults can be committed with impunity if one has sufficient political power to silence and discredit one's accusers. I have no doubt that the lives of many American women working for and with powerful men had been made more difficult by Clinton's conduct.

In my view—and that of many other observers—Bill Clinton is a felonious sexual predator who used the power entrusted to him by the people of Arkansas and then the United States to cover up his actions. During Clinton's past campaigns, his gubernatorial chief of staff Betsy Wright described one of her major job duties as managing "bimbo eruptions." The goal of such management was preventing the women Clinton attempted to seduce—forcibly and otherwise—from talking. If they could not be prevented from speaking out, the mission was to discredit them by any means necessary. The same pattern followed Bill Clinton into the White House. In affidavits submitted in the closing days of Clinton's Senate trial, *Vanity Fair* columnist Christopher Hitchens and his wife recounted how Clinton operative Sidney Blumenthal shared malicious information on Monica Lewinsky with them to support the case that she was a "stalker" who had victimized Bill Clinton. Blumenthal presumably hoped Hitchens would publicize this information.

The women Clinton targeted were alternately described by the White House as stalkers, whores, liars, and psychologically troubled. In the case of these women, who were victimized by arguably the most powerful man in the world, one would think liberal feminists would be outraged. Yet the allegations were met largely with a deafening silence from the left. The message here from Clinton's core constituency was that he could do whatever he wanted to individual women as long as he continued to toe the liberal line on a handful of policy issues they deemed politically important, such as abortion. The victims of Clinton's unwanted advances and smear campaigns were treated like roadkill by so-called women's rights organizations. They were something to be driven by and perhaps pitied, but no one was going to go out of their way to see they were okay or prevent the same thing from occurring again and again.

The point here is not that Clinton had extramarital affairs while in office. He was not the first president to cheat, and he will not be the last. Bill Clinton's adultery was—in my view—something that was between him, his wife, and God. I am amazed that any spouse would tolerate his brazen behavior, but it is none of my business. However, what was my business as a member of Congress is that the evidence clearly showed that the president of the United States was a sexual predator (and, of course, a perjurer and obstructor of justice). There was a clear pattern. First, Clinton targeted women he believed were vulnerable to his advances and who could not say no due to their station in life or their personal circumstances. When some of these women did say "no," they were subjected to a carefully orchestrated and brutal campaign that involved lawyers, political operatives, donors, and White House staff, with the clear goal of threatening or pounding them into silence.

The Clinton way of doing business was not limited to women who were the objects of Bill's sexual desires. Another person who was run over and flattened by the personal whims of the Clintons was Billy Dale, who had the misfortune of being assigned to run the White House Travel Office at the start of the Clinton presidency.

Bill Clinton and Monica Lewinsky in the White House.

Initially, the "Travelgate" affair appeared to be typical of the kind of small-time corruption that occurred so frequently in the early days of the Clinton administration. As you might imagine, the White House staff does a large amount of traveling to destinations in America and abroad, often under short notice. Consequently, it operates the White House Travel Office, which is responsible for handling these constant and complex arrangements. After winning the election, the Clintons were eager to reward some of their cronies by putting them in charge of this office.

The only problem is that the Travel Office was manned by a nonpartisan staff and led by a man with twenty years of experience and an unblemished record, Billy Dale. The Clintons wanted to get rid of Dale, insofar as he was seen as a professional government employee not subject to their complete control, but they did not want to be accused of firing government workers simply to reward some of their pals. So they decided that destroying Dale's reputation would have to be their first priority, which they did by having him indicted on trumped-up fraud charges. Not coincidentally, the Clinton White House obtained his confidential FBI file—and that of at least one other Travel Office employee—at the same time. Dale was later exonerated of any crimes and was even awarded attorneys fees for the funds he spent defending himself against the baseless accusations. Yet again, the Clintons thought nothing of trampling an innocent person who got in their way over an issue that was hardly worth ruining someone's life. This was the kind of capricious and narcissistic behavior one might expect from, say, Marie Antoinette, not from the elected leader of the world's greatest democratic republic. It was a small issue, but it was far from an isolated one, and it indicated a pattern that would become all too familiar as the Clinton administration progressed.

The Libertarian Party actually seemed to grasp the significance of Clinton's assaults on individual freedom. In a public call for impeachment in July 1998, the Libertarians argued that Clinton "has the worst record on civil liberties since Richard Nixon, and the worst record on economic issues since Fidel Castro. What he's done to the Constitution should be classified as a hate crime."[10] Specifically, they cited the administration's systematic assaults on cherished constitutional principles, most notably those contained in the Bill of Rights. I found myself fully in agreement with their logic, and we became close allies in the impeachment effort, although I still disagreed with the party's position on several issues such as abortion and drug legalization. Interestingly, this disagreement would surface four years later when, in running for election in a new district, the national Libertarian Party, in a move reflective of the old adage about "cutting off your nose to spite your face," worked hard to defeat me over the drug issue, even though on privacy and civil liberties I was—in the words of many of the party's own members—one of their best friends in office.

4

Investigating Clinton: What Went Wrong?

Looking back on the Clinton administration from the perspective of someone personally involved in investigating basically every public corruption case raised against Clinton, I am most amazed that the Monica Lewinsky case is ultimately what got the president impeached. This is not to say that lying under oath and obstructing justice are not impeachable charges or that the remedy we chose was inappropriate. However, these charges pale in comparison to the systematic damage Bill Clinton did to American national security, the office of the presidency, and the civil liberties of individual American citizens. The reason we ended up talking about a tawdry sexual affair instead of these issues stems from a failure of the institutions constructed to prevent the president from abusing his office.

The first bulwark against presidential abuse of power is one the Founders understood quite well. By setting up separate branches of government that would compete with each other for power, they intended the ambitions of one branch to counteract the ambitions of another, resulting in a balanced system of government that protected freedom and governed effectively through competition, tension, and self-interest. As the executive branch has grown dramatically in recent years, the only way for Congress to exercise its power to check the president and federal agencies is through effective oversight. In order for we the people to exercise any of our constitutional prerogatives, we must at least know what the president is doing, and the only way to obtain that knowledge is through holding oversight hearings. Oversight is a critically important function because as the federal government continues to grow in size and responsibility, the *only* way Congress can know whether bureaucracies are faithfully implementing laws is to repeatedly hold focused and effective oversight hearings. Failure to do this amounts to allowing the executive branch to apply laws in virtually any fashion it wants, so long as it is not limited by court action (which occurs relatively infrequently in practice).

Those of us who were elected in the 1994 GOP congressional landslide and believed in the importance of oversight when we arrived in Congress were quickly disappointed. Time and again, the Republican majority in Congress let Clinton and his defenders turn such hearings into discredited circus acts, often within a matter of hours. This was disappointing because we had experienced years of watching the Democrats run masterfully orchestrated oversight hearings that made a real difference in changing policy outcomes or in putting a certain spin on major political issues. Our new majority was bursting with experienced members from state legislatures, local government, and even high federal office. We should have known how to run oversight if for no other reason than that we had watched the Democrats do it for years. Yet we systematically and repeatedly failed to do it right. Worse yet, we never seemed to learn from our mistakes.

Many of us who ran for Congress in 1994 had watched the Democrats in the House systematically sweep under the rug the gross mismanagement that resulted in the deaths of more than seventy men, women, and children in the Waco incident. When we gained control of Congress, it was understood that our first major oversight hearings would focus on uncovering this injustice and holding accountable those responsible for the deaths. The Waco hearings were chaired by Bill Zeliff, yet another VNG or "very nice guy" (the GOP seems to have an abundance of VNGs). Zeliff's pre-congressional experience consisted of running the Christmas Farm Inn, a lovely bed and breakfast in New Hampshire.

Assisting Bill in conducting the hearings was Florida congressman Bill McCollum, who would later attract widespread attention for being perhaps the single most boring speaker to take the Senate floor during President Clinton's impeachment trial. I served on the Crime Subcommittee of Judiciary, which McCollum chaired, so we worked closely together. In one of the final in a series of meeting we held among members to plan strategy for the 1995 Waco hearings, McCollum told us his top goal at the end of his process was "to be remembered as a gentleman," in the mold of Senator Sam Erwin (of Watergate hearings fame). I realized early on we were in big trouble.

On the other side, the two Bills were faced by Democrat Chuck Schumer, a formidable street-brawling Brooklyn politician (who is now the senior senator from New York), and Massachusetts congressman Barney Frank (one of the Hill's sharpest debaters). If the Democrats put together a dream team for a debate tournament, I have no doubt they would choose these two guys to chair it. At the outset, our decision to employ alternating chairs on different days (each with their own staffs) virtually ensured a lack of continuity in our work. Needless to say, Schumer made mincemeat of the Republicans in this case by turning the issue into a debate over gun control and whether or not David Koresh was a good guy. Koresh, of course, was most definitely a sick and evil person; every member of the Waco hearing panel on both sides of the aisle knew this. But that still does not absolve the Clinton administration of its responsibility in the deaths of more than seventy men, women, and children, most of whose only crime was having the bad judgment to follow Koresh. Despite this, Chuck Schumer quickly sidetracked the hearings into a debate over child abuse and banning assault weapons.

Giving Schumer an added boost, the Republicans allowed him to schedule his parade of pro-Clinton witnesses in the middle of primetime live broadcast coverage of the hearings. If the Democrat staffers of the 1980s had been in charge, that part of hearing would have taken place at 2:00 AM. Our leaders, on the other hand, were trying to be nice guys and give the appearance that they were deeply devoted to bipartisanship. Predictably, Clinton's congressional allies took the olive branch we extended them and whipped us raw with it. I also suspect this experience discouraged the Grand Old Party from attempting serious oversight on other matters down the road.

No matter how our party managed to bungle a hearing, it always seemed we did things even worse when the next one came along. Take the Whitewater hearings, for example, that closely followed the Waco oversight debacle. The House Republican leadership decided that conducting the hearings in the Banking Committee would be a great idea. Bear in mind that Banking does not attract the most aggressive members of Congress, at least on the Republican side of the aisle. On the Democrat side, however, many of the same ideological firebrands who would run circles around us in Judiciary were present in Banking, drawn there largely by their hatred of any financial institution that had the temerity to make money by providing financial services to their constituents. Additionally, the panel regulated much of the nation's public housing efforts, another area that tended to attract hardcore left-wing partisans. Thus the Republicans were left with a roster top-heavy with VNGs, while the Democrat battalion included a number of disciplined hardcore partisans.

Banking is an important committee to be sure, but one that usually works out of the spotlight, dealing with financial services laws and federal housing policies. Sitting in Banking hearings was often about as interesting as plopping down in the middle of a Midwestern farm and watching the corn grow for eight hours straight. Fortunately, I also served on the Judiciary Committee and Government Reform Committee, which were usually so contentious that Banking often seemed a welcome chance to relax and pour over other files while financial services bureaucrats droned on about obscure statutes or showed us econometric graphs of supply and demand curves. Needless to say, this was not a group of members or staff accustomed to dealing with high-profile public corruption inquiries.

Sending Whitewater to Banking also meant that Jim Leach, an Iowa Republican and former Peace Corps volunteer and diplomat to Russia, would chair them. Jim has what I suspect is a genius-level IQ, and he was one of the most thoroughly decent human beings I have ever known. Unfortunately, to use a canine analogy (which seems fair since I have so often been called a bulldog), Jim had the prosecutorial instincts of a fourteen-year-old basset hound.

The staff on the Banking Committee took the investigation seriously and wanted to present the case in such a way that the public could understand how Bill and Hillary Clinton had illegally manipulated financial institutions to their personal advantage in Arkansas. As a former federal prosecutor on the committee, this task often fell to me. In this area, most of my assigned focus was on building a case that the Clintons had systematically obstructed justice in the Whitewater matter, which was undeniably the case. The stakes were high in this area; if we could develop this kind of evidence, then some of the worst administration officials could be prosecuted for their behavior and removed from office, saving the government from sustaining further damage as a result of their actions.

One of the high points of testimony in the hearing came from L. Jean Lewis, a courageous federal financial investigator who knew something was deeply amiss with the Clintons' business activities in Arkansas, especially those involving Jim and Susan McDougal. When Clinton was elected, Lewis was a federal investigator working for the Resolution Trust Corporation, charged with looking for evidence of criminal conduct that led to the catastrophic failures of Savings and Loan institutions around the United States. Lewis uncovered evidence of such conduct in the failure of Madison Guaranty, an Arkansas Savings and Loan that was involved in the

Clintons' failed Whitewater land development. Some of the evidence indicated that the Whitewater partnership had stolen large sums of money from Madison, contributing to its failure.

This is a complex financial picture, but Lewis concluded—in her professional opinion—that there was more than enough reason to refer the matter to the Department of Justice for prosecution. Predictably, Justice not only sat on her case, but actively obstructed her efforts to move forward. Fortunately for America, this lady was not easily deterred. She had the courage to come tell her story to Congress, even though she knew she would suffer retribution for doing so. Though Lewis is now a high-ranking Pentagon official, she is still being pursued by critics, suffering attacks from liberal journalists who apparently intend to hound her at every new job she takes in retribution for what she "did" to "their" president. In light of the results she achieved and the attacks she faced, Jean Lewis is another example of the way a single courageous American can make a real difference if they care more about what is right than about what is expedient.

Throughout the lengthy hearings, I spent a substantial amount of time carefully building the record on several fronts, notably in showing perjury by administration witnesses. Then, on the last day of the hearings, Leach addressed the witnesses and complemented them profusely, thanking them for doing their best and letting them know he understood their memories were not perfect. In other words, our chairman completely gutted any case for perjury or obstruction we might have. In our leadership's maddening effort to burnish our "nice-guy" image, he gave them a pass on all the issues his own staff had urged me to raise and develop on the record. In so doing, we once again wasted our effort and showed the Democrats in Congress and in the White House that we were paper pussycats. Jim was, of course, being a thoroughly decent guy, but at the time I contemplated taking a few steps up the dais and politely urging him to shut the hell up. At that point, though, the damage was done, as witnessed, I am sure, by the stifled guffaws on the other side of the aisle.

I was still wrapped around the axle about the whole series of events, so I unloaded with both barrels on the Banking staff that had asked me to question the witnesses in the first place. They felt the same way and apparently talked to Leach about it. I had barely returned to my office across the street when the phone rang. It was Chairman Leach calling to apologize. This fiasco taught me the important lesson that I was pretty much on my own in developing such evidence through any formal oversight process in the hands of the official GOP power structure. It was a lesson I would keep foremost in mind and one that would serve me well in developing the case for impeachment.

The Government Reform and Oversight Committee made one of the few other serious efforts to conduct oversight of law violations during the Clinton administration in the House. The committee was chaired by Indiana congressman Dan Burton and was granted a massive budget to hire investigators and hold hearings on numerous matters related to national security, campaign finance corruption, and other issues. Dan was also a good guy, and he was one of the most loyal people I have ever met, almost to a fault. By way of illustration, he once stood up in a meeting of the entire Republican caucus and defended an extremely incompetent aide, sending Newt Gingrich over the edge and earning a blistering rebuke from the Speaker. Dan would be a great guy to have with you in a foxhole, but unfortunately he had no legal or prosecutorial training, having spent most of his professional career in the insurance business.

On the other side of the aisle, we were faced with Henry Waxman. Henry—familiar to many C-SPAN watchers as the man who looks like a chipmunk—fulfills the important responsibility of representing Beverly Hills in the United States Congress. In a House full of Democrats who were extremely skilled at obstructing oversight investigations, Waxman was—bar none—the champ. There was no detail too small for him to pounce on and spend an hour discussing as a grave violation of the most basic standards of American jurisprudence and human decency. He consistently refused to cooperate in authorizing committee action, interfered with subpoenas and depositions, and stuck up for Bill Clinton no matter what he did.

Dan Burton hired an experienced staff of investigators but made the mistake of including among them a number of people with only political rather than legal experience. This resulted in a committee preoccupied with doing what you do during a campaign, namely focusing like a laser on winning each day's news cycle and paying little or no attention to the big picture. This often led to silly and juvenile PR stunts, like mocking up a plywood "wall of shame" across the back of the committee room. Burton also got himself into trouble early in the game by telling the media about the backyard ballistics tests he conducted by shooting at a melon in an effort to prove White House staffer Vince Foster was murdered. While much about Vince Foster's death remains unresolved and Burton raised legitimate questions, the spectacle of him pumping rounds into a melon dogged him throughout his six-year chairmanship of the committee.

The most notable case of how this problem played out with the Government Reform and Oversight staff was in the release of taped phone conversations of long-time Clinton confidant and former associate attorney general Webb Hubbell. At the time, Hubbell was serving a jail sentence, and most of his phone conversations were being recorded (as they are for most inmates). The tapes contained damning evidence that Hubbell had accepted $700,000 in bribes for his silence on matters important to Bill and Hillary. The committee obtained the tapes and began releasing them to the media.

One of the worst mistakes the committee made in releasing the tapes was letting giggling staffers literally toss them out to reporters like candy bars from a cardboard box. Needless to say, this image was recorded and replayed by the media, underscoring the impression that we were rank amateurs in the oversight game who though the whole thing was a big joke. Adding insult to injury, the tapes were selectively edited—not illegally or even unethically, but selectively—to emphasize their incriminating nature. This occurred despite the fact that the tapes were already incriminating without a shred of editing. As one might imagine, this meant that what should have been a story about the Clintons bribing a former DOJ official became one about dangerously obsessive Republicans bending the rules and manipulating evidence to get Clinton.

Sadly, this kind of thing happened time and time again on Government Reform. Adding insult to injury, Newt Gingrich and the other Republican leaders in the House repeatedly pulled the rug out from under Dan Burton. The most damaging example was when they assured him they would back him up if the Government Reform Committee voted to hold Janet Reno in contempt for refusing to provide subpoenaed information (the so-called "Louis Freeh Memo"). When, under Dan's leadership, all of us Republicans on the committee voted to do so (following a vexing day of listening to Waxman rant and rave), the House leadership abruptly reversed course and left Burton and the rest of us holding the bag. In the end, the committee succeeded in revealing large volumes of information that should have been acted on by Judiciary or an independent counsel but were not due to mismanagement, lack of support, and inconsistent proceedings. All things considered, for a situation in which he got insufficient support from both his staff and his leadership, Burton did a remarkable job of uncovering much of the information that Clinton desperately wanted to keep hidden.

The other way in which the system set up to prevent public corruption after Watergate concerns the independent counsel statute, which was proving to be a miserable failure. Although it took until the Clinton administration for Congress to figure this out, several fatal flaws in the law made it worse than having no independent oversight mechanism at all on the books. In the end, the law intended to be used as a sword against wrongdoing would be turned into a shield to cover up wrongdoing.

First of all, putting the attorney general in charge of invoking the independent counsel statute meant that it would only be applied when public pressure reached such a high pitch that its use could not be ignored. In the Clinton case, there were so many scandals that simply ignoring them was not an option. The range of scandals was impressive in and of itself, with everything from small-time corruption to major national security violations. An honorable attorney general would have investigated the serious problems, but this description clearly does not fit Janet Reno. Early in her tenure, Reno figured that the best way to deal with this problem was to appoint independent counsels on small, irrelevant issues and avoid threatening the administration on real cases of corruption. The name of the game was focusing attention on small brushfires, hoping folks would not see the inferno blazing away in the background. So Reno's boss at 1600 Pennsylvania Avenue was investigated—sort of, anyway—for aspects of Whitewater (which was fairly stale and extremely boring) but not for encouraging foreign contributions or for allowing agents of Communist China to infiltrate the United States government at the highest level. Of course, we only got an independent counsel in Whitewater when a kicking and screaming Reno was forced to appoint one.

In other cases, small-fry people like Mike Espy were subjected to massive investigations for—in his case—illegally accepting tickets to sporting events while serving as agriculture secretary. This may have been unethical and illegal behavior, but probably not the kind of thing that needed a $17-million, multi-year investigation. Still, Reno allowed these and other investigations to proceed because she wanted them as cover. By overreacting to small matters, the attorney general bought room and time to ignore larger, truly damaging ones. In addition to the American people and the legal system, the biggest losers in this strategy were the second-tier administration officials who found relatively minor charges inflated to major felonies of national significance. In essence, they were nothing more than chum thrown overboard to draw the prosecutorial sharks away from more tempting targets. As these folks learned, if you were a supporter of Bill Clinton, you had better watch your back at all times because you were always subject to being sacrificed for the "cause."

Reno's behavior left Congress with only a handful of choices, most of which revolved around holding her in contempt of Congress or removing her from office. Although I and others pushed for a contempt resolution, it clearly was not going to happen given that Democrats were united in supporting her and many Republicans did not have the stomach for such an effort. With Congress unwilling to respond, an independent counsel was never appointed to investigate the most serious abuses in the administration, despite the view of Clinton's own FBI director, Louis Freeh, that the independent counsel statute had clearly been triggered in these cases. We were left with a Mexican standoff, and Reno was more than willing to stare us down from the Main Justice building until hell froze over or Bill Clinton became a former president, however that might occur. This strategy actually would have worked out well for the attorney general, except that Clinton violated so many ethical and legal standards so quickly that sheer statistical odds eventually caught up with him, resulting in the Starr report. Ultimately, the only reason Janet Reno did not succeed in completely turning the Department of Justice into Bill Clinton's private defense firm was not lack of effort but lack of competence.

There were also other holes in the independent counsel law that made it easy for a sufficiently corrupt administration to work its way around. For example, the law creating the independent counsel defines which individuals are covered by its provisions based on the salary they are paid. To the writers of this law in the 1970s, this undoubtedly seemed like a reasonable way to limit its application to senior officials. After all, we did not want independent counsels being assigned to investigate, say, the White House gardening staff for a conspiracy to steal a pair of hedge clippers. The Clinton administration took advantage of this hole in the law by simply hiring far fewer people at top salary levels than it was authorized to do. Clinton still hired people for all the positions; he just paid them right below the level that would trigger the statute. As FBI Director Freeh put it, "officials have avoided coverage simply by accepting a salary below level II."[1] Of course, all of these individuals knew they were only getting their big paychecks briefly delayed. They knew full well they could leave the administration and, like other "Friends of Bill," count on presidential assistance to pad their bank accounts. Once again, Bill Clinton, clever boy that he was, had figured out a way to game the system.

Many independent counsels really did come to view themselves as a fourth branch of government. Robert Fiske, the independent counsel appointed by the Department of Justice to "investigate" the Whitewater matter, actually had the nerve to insist that Congress should not be allowed to conduct hearings on the topic because they would interfere with "his" investigation. Amazingly enough, my copy of the Constitution and the *Federalist Papers* express great confidence in the ability of Congress, the executive branch, and the Court to act as checks and balances on one another, but they do not seem to mention the right of an independent counsel to curtail the actions of Congress. White House officials often viewed independent counsels as a threat to their constitutional authority, but what often goes overlooked is that they threatened the prerogatives of the other branches as well.

The independent counsel statute itself (almost as a footnote) mandates referral to Congress of any information deemed by the counsel to constitute a possible impeachable offense. This seems logical at first glance. However, because of congressional deference and confrontation-avoidance, its net effect is to give the independent counsel the power to set the congressional agenda on impeachment. We basically found ourselves sitting around for months, waiting for Starr to make a referral. As America burned, the Republican Party was fiddling away. When Starr's report did arrive, GOP leaders felt bound to consider *only* the information it contained when it arrived. After all, we had waited so long for this report and put so much else on hold that there was no way we could set it aside and move on to something else. This meant that all of the national security related charges against Clinton were ignored, and we were left focusing on the Lewinsky matter alone.

A further problem was that linking the independent counsel statute directly to impeachment meant that the charges we would ultimately be responding to would be criminal charges. This occurred because independent counsels have a mandate to build only criminal cases but are required to refer those cases to Congress when they rise to the level of impeachment (in the judgment of the counsel). Keep in mind, however, that the impeachment process was set up to deal with political charges, which could include criminal charges, but not necessarily. All impeachable offenses are not criminal, and all criminal offenses are not impeachable. The impeachment provisions in the Constitution are set up to deal with what can broadly be described as abuse of power. Impeachment—in the presidential context—is essentially a mechanism for reversing a popular election, and it is designed to be applied when a president is doing so much damage to the country that the only way to stop the bleeding is to remove him from office before the next election. As a report prepared by the Peter Rodino Judiciary Committee during 1974—on which young Hillary Clinton worked—aptly put it, impeachment is "not so much designed to punish an offender as to secure the state against gross official misdemeanors. It touches neither his person nor his property, but simply divests him of his political capacity."[2] Further, impeachment was meant to cover a "course of conduct more than individual acts that have a tendency to subvert constitutional government."[3] In short, impeachment as a constitutional remedy fit Bill Clinton's pattern of conduct in office like a glove. I could not have said it better myself.

Therefore, making a solid case for impeachment meant proving President Clinton was systematically abusing his office and doing grave damage to the nation in the process. In my view, his conduct on national security issues alone was sufficient to merit impeachment. And, as we will soon see, his politicization of the White House and his disregard for the constitutional rights of American citizens provided significant causes for impeachment as well. But because we were essentially stuck making a case that related only to what Ken Starr had sent over, we were limited to arguing about a criminal matter that, while serious, simply did not allow the American people to see the full extent of Clinton's abuse of power. This would come back to haunt us in the Senate trial, and it severely constrained our ability to make a compelling case to the public.

It was easy for the public to see what Clinton had done but more difficult to understand its consequences to the nation as a whole. Those consequences were there, but they were camouflaged by the tawdry details of an extra-marital affair with a White House intern. This was not true of some of the other information. Taking bribes from agents of a foreign power, making violent felons citizens, destroying the U.S. National Security apparatus, and systematically violating the constitutional rights of numerous citizens were clearly official acts with consequences that were undeniably real and serious and that led directly to Bill Clinton's doorstep. But the Republican leadership forgot to ring the doorbell.

Unfortunately for our nation's future, the Republican Party found itself inexplicably drawn away from the national security aspects of Clinton's conduct and pulled toward the more easily digestible charges related to his personal conduct. Everybody— every man, woman, and teenager—understands sex. Few, however, understand the intricacies of national security decision-making, of intelligence policies, or of satellite and weapons system technology. Fewer still—including members of Congress—have the desire to take the time needed to understand these matters.

Consequently, much of what we do know about the depths of Clinton's neglect on national security issues comes from these sources. The first category of information comes from a handful of intrepid beat reporters, most notably Bill Gertz, Pentagon reporter for the *Washington Times*. His efforts deserve a Pulitzer Prize and probably would have received one if he had written the same articles for a left-leaning paper such as the *New York Times*. Of course, given the rate at which reporters for major media outlets are being forced to admit making up their stories out of thin air, Gertz may end up getting such recognition out of sheer attrition among his counterparts.

The second reason we know what we know lies with the efforts of former DOJ attorney Larry Klayman and the organization—Judicial Watch—that he founded. Larry's critics (of which there are many) argue that he is excessively litigious, as evidenced—for example—by the fact that he once sued his own mother. They may be right about that. But there's no getting around the fact that Larry's efforts to carpet-bomb the White House with civil lawsuits brought information to light that would otherwise have gone unobserved.

It is also interesting that Judicial Watch was supported largely by small checks mailed in from people all across America who had become sick and tired of watching Clinton's systematic abuse of power. Depositions and trials are hugely expensive processes, and conducting them from a group that has neither wealthy corporate clients nor taxpayer support can be nearly impossible. The fact that Judicial Watch accomplished as much as it did through the support of so many small donors is itself testament to the national disgust with Clinton, at least among people who were actually paying attention to what was going on.

Finally, at least one sliver of the official Republican Party apparatus expressed some level of consistent concern about these issues. That sliver was Dan Burton's Government Reform and Oversight Committee. Despite the enormous roadblocks put in his way, Dan bravely soldiered on, and he never lost his focus on getting to the bottom of illegal activities and national security breaches during the Clinton administration. The committee's work was not always perfect, but it is the only institution in Congress that seemed able to stay focused on these issues long enough to develop a consistent record of evidence.

If you find yourself surprised and somewhat outraged that a limited segment of the news media and a small outside interest group did much of the early digging that first showed America the truth about the Clinton administration, you should be. Virtually all of the bulwarks we had constructed since the Nixon Administration to limit presidential abuses were failing.

In sum, both official mechanisms set up to prevent presidents from doing things like undermining national security failed in the Clinton case. The results of this failure were significant. Instead of being removed from office when it became crystal clear that he was neglecting his constitutional responsibilities and abusing the powers entrusted to him, Bill Clinton was allowed to remain in office for the remainder of his second term. The resulting damage to America and our national interests is significant.

5

On the Road to Impeachment

As 1997 rolled around, everyone in Washington knew already that Bill Clinton was one of the most formidable political operators ever to occupy the White House. He had no core dedication to principles or moral compass that would limit or hamper his actions, and he possessed an uncanny ability always to take the right political step to cover himself, no matter what. Many people disliked Bill Clinton, and others truly believed he had violated his oath of office and deserved to be impeached. However, practically no one with any status to lose was interested in tangling with someone who had such a robust batting average and a demonstrated propensity for destroying his political and personal enemies before they could inflict serious damage on him.

At the time, we had never heard of Monica Lewinsky. It was, however, common knowledge that Clinton was a compulsive philanderer. All the world knew of Gennifer Flowers. Everyone knew the president's personal life was a disaster zone. But all this was more often laughed at over drinks or at political gatherings than discussed in any kind of serious public forum. What we did know, however, is that Clinton and his allies had damaged national security, violated the rights of individuals, taken away freedoms, and systematically abused the presidency. To my mind, this was exactly what the Founders were thinking of when they inserted impeachment provisions into the Constitution. In *Federalist 65*, Alexander Hamilton wrote that impeachment is directed toward "those offenses which proceed from the misconduct of public men, or in other words from the abuse or violation of some public trust. They are of a nature which may with peculiar propriety be denominated POLITICAL, as they relate chiefly to injuries done to the society itself." In a real way, Clinton (like Nixon) had committed crimes against the nation, and he deserved to be held accountable and punished for them. More importantly, it was critical to stop him from destroying more of our national fabric as quickly as possible.

As a second term member of Congress, deciding to engage in a titanic struggle with the White House is not something you do lightly. If you make an effort to suck up to everyone who passes by your office door and devote a reasonable amount of time to campaigning, regularly trek over to your party headquarters and dial for dollars, you can basically expect to stay in office forever. Of course, for this strategy to work, you also have to avoid making waves and routinely vote with your party (although it is a good idea to vote against the party 2 or 3 percent of the time when your vote isn't really critical so you can say you're "independent"). That said, if you do these things, you can park yourself in Congress almost indefinitely once you get there.

In the most recent election, more than 98 percent of incumbent House members were voted back into office by their constituents. Many of these members have almost no real legislative accomplishments to speak of, yet the people they represent send them back again and again. They are the non-threatening smiling faces that gild Rotary and Kiwanis lunches regularly, visit VFW halls and Moose Lodges, and beam at us from sappy TV commercials every other year.

This situation poses significant problems for you if you think the president has committed such grave offenses that he deserves impeachment and removal. First, you know full well your job can be a cushy one if you sit back, relax, and go with the flow. Jumping into the national spotlight invariably reduces your chances of getting reelected and severely restricts your ability to get a high-paying job as a corporate lobbyist or Washington super lawyer—who rarely or never actually enters a real courtroom—when you leave Capitol Hill. Rather than coasting to reelection year after year, you might actually have to fight to go back, and you could possibly lose. Furthermore, the cocktail party circuit so important to many congressmen is willing to tolerate almost anything except questioning the establishment. And trying to impeach a president would most definitely constitute "questioning the establishment."

Let's take, for example, a typical night in the life of a House member. Walking out the front door of your office, it is difficult to miss the large receptions happening at both ends of the building. Looking back on my schedule for one random night in early 1997, there were sixteen receptions featuring everything from Billy Joel and Garth Brooks lobbying for the recording industry to the Southern Cotton Growers asking for more farm subsidies. You can wander to the nearest one, eat shrimp the size of your fist, drink as many free beverages as you want, and chase desserts from trays as large as Ferris wheels.

This probably explains why many of my Republican colleagues responded to my mention of the word "impeachment" in early 1997 with puzzled stares. It was as if they wanted to tell me something.

"Now, Barr" they seemed to be thinking, "why do you want to go and mess everything up? If you start talking about impeachment, the liberals in my district are going to get energized. I'll have a real race on my hands, and my second career as a lobbyist could get derailed. Ski vacations in Aspen are not cheap, and my new beach house needs a roof. So, you need to just shut the hell up and go find a nice project to fund."

It quickly became the case that impeachment was referred to as "the I-word," and I was the eager youngster who had the temerity and "bad judgment" to utter it on a regular basis. I kept waiting for the hostess from one of the better drawing rooms in a fashionable Georgetown neighborhood to come and attempt to wash my mouth out with soap for saying it, but that moment never arrived. What did arrive—though not unanticipated—was far more brutal.

Fortunately, I was relatively experienced at ignoring the advice of political insiders who prefer what is expedient to what is right. During my days as a United States attorney, appointed by President Reagan a decade earlier, I received evidence that a sitting Republican member of Congress—Pat Swindall—was involved in a money laundering scheme. There were not many Republican elected officials in Georgia at the time, so I anticipated a less than positive reaction to my announcement that I was prosecuting one of them.

Swindall initially went to Attorney General Ed Meese and then his successor, Dick Thornburgh, neither of whom were willing to make any effort to get him off the hook. However, Republican Party officials were less than pleased to see one of their own indicted, and a young congressman named Newt Gingrich was publicly critical of the case my office was building, calling me a "rogue U.S. attorney" on local television. Perhaps the strangest part of the whole episode was that Swindall flew in Massachusetts Congressman Barney Frank to argue that most members are not aware of what they are voting on when they pass laws (in this case amendments to money laundering laws). Although the judge limited much of Frank's testimony, the episode was certainly an interesting one. In the end, most of the critics were silenced when Swindall was convicted by a jury and sentenced to federal prison on charges of perjury, nine counts in fact.

Although Clinton's defenders often argued that prosecution of perjury in civil cases was rare, I knew a thing or two about that as well. When I served as a U.S. Attorney and anti-racism groups brought me some interesting allegations on a top leader of the Ku Klux Klan. This particular individual had led an attack against civil rights marchers in a north Atlanta county. The marchers sued him in a civil case for the attack and he made the mistake of lying about his personal wealth in order to obtain a free transcript of the trial from the federal judge. It turned out that he was not, in fact, poor, but rather had numerous assets. My office then moved forward with a case against him and won a federal conviction for lying under oath in a civil trial, which led to him going to jail. The Klansman's actions were very similar to what Clinton had done, so I knew full well that such cases could be—and were—prosecuted.

I had prosecuted other high-profile cases—particularly in public corruption—largely because the political world in and around Atlanta at the time was ripe with such opportunities. The lesson in all of them was to be sure of your charges before you made them and then relentlessly stay the course.

So I reached a difficult decision different from the traditional wisdom prevalent in Washington, D.C., circa 1997. I resolved to be the first member of Congress to call for the impeachment of William Jefferson Clinton.

I knew this was going to a difficult fight, one that we would have to wage across a range of fronts. I knew I would be outgunned at every turn. My staff consisted of anywhere from fifteen to twenty people, the majority of whom were dedicated but inexperienced young people, often working their first real job in the government. Furthermore, most of their time would continue to be focused on the many other things I was elected to do in addition to upholding the law and the Constitution: handling constituent inquiries, reviewing the masses of legislation emanating from our colleagues daily, and preparing for the multiple committee hearings I generally attended. We were up against one of the most hardcore, experienced, and talented packs of political operatives ever to wander the streets of our nation's capital. The other side had unlimited money, a national media that tilted sharply in their direction, and numerous other assets that go along with holding the most powerful office in the world. Never in my life have I had a deeper and more personal understanding of the way General George A. Custer felt on that western battlefield long ago.

In this effort, our battlefield would be the court of public opinion. One thing I knew with absolute certainty is that Congress would never act on a matter of such potential controversy as impeachment unless forced to do so by the citizens they represent. However, I had great confidence that—if they really learned what was going on in the Clinton White House—many Americans would back House members who had the courage to vote the right way on impeachment. The group of people most likely to respond in this way were those who pay the most attention, the activists who vote in every election, volunteer in campaigns, donate to candidates, and fill the ranks of interest groups.

I adopted the basic strategy encapsulated more than 2,000 years ago by the Chinese military strategist Sun Tzu in his famous work *The Art of War*, a book I kept handy throughout my years in Congress but at no time closer than during the impeachment years. In his book, Sun Tzu wrote that "opportunities multiply as they are seized." In other words, we would concentrate on achieving one step at a time and then use our achievements to further fuel the campaign to get Congress seriously thinking about impeaching the president.

The reaction of many media outlets to my initial call for impeachment was, predictably, vicious. One of my hometown papers, the left-of-center *Atlanta Journal-Constitution*, accused me of being so "blinded by partisanship that he is willing to use any means available to inflict damage on his enemies."[1]

The attacks certainly did not begin or end in my home state or even at our nation's shores, nor did they take place merely in print. One of my personal favorites were the talking heads who simply laughed at what we were doing, saying things like "[i]t is delusional to think that Clinton will be impeached."[2] Then there was the Malaysian paper that called me "one who creates a lot of noise but accomplishes little."[3] So the attacks came in from across the oceans as well, from countries in which Bill Clinton's macho behavior is still admired. The attacks were not just confined to liberals or foreign newspapers. One of my colleagues and a member of my own class of 1994, Ray LaHood of Illinois, made personally disparaging remarks about me in public. In a flash of misguided foresight, GOP pundit Laura Ingraham—a member of the legion of smart, young blonde commentators who took the airwaves by storm during the Clinton scandals—said that impeachment "won't go much further but it is succeeding in making Republicans look disjointed."[4]

Being a mild-mannered guy, I decided to take all of this sitting down, right? Well, not exactly. Actually, I fired back in as many written venues as possible, aiming to take the legs out from under smarmy pundits on their own ground. One of the first articles I published was a long open letter to Hillary Clinton that appeared in the *Wall Street Journal,* which had itself done a great job of systematically laying out the case against Clinton on Whitewater. Basically, I reminded her that, as a young lawyer, she had been assigned by Bernie Nussbaum (who later became a White House counsel) to write a brief on the constitutional grounds for impeachment. In her zeal to go after President Nixon—whom she clearly despised—she interpreted the impeachment provisions in the Constitution in a fairly wide manner, essentially arguing that a criminal offense was not necessary to impeach. She concluded impeachment was about violating the public trust and did not have that much to do with the criminal law. I agreed with her assessment, although I can only imagine how much it annoyed her to be reminded of the words she wrote in such a public fashion in the context of her husband's pending impeachment.

Apparently, Hillary Clinton remembered her prior life well but chose to put a completely different spin on the words she wrote back in 1974, recently reminding CNN's Larry King that she "had been on the impeachment staff back in 1974" and "had actually researched the historical and legal grounds for impeachment." However, Hillary went on to add that she knew "what was being attempted against this president [Bill Clinton] was absolutely out of line with what the founders had thought, what people had always believed was the basis for Constitutional impeachment."[5]

Apparently, for both Clintons, not only does it matter what the meaning of "is" is, but the meaning of "is" can also change dramatically over time.

Another article that played a key role in our impeachment effort was an extensive law review piece that I authored for the *Texas Review of Law and Politics*. This is not a publication that would appear on most coffee tables in America, but it is a well-respected conservative law review read by the kind of legal scholars we could use on our side if we wanted the impeachment campaign to gather steam and succeed. More importantly, walking through the process of generating an extensive, footnoted, scholarly article on impeachment would force my staff and me to hone our case down as sharply as possible.

Probably the single most important blow struck by a commentator came from a piece published by Mark Helprin in the *Wall Street Journal*. The prose is so well done that it would have been persuasive no matter who penned it. However, Mark's reputation as one of the greatest living American authors—whose novels occupied prominent places on home and library bookshelves across America—added extra credibility to what he wrote. When I met with Newt Gingrich at a corner table in a Cracker Barrel in Marietta, Georgia, shortly after Mark's piece was published, Newt too spoke favorably of it, and I believe it played a significant role in his decision to encourage my initial efforts. One of the more encouraging things that occurred during impeachment was seeing this and a handful of other cases prove that everyone in America was not held hostage by the siren song of the television sound bite. Words, carefully written and eloquently spoken, could still influence the political debate just as they had when America was founded.

A short example of the written eloquence of Mark Helprin that helped to move so many toward impeachment follows here. I would encourage all patriotic Americans to find and read the entire article:

The task is to address the question of President William Jefferson Clinton's fitness for office in light of the many crimes, petty and otherwise, that surround, imbue, and color his tenure. The president must be made subject to the law. When that moment arrives it will signify the rejection of flattery, the rejection of intimidation, the rejection of lies, the rejection of manipulation, the rejection of disingenuous pretense, and a revulsion for the sordid crimes and infractions the president has brought to his office. It will come, if it does, in one word. One word that will lift the fog to show a field of battle clearly laid down. One word that will break the spell. One word that will clarify and cleanse. One word that will confound the dishonest. One word that will do justice. One word. Impeach.[6]

There is no doubt that the heroic efforts of the *Wall Street Journal* to expose the Clinton scandals played a significant role in our ability to generate a high level of public understanding about why these issues were important. The *Journal*'s editors were some of the sharpest minds among the ever-growing assortment of conservative intellectuals who were interested in and capable of communicating ideas to the general public. If anything made it onto their pages, it was carefully crafted, absolutely accurate, and widely read. The paper's willingness consistently to tackle these issues provided a measure of credibility among American opinion leaders that would have been impossible absent its efforts.

As I continued to discuss impeachment publicly through printed words, letters, television appearances, and speeches, I started to learn that a handful of other constitutionalists in Washington had reacted the same way I did to Clinton's repeated abuses of power. In early 1997, under the auspices of *The American Spectator* founder and honcho R. Emmett "Bob" Tyrrell, Jr., I met with a handful of influential conservative opinion leaders—including conservative icon Grover Norquist—at the fashionable Capitol Hill restaurant Le Brasserie to discuss a possible impeachment resolution. It seemed an odd setting for an issue so serious, and it was one of the first occasions when I would publicly discuss impeachment. More than anything else, I was surprised by the degree to which others at the table had been thinking the same things I was thinking. They had also started to see the outlines of a pattern at the Clinton White House that was eerily reminiscent of the Nixon administration. As we went around the table, each of those present offered support for what I was doing, and many of them announced their own plans to begin working to build public support for an impeachment inquiry.

We further honed our message and focus at a private meeting that took place at a conference of a group called the Council for National Policy or CNP held in Charleston, South Carolina, in 1997. That group calls as its members many of the leading grassroots activists in conservative America, ranging from Howard Phillips of The Conservative Caucus to Phyllis Schlafly of Eagle Forum to Larry Klayman of Judicial Watch to direct mail legend Richard Viguerie, as well as several former top officials from the Reagan and Bush administrations, like former attorney general Edwin Meese. At this meeting, separate from and unrelated to the official functions of CNP, we discovered we were in near universal agreement that President Clinton's greatest abuses of power had occurred on the national security front. It was at this event that we agreed the best step to take would probably be putting together an inquiry of impeachment, which was one of the first steps taken against President Nixon. Almost all of the leaders present at this meeting agreed to go back to their respective organizations and begin building support for the impeachment inquiry.

This was a key element of our effort and it would remain a constant until at least the House impeachment vote. Most of the groups represented at the CNP meeting had members in every state in the U.S. We resolved to contact each of those Americans and convince them that they could make a difference by getting person-ally involved in standing behind the impeachment inquiry.

After working the ground by talking to my fellow House members and as many of their constituents as possible, I decided it was time to establish a formal legislative vehicle to carry the impeachment forward. There were several possible vehicles for doing this, and we studied each of them in great detail. In the end,

Bob Barr with Phyllis Schlafly.

we decided on a simple resolution directing the House Judiciary Committee to conduct an inquiry into President Clinton's impeachment. We intended this resolution to start settling some of the questions that were being asked as the nation started incrementally to take the idea of impeachment more seriously. It was a serious step, a formal request for an inquiry. Importantly, it was also based on sound precedent. No less a Clinton diehard than John Conyers, the ranking Democrat on the Judicary Committee, had filed a similar resolution against Richard Nixon early in the Watergate scandal. Moreover, in the list of formal impeachment related steps, it was actually the smallest step one could take.

First of all, our resolution established the Judiciary Committee as the place where the inquiry should be conducted. Interestingly, neither the Constitution nor the House rules specify a particular mechanism for conducting an impeachment inquiry. Judiciary had historically been the venue for most such inquiries, but that was largely because most prior impeachments were responsive to misconduct by federal judges, clearly the province of the Judiciary Committee.

However, having the inquiry conducted by the Judiciary Committee gave us one asset of immeasurable value. On Judiciary, members on both sides were deeply principled. Judiciary is not a committee where members go if they want to deliver pork to their districts or rake in piles of lobbyist cash for their campaigns. We dealt with issues like constitutional amendments, affirmative action, gay marriage, gun control, hate crimes, abortion, and other vitally important but highly divisive issues.

In many cases, the level of feelings held by members on the Judiciary Committee boiled over into fairly personal conflicts. Given that I am quite outspoken, I was involved in more than my share of such conflicts. In an interview with *Rolling Stone*, Barney Frank—one of President Clinton's leading defenders—said that "for many years now my feeling has been that if Bob Barr caught on fire and I was holding a bucket of water, it would be a great act of discipline to pour it on him. I would do it, but I would hate myself in the morning."[7] Barney is normally a good-natured fellow, but I do not think he was ever quite able to forgive me for leading the fight to pass the Defense of Marriage Act, which prevented judges from forcing states to recognize homosexual marriages performed outside their borders. As a gay man, I am sure Frank resented the effort, although he was noticeably less critical of Clinton, who had not only signed the act but had taken out ads on religious radio stations taking credit for doing so. Perhaps Frank's selective application of principle in this case had a little something to do with the fact that his sister, Ann Lewis, worked in the White House for much of the Clinton administration.

Another hallmark of the Democrats on the committee was that some of them were so rabidly anti-Republican that they made me appear moderate and benign by comparison. Take Maxine Waters. At the time, she was obsessed with the idea that the Central Intelligence Agency had played a major role in creating and sustaining the cocaine market in Los Angeles. Maxine was one of those people who always seemed to be angry or bitter about something, significant or otherwise—in the mold of Bela Abzug, for those political observers who recall the Watergate era. In fact, during the entire time I served with her on Judiciary, I cannot remember seeing Maxine express a single positive thought. Her face seemed to be permanently etched in a menacing scowl, more frequently directed at me than any other member on our side of the aisle. While I was frequently derided throughout my congressional career for never smiling, next to Maxine Waters I was the Cheshire Cat.

Later in the process, as the Judiciary Committee was conducting its impeachment inquiry, Maxine would repeatedly lose her cool over the slightest provocation. For example, in some of the most eloquent words spoken during the hearings, our Chief Counsel David Schippers quoted St. Thomas More in *A Man for All Seasons.* Specifically, he reminded us that "the laws of this country are the great barriers that protect the citizens from the winds of tyranny. If we are to permit one of those laws to fall, who will be able to stand up in the gusts that follow?" These seemed to me to be fairly non-controversial words that most Americans would support. Plus, they came from a trial lawyer who was a partisan Democrat who had twice voted for Bill Clinton. However, they sent Maxine and several other Democrats over the edge. Hyde was able to talk Maxine away from the ledge by promising to have the remarks stricken from the record, but I decided they needed to be a part of the historical record, so I added them under my own name. This really set Maxine off, but there was not much she could do about it.

Initially, I was also encouraged by the presence of liberal Democrats on the Judiciary Committee who still seemed to care more about principle than politics. That short list included such members as Bobby Scott of Virginia, whom I had come to respect as a studious and quiet legal scholar and a strong advocate of civil liberties. Bobby is liberal, but he always listened to both sides of every argument I made to him, and he seemed to weigh things on the merits. Of course, saying anything negative about Bill Clinton in

Bobby's district would have been political suicide, and I had no expectation that he would do so.

On the Republican side of the aisle, Judiciary members were generally much less flamboyant than the Democrats in their manner but no less firm in their ideological beliefs. We counted among our number several former prosecutors, as well as many members who had practiced law in other contexts. We knew each other well, and given the "five-minute rule"—limiting the time within which any one of us could make an argument during our public deliberations—that essentially forced us to "borrow" time from each other, we were used to making our legal arguments as a team. At that time, I did not know just how tight of a team we would become as the impeachment idea caught on with the American public and emerged on the national stage.

One might expect that having such a sharply divided committee handle the impeachment inquiry would impede its success. Exactly the opposite was true, in my estimation. The one thing that would kill impeachment in its infancy was a compromise, a deal. Left to their own devices, the leaders of both parties would invariably gravitate toward negotiating one; this was the time-honored environment in which they operated—compromise whenever possible. They would do so because they feared—or would come to fear—the electoral consequences of impeaching President Clinton. The deal I feared would be something like a censure motion combined with the possibility of post-presidency prosecution. The likelihood of any prosecutor bringing charges against Clinton after he left office was nil, but the argument would be enticing to Republican leaders seeking to avoid a messy impeachment. If we went the censure route, we would be letting Clinton off the hook, ensuring he received no punishment at all for his misdeeds. For my part, I wanted nothing to do with a process that culminated in a political fix. This debate was about justice, not compromise.

However, because consistent partisans filled the ranks of the Judiciary Committee on both sides of the aisle, it was unlikely the committee would approve a deal. And, if party leaders negotiated a deal, there was little chance the committee would rubber stamp it. With Judiciary actively criticizing a deal, neither party would move forward for risk of alienating its base constituency. While the outcome of the Judiciary debate was not certain, the fact that a vigorous debate would at least occur was beyond question. For this reason, one of my top priorities was focusing attention on Judiciary as the one committee suited to address these charges.

At the time, I deeply believed—and still do—that any successful impeachment inquiry would have to focus not on any single narrow case, but rather document a widespread pattern of systematic abuse of power. My initial resolution was simple, therefore, and made up of only the following three sentences:

> Directing the Committee on the Judiciary to undertake an inquiry into whether grounds exist to impeach William Jefferson Clinton, the President of the United States. Whereas considerable evidence has been developed from a broad array of credible sources that William Jefferson Clinton, President of the United States, has engaged in a systemic effort to obstruct, undermine, and compromise the legitimate and proper functions and processes of the executive branch: Now, therefore, be it *Resolved*, That the Committee on the Judiciary is directed to investigate and report to the House whether grounds exist to impeach William Jefferson Clinton, President of the United States. Upon completion of such investigation, that Committee shall report to the House its recommendations with respect thereto, including, if the Committee so determines, a resolution of impeachment.

In putting the inquiry resolution together—and working through the entire legal basis for impeachment—I received assistance from two outside lawyers who were very different in partisan background, experience, and personality but who shared a deep dedication to the Constitution. The first was Jerry Zeifman, who had served as chief counsel to the House Judiciary Committee during President Nixon's impeachment. Jerry was, as he describes himself, a "classical liberal" who deeply believed in living the principles one wanted to enact through the political process. There were probably few elements of domestic policy on which the two us would have agreed, but in the impeachment endeavor we found common ground.

Jerry bore the distinction of being one of the few voices crying in the wilderness before the 1996 election, warning American voters that "there is now probable cause to consider our president and first lady as felons."[8] This was a man who knew better than most how damaging abuse of power by the president could be; he played a key role in holding Richard Nixon accountable for such behavior. Jerry also possessed a sharp legal mind and wide experience in an important—but infrequently practiced—area of law that made him a critical asset in our work to develop the legal underpinnings of our case.

The other lawyer with whom we worked closely is a brilliant constitutional scholar and lawyer named Bruce Fein. Bruce is one of those characters one encounters in Washington who could undoubtedly have made large amounts of money in the private sector if he could give up his compulsion to try and make a difference in the national debate. However, Bruce has a rock-solid belief in the Constitution that propels him to work on issues that are far less lucrative than, say, intellectual property or mergers and acquisitions. Bruce had served as a top Senate staffer and a Justice Department official under President Reagan. He is a world-renowned expert in constitutional draftsmanship as well as a newspaper columnist and frequent guest on national television programs. Fortunately for us, he was willing to work with us on many of the difficult legal issues involved in structuring the impeachment inquiry. While I did not always take his advice, he could be counted on to shoot straight and vigorously defend his opinion. These were (and still are) both short commodities in Washington, so we benefited greatly from having Bruce on our team.

When I introduced the resolution on November 5, 1997, I gathered with a handful of supporters of our impeachment inquiry legislation in the radio and television gallery in the U.S. House side of the Capitol. All told, in addition to myself, we had secured seventeen supporters for the resolution. By the time things really started to pick up steam, my resolution would garner thirty-one cosponsors, but we began with seventeen. The names of those brave individuals who stepped forward before the world had heard of Monica Lewinsky and no one else had the guts to move against Clinton were Roscoe Bartlett of Maryland, Helen Chenoweth of Idaho, Barbara Cubin of Wyoming, John Doolittle of California, Lindsey Graham of South Carolina, Duncan Hunter of California, Sam Johnson of Texas, Jack Kingston of Georgia, Jack Metcalf of Washington, John Mica of Florida, Ron Paul of Texas, Pete Session of Texas, Chris Smith of New Jersey, Linda Smith of Washington, Mark Souder of Indiana, Bob Stump of Arizona, and Todd Tiahrt of Kansas. Although I am sure each of these members took some shots for supporting my resolution, they are the kind of people who stood for principle and who learned that doing so—if done consistently—earned them respect. Of this list, one is now a member of the House leadership, another chairs a powerful committee, and a third won a

Bob Barr at House Press Conference.

seat in the United States Senate. These folks were conservatives, but they were certainly no slouches.

The press gallery—where we chose to make this historic announcement—is an odd place, added as an afterthought since radio and television were not foremost concerns when the House was built. It is a tiny room, a cramped space with a small stage used by House members on many days to act out a series of plays for the dozen or so network news cameras that cluster in front of the stage. Typically, the gallery is half filled with tired reporters. There's usually someone lounging around drinking coffee or fiddling with media gizmos. Around deadline, things start to pick up as reporters scurry to file stories. This morning, however, we had a packed house and everyone was paying close attention.

As I prepared my remarks for that event, I had no doubt that I was doing the right thing. This was important to me because moral certainty is a feeling so rarely experienced in Washington. It is a town full of compromises, deals, balancing acts, and tough choices where you almost always get only some of what you want as an alternative to getting nothing. Nine times out of ten, you held your nose and voted for things that fell far short of your expectations because they were better than the alternative. Impeachment was different. My conscience was crystal clear as I introduced this bill because I knew this process was working exactly as the Founders had intended. At not one single moment in the entire process (or since) did I have any doubt that I should be doing what I was doing.

I went into the event expecting to be skewered by a relentlessly critical media. I knew most members of the national press corps clearly did not share my outlook on policy issues, and I expected that to show through in the questions at our press conference. When we actually began, I was surprised by the degree to which we were taken seriously. Clearly, the close exposure of many reporters to scandal after scandal emanating from the White House had softened the terrain. The questions were tough, but they were also generally fair. As we left that press conference, I knew that, for the first time, a large number of reports would reach people in real

America, letting them know that there was hope for bringing Bill Clinton to justice.

In addition to the news media, the White House was clearly watching what we were doing. At a White House press briefing a few blocks down Pennsylvania Avenue, a reporter asked President Clinton for his "reaction to the announcement by Congressman Bob Barr this morning that he will ask for a resolution for a preliminary inquiry by the House Judiciary Committee into possible impeachment proceedings against you for, among other things, possible abuse of presidential power."

"Well, Congressman Barr, as I remember, was the man who carried the NRA's water to try to beat the Brady bill and the assault weapons ban, and he's always had a rather extreme view of these things. I don't really have any comment on that," Clinton answered, before moving on to explain why the U.S. was not going to keep flying U-2s over Iraq.

I guess I was somewhat flattered that the president thought it was a good use of his time to take a swipe at me. The words he chose to use in his attack are notable because they show a now-familiar pattern in the response of the Clinton team (and its leader) to anyone daring to question their activities. First of all, you attack the attacker. Clinton did this by basically making the allegation that I wasn't thinking for myself and that the National Rifle Association— one of his all-time favorite whipping boys—had put me up to trying to impeach him. Secondly, you refuse to discuss the substance of the allegations. Here again, Clinton says nothing about the charges except that—by implication—they aren't worthy of his time to address because they came from someone who was "extreme" and "carried the NRA's water." Finally, you shift to talking about something else. If at all possible, you want that something else to be esoteric and "presidential," usually a foreign policy issue. And, of course, you do not let the facts get in your way—though the president gave me credit for leading the effort to defeat the Brady bill and the so-called assault weapons ban, I was not yet in the Congress at that time.

The odd thing about this kind of response, and the frequency with which it emanated from the White House, is that it did not work that well. Every time the administration tried to stonewall and attack its critics, it ended up in a worse position than if it had simply addressed the criticism on the merits. Reporters aren't stupid, and they weren't going to give Clinton a pass on questionable conduct just because he said everyone who attacked him was an idiot. The message to reporters was "I'm not gonna waste my time discussing this issue, so if you want to write about it, you're going to have to do it without my help." On more than one occasion, that's exactly what they did. Even though some editorial pages and television commentators were essentially wholly owned subsidiaries of the White House, many other journalists picked up the gauntlet Clinton threw and tracked down the information themselves. When they did, you better believe the White House was not going to get friendly coverage. Liking Bill Clinton is one thing, but winning a Pulitzer Prize is entirely another, and the White House press corps was nothing if not self-interested.

Watching the ripple effect from White House attacks and obstruction in response to legitimate inquiries, I had come to the conclusion that a key asset we could field in our fight was our ability to force the White House to respond directly to questions. Clinton's tendency to respond with emotion rather than facts had infiltrated throughout the White House, and the more facts we could throw at them, the more likely they were to respond poorly. This would form a core part of our strategy.

The initial reaction of official Washington—both Republicans and Democrats—was to view what we were up to as a fringe effort. It was something to chuckle at over drinks, but it was not to be taken seriously. Almost no Beltway insiders thought there was any chance the president was going to be impeached.

The Republican leaders in the House did not know what to make of the impeachment inquiry resolution I introduced in fall 1997. I met with Newt Gingrich several times to discuss the issue with him, and he seemed persuaded by my arguments during our meetings. In fact, I noticed an observable shift in Newt's attitude toward the prospect of impeachment after several of our meetings. The most memorable such case was our meeting at the Legislative Office Building adjacent to the Georgia State Capitol on Monday, April 27, 1998, at 10:00 AM.

I had worked for a long time to get that meeting with Gingrich because I wanted to impress upon him the seriousness of the emerging pattern of corruption we were seeing. At the time, it was widely expected that we would at some time see a referral from Ken Starr. Therefore, my goal was to make sure we were able to investigate and organize as much material as possible *prior* to the arrival of the Starr report. I also wanted badly to make sure the inquiry was handled by the Judiciary Committee, since its staff of legal professionals and the sterling reputation of its chairman, Henry Hyde, made it the most credible and effective venue for conducting such an investigation.

In our meeting, Newt seemed to listen unusually intently to what I said. Still, even I was not prepared for what happened immediately afterward and continued over the next several days. At a speech he made to the Atlanta Rotary Club at the Peachtree Plaza

Bob Barr with House Judiciary Committee Chairman, Henry Hyde.

Hotel—which I also attended—immediately after our meeting, Newt made his famous pledge never again to make a speech without mentioning Clinton's crimes. An early article published a few days later in the *Atlanta Journal-Constitution* put it:

> For three months, Gingrich had uttered little more than "no comment" when asked about Clinton's problems. He has counseled patience in waiting for independent counsel Kenneth Starr to report the results of his investigation. And, after Starr's recent statement that he has much work still to do, members of Congress had generally concluded that prospects for impeachment hearings this year were remote. Yet, Gingrich used several appearances—a Rotary Club appearance and a Monday evening speech to GOPAC, the political action committee he once led, a Tuesday address on the floor of the House, and his two sets of comments Wednesday—to assail Clinton and Democrats in the House for working in concert to keep investigators from getting at the truth. Gingrich's sudden shift has puzzled even conservatives who have been eager for Republicans in Congress to take a firmer stand on campaign finance, potential hush payments to Hubbell, and allegations that Clinton had an affair with former White House intern, then encouraged her to lie about it.[9]

Unfortunately, the strategy did not play out as well as he had apparently hoped based on early polling data, so he changed course shortly thereafter, doubtlessly under tremendous pressure from political operatives and pollsters working for the Republican Party in Washington. However, the mere fact that Newt had devoted such a focused and concentrated level of attention to underscoring the seriousness of Clinton's behavior provided invaluable credibility and momentum for our effort to get Washington to take these issues seriously. In this area, he was doing what he did best, making a strongly principled and intellectually tight argument. The problem was that Newt was now such an important person that he had a legion of political operatives attempting to pull his strings on a daily basis. The net result is that it was difficult for him to stay the course on something that was unpopular in the short term, even if he thought the country was likely to come his way over the long run. Anyhow, it was encouraging to many conservatives to see the old Newt of 1994 return, even if only briefly. Newt's work also helped pave the way for the arrival of Starr's report among rank and file Republican activists, focusing their attention on the matter.

In 1998, Speaker Gingrich further signaled his interest in the impeachment question by assigning an informal but permanent liaison from his staff to work with our office. Newt's staff member was officially assigned to help us, but I have no doubt her role was just as much to keep an eye on what we were up to and report back to Newt. Even if Newt seemed to be personally with us, there was a platoon of "leadership staff" who, like many others in Washington, D.C., imagined that they—not the members elected by American voters—were in charge of the House of Representatives. These establishment denizens wanted to know exactly what I was doing, because it made them nervous. I met several times in my office to discuss the inquiry with Newt's emissary, and it was always difficult to know exactly what was happening to the information she collected. Nonetheless, it is impossible to achieve much of anything in the House without leadership support, so we did whatever we could—or had to—to keep the lines of communication open.

Although many leading Republicans chose to ignore our work, there were ways to force them to address it. One asset we had at our disposal was the GOP presidential primary process that was starting to pick up steam as candidates jockeyed for the nomination in 2000. At that time, George W. Bush was the presumed frontrunner with John McCain also a frequently mentioned candidate, but neither was running actively. The primary candidates in the race at the time were John Kaisich, Dan Quayle, Alan Keyes, Steve Forbes, Gary Bauer, Bob Smith, and John Ashcroft. I knew that if we succeeded in getting these folks talking about impeachment, the message would continue resonating as they visited groups of key Republican activists and donors in battleground states around the country. Even if none of these candidates became serious competitors, their rhet-

Bob Barr with Alan Keyes.

oric would echo in the months ahead as the fight for the nomination continued. No battleground states are more important to early
candidates for the nomination than Iowa and New Hampshire.

This is how I found myself in Cedar Rapids, Iowa, where the
White House press corps—who were visiting the town for the Iowa
GOP "First in the Nation Gala"—assumed I was planning to
announce my candidacy for the nomination. For example, the *New
York Times* reported that I planned to ride my "outspokenness on
the President to the White House," which was certainly news to me
since I had no such plans.[10] Rather, my goal was to use my presence
on the stage to force the early pack of candidates to address the
threat Bill Clinton posed to our nation. With me on the stage,
pretending that impeachment was not an issue would be at least
difficult. At least *USA Today* seemed to get the point of my presence
at the presidential cattle call, quoting me accurately as asking the
audience, "I didn't hear the I-word out there, did I? Impeach!"[11]
The tactic actually seemed to work well, judging by the audience
reaction when the candidates confronted Clinton head-on. Anyone

who can get a crowd of Iowans excited—I think I can get away with saying this because I was born in the state—knows he has struck an extremely strong chord. Iowans are quite possibly the most even-tempered and slow-to-criticize citizens of the United States, so getting them fired up was a public speaking achievement of Olympian proportions. Among GOP activists, there was clearly a political benefit associated with the issue.

This is not the only trip I took to advocate impeachment. I visited many other states, from Idaho to California, Florida to Alaska, and spoke to virtually any group, large or small, that would listen. I would find myself in one weekend talking with students and professors at Yale University, then talking to conservatives in rural Ohio, and then making the same points to wealthy money managers and leading newspaper editors in posh Manhattan high-rise build-ings shortly afterward. This often meant that one night I would find myself sleeping on the couch in my office, and the next night I would be parked in a $400-a-night hotel paid for by major GOP donors. I drifted off to sleep in a bed that cost more than my car back home, wishing more than anything else that home was where I was. I would then leave, spend one night at home—where I was too tired to do anything other than sleep—and then hop on another airplane to speak to a small group in a rural community, sleeping in the local Motel Six furnished with 1960s furniture, cigarette holes, and mildew—again wishing that I was home—before returning to Washington.

All the travel rapidly outstripped the ability of our small staff to handle it, meaning I often jumped on a plane with a few half-completed files and a cell phone. It also meant we did not always screen groups sufficiently before I spoke to them, resulting in one awkward situation in South Carolina. I had been invited by the top Republican official in South Carolina to speak on impeachment to a particular group, so we made the reasonable assumption based on his recommendation that the group was legitimate. It turned out the particular group—which innocuously called itself the Council of Conservative Citizens—was united largely by its advocacy of racist views with which I and most Americans deeply disagree. Needless to say, that was one meeting I left as quickly as possible, but it was not surprising to see the president's defenders later track it down and use it to attack me during the impeachment inquiry. It hardly mattered that Dick Gephardt had spoken to the same group in Missouri years earlier. What mattered was that it was a quick sound bite with which the White House spin machine could personally attack the messenger of bad news.

As 1998 wore on, there were still not many people living in Washington's fashionable zip codes who took impeachment seriously. But there were large numbers of American citizens living in less ideologically warped communities around the nation who took it very seriously. In fact, they viewed it as their constitutional duty as citizens to support the impeachment process. Since they didn't live in Washington, we decided it would be a good idea to bring some of them into town for a visit (a lot of them, in fact).

One of the most unusual groups to coalesce during the impeachment called themselves "Freepers." This self-created name traces its etymology to the name of the website from whence they came, named *FreeRepublic.com*. I say they came from this website because they did. It became an online community for people in America who believed deeply in the Constitution. In an increasingly relativistic society, such patriots naturally wanted to meet others who shared their sense that something was deeply amiss in the Clinton White House. So they set up this website, where they started off posting information on Clinton scandals as they broke and then posted follow-up comments. Soon, however, the site morphed into a clearing point for online activism.

Most established Republicans sneered at what the Freepers were doing, but I welcomed them with open arms; they were my kind of Americans—unpretentious, informed, unafraid, and committed. I soon discovered that alerting their network could trigger a rapid-fire barrage of phone calls to any target that needed a little softening up. On more than one occasion, a member who seemed unsure of where to break on impeachment was deluged with calls, e-mails, faxes, and mail from people who lived in his home district and wanted action.

It was also an excellent vehicle with with to deluge offices of Republican leadership in Congress with calls to support the impeachment effort. In fact, this proved so effective, our leaders began to complain to me that their offices were getting tied up with grassroots petitions, faxes, emails, and calls. While outwardly I commiserated with them, in fact this was great news, since I knew that if a matter reached the point at which our leaders could no longer ignore the problem, we definitely stood a chance of having it addressed.

In another case, my staff used such an online campaign to tie up the phone lines of Harvard professor Alan Dershowitz for a significant amount of time after he leveled personal attacks at me. It was a guilty pleasure for them, and I would have probably tried to talk them out of it at the time, but I must admit to chuckling under my breath when I heard the story later.

The greatest achievement of the Freepers was putting on a massive rally at the foot of the Washington monument on Halloween Day (a Saturday) in 1998. This was a critical time for impeachment because we knew the election in a few days could change everything. We wanted to ensure the Republican Party was as strongly bolstered as it could be going in to the election, so that no matter the outcome, impeachment would move forward. One way to do this was to vote with our feet, coming to Washington and showing Republican power players that there really was a constituency for impeachment in real America.

As you might imagine, putting on a massive rally on the mall of the nation's capital is no easy task. There are numerous government permits to secure, and those permits have specific requirements. For example, the National Park Service requires a certain number of portable toilets at the event, and so on and so forth. If the media also decides to cover the event, it also has its own list of demands, ranging from elevated platforms to reliable electric supplies to phone lines. Out-of-town visitors need help with parking, trans-portation, and lodging. Most groups who put on such events have large staffs of trained professionals who deal with these kinds of details. The Freepers, very much a group of grassroots citizens of modest means, had only volunteers, many of whom had never met in person before, and all of them had other responsibilities in life besides setting up this "March for Justice."

Somehow or another, they managed to pull off the event. The list of speakers included yours truly, Larry Klayman, Gary Aldrich, Matt Drudge, Alan Keyes, and Lucianne Goldberg. We all had inter-esting things to say, I'm sure, but the real point was to show the world that people in real America actually gave a damn about these issues and were ready to put their money where their mouths were. The total crowd in attendance on a beautiful October day ranged well into the thousands, and I am sure their shouts were heard loud and clear at the White House located just across the mall and down the street. The Freepers also did other things, including putting together one of the most effective printed political ads I have ever seen, which featured George Washington shedding a single tear over the state of affairs in the nation he fought to build. I still proudly display a framed version of that ad in my office. The group would later play a prominent role in other chapters in American political history, making a significant contribution to such battles as the Florida recount following the 2000 election.

A second rally after the 1998 election was held right at the Capitol and attracted another large crowd of activists. I was joined at the podium by Bob Tyrrell, and as we left I noticed a few non-Freeper flyers littering the ground. The flyers identified me in a photo in the center of a target as "the most dangerous man in America." I presumed this was a label resulting from my push to impeach Clinton. A closer examination revealed that my "threat" to America was based not on my advocacy of Clinton's impeachment, but the result of my stance against relaxing anti-marijuana laws in the District of Columbia; at least the residents of our nation's capitol had their priorities straight!

Another unconventional ally in the impeachment effort was the oft-maligned John Birch Society, which many Americans remember for its role in the communist scares of the 1950s and 1960s. Since then, the Birchers had managed to survive as a reincarnated organization, claiming a membership that—while not large—was extremely predisposed toward political activity. For this reason, I visited a few of their meetings and agreed to be interviewed for one of their publications. While I did not agree with every position taken by the organization, their high level of intensity about political issues made them a useful ally in generating grassroots activism.

We worked with many other groups over the course of our campaign to get the House to move on impeachment. One band of conservative activists had made impeachment a part of their fundraising campaign, generating tens of thousands of signed petitions from American voters demanding an inquiry. The petitions were addressed to Republican leaders in the House, and the spectacle of listening to their staffs create excuses not to have the wheelbarrows of signed petitions delivered in person to their offices is one I will always remember. Still other groups orchestrated calls to talk radio shows or sent letters to their local papers. The point was to generate activity on as many fronts as possible. In a complacent nation, merely taking the time to get involved in a visible and personal way can make all the difference, as it did in this case.

It was often argued that succeeding in removing the president would require bipartisan support. So we focused a great deal of effort on building support for our case among Democrats we thought would be predisposed to think independently and let the Constitution be their guide. We were frequently disappointed to find out that fear of retribution from the Clinton political machine was sufficient pressure to coerce most members of Clinton's party into silence. Fortunately, one Democrat who wasn't interested in being silenced was Congressman Gene Taylor of Mississippi. A somewhat idiosyncratic and unfailingly independent guy, Gene usually sat near the aisle on the Democratic side of the House. As I walked by one day, he turned my way and barked "Barr!" As I turned toward him, he said only three words: "Put me on." He was added as a co-sponsor of the impeachment inquiry right away.

Gene Taylor was one of the few Democrats holding political office who was willing to be identified with us. Although we worked hard to make our case to them, Congress in 1997 and 1998 was a vastly different place than it had been more than two decades earlier during the Nixon impeachment. In the new Congress, partisanship was everything. You played on a team and you were loyal to that team no matter what. Independent thought was strongly discouraged, and loyalty was enforced through a system that rewarded lemmings and punished mavericks. If you towed the line, you got campaign cash, action on your bills, and perhaps a shot at a committee chairmanship. If not, then the party leadership was not going to lift a finger to help you get anything done, either in your home district or in Washington. The same system was enforced in both parties, and it ultimately made it difficult for anyone to cross partisan lines, as many Republicans had done during the Nixon impeachment debate.

Pushing against the weight of a system this powerful wasn't going to be easy. We stared out slowly, talking about impeachment quietly. I met frequently with other members individually and in groups, explaining the constitutional history of what we were doing and how it fit with the case at hand. This initial approach selected a sample of the most courageous members. These were folks who believed they were elected for a reason. They felt their constituents had chosen them not merely to swipe a voting card and attend receptions, but to use their judgment and reason. When they saw the case, they quickly agreed to support our work or offered a substantial reason why they felt a different course was more appropriate. It would be nice if all of Congress worked this way, but it does not. This description now fits only a handful of members. The Founders had vacated the Capitol, and only their pale ghosts now lingered.

At the opposite extreme, we had members who cared for nothing so much as the status quo. They liked things exactly the way they were. They had invested large parts of their lives, huge sums of money, and a great deal of effort in feathering their nests. They were mortally afraid of any kind of change that might upset the spot in the Washington pecking order they had worked so long to secure. These people would sign up for something as controversial as an impeachment inquiry about the same time Satan and all the demons strapped on ice skates and went merrily scampering across the frozen fires of hell. The only way we would ever get these people on our side was by dragging them there kicking and screaming. My attitude toward this category of members was that they were not worth expending an ounce of effort on.

After talking to the handful of independent thinkers left in the House and writing off the rabid defenders of the status quo, we were still left with the majority of House members who fit some where between these two extremes. Reaching them meant working on their intellects and consciences as well as giving them political cover. On the intellectual side, the newspaper columns I published in such outlets as the *Wall Street Journal, USA Today,* the *Washington Times,* and numerous other media outlets were focused largely on this goal. So were my numerous appearances on the more "respected" television talk shows, which boast small audiences but reach a large number of so called "opinion leaders" who tend to be influential in spreading carefully reasoned arguments to people like wavering members of Congress. Additionally, I continued personally to reach out to as many of these members as I could, making our case as often as possible. Finally, we bombarded these members with letters, focusing on persuading both the members themselves and their staff.

We started publishing a weekly "Impeachment Inquiry Update" to give these members quick news about our progress in building support for our resolution to begin an impeachment inquiry. Every new endorsement we secured, every newspaper endorsement we won, went into the update, so that we conveyed a sense of momentum that would attract wavering sponsors. These updates were then "blast-faxed" to hundreds of House offices, grassroots organizations, media outlets, and opinion leaders. Typically, such "legislative" information goes only to the Washington offices of House members, but we realized that staff in home district offices out in real America would be less likely to advise their bosses to defend the status quo and more likely to advise doing the right thing. Plus, district staff are generally less arrogant and protective of the members they serve, so there was a greater chance our communications would arrive on the boss's desk if we sent them to offices outside the Washington Beltway.

The other side of our work in shifting wavering members into the impeachment column consisted of making sure they got as much political cover as possible. For better or worse, all but a handful of congressmen were not going to touch this thing unless they thought they could still win reelection after doing so. As I have mentioned, bombarding members with mail, phone calls, and faxes was an important contribution made by the many groups who backed our impeachment inquiry drive. Some of the groups even sent their members to town hall meetings or got them to make personal visits to their local congressman's office. There may not have been thousands of activists in every congressional district, but even in the most liberal districts there were dozens, and they made their presence known loudly and frequently.

As the noted political scientist Richard Fenno has explained, House members do not just structure their behavior in order to please one set of constituents.[12] In reality, they see several constituencies, ranging from the core group of supporters who make up their inner circle to the entire electorate. In this case we were after the "primary constituency" or what House members commonly call "their base." When House members sit around and plot out our reelection campaigns, we always wonder who will actually turn out to vote. In many ways, this is the most important thing we have to figure out in order to win. You always find yourself questioning whether so-called "swing voters" will turn out, because generally these folks aren't tuned in to politics on a regular basis.

Sometimes they vote in large numbers and sometimes they don't. Consequently, you do everything you can to reach out to these often-moderate and indecisive lackadaisical voters, but you certainly do not bet all of your chips on them. Every candidate who has tried to do so—just ask George H. W. Bush about his 1992 campaign—has failed.

In politics, there is one group you absolutely cannot afford to ignore, and that's your base. These are the loyal foot soldiers without which no political candidate has a prayer of succeeding. They stuff the mail, staff the phone banks, put up the yard signs, knock on doors, write campaign checks, persuade others to vote, and do the countless other things that make a difference in political campaigns. When everyone else stays home, these people will vote. If you get into a runoff election, they will vote again.

To my knowledge, no other office during the time I served in Congress engaged in an effort anything like this impeachment effort, both in terms of the volume of paper we generated and the length of time we sustained the effort. There is a reason no one else had tried this. It took an enormous amount of work. For example, sending out an impeachment update meant researching it, writing it, and programming a list of thousands of fax numbers into computer code so an automated system could process the "blast-fax." It also meant removing people who got angry about the faxes from the list and adding new people who said they wanted to get them. That's only a small portion of what we did. The total sum of our effort is obvious in the archive that now holds my congressional paper. Merely storing the files of information we saved—which is only a fraction of what we did—consumes more than an entire room of file boxes stacked from floor to ceiling.

In a typical congressional office, you get a staff of about fifteen to twenty people, which sounds like a lot. But merely assisting constituents with problems they encounter with federal agencies, analyzing pending legislation, ordering office supplies, managing the office budget, drafting your own bills, greeting visitors, planning the schedule, and handling the range of tasks the public expects a

congressman to conduct requires the full-time attention of every
one of your authorized staffers. Consequently, attempting an effort
this large essentially meant asking a handful of underpaid young
people to work an additional ten to twenty hours a week on top of
the fifty hours or more they—like most congressional staff—regularly worked. It also meant I could pretty much expect to sleep four
or five hours a night and spend the rest of the time working.

Yet, despite these demands, we somehow managed to pull it off.
The worst days were those that began at 5:00 AM in Washington, an
early start necessitated by my desire to reach audiences on morning
television. Since I slept in my office, I had to wake up early in order
to shower at the House gym in the building next door. I often got
strange looks from the handful of early birds and custodial staff as I
shuffled down the hall half asleep wearing slippers. Fortunately, a
fair number of other members did the same thing, so no one was
too confused. After reading through two or three newspapers, I
would try—often without success—to scrounge a cup of coffee
somewhere. Reading the papers was a tiresome but essential process.
During impeachment, I regularly digested the better part of four
newspapers—the *Washington Times*, the *Wall Street Journal*, the
Atlanta Journal-Constitution, and the *Marietta Daily Journal*, as well
as several key magazines including the *Weekly Standard* and *The
American Spectator*. Early in my term, I had banned the *Washington
Post* from our office since it tends to be—putting it mildly—less
than sympathetic to conservative political views. However, even it
became essential reading during impeachment in order to keep up
with the torrent of information surrounding the various Clinton
scandals. Finally, my chief of staff insisted on reading the *New York
Times* every day, so I would often get clips from that newspaper as
well. Reading newspapers is like listening to witnesses at a trial; you
assume no one is actually telling you the truth, so you listen to all of
them and glean out of their words whatever nuggets of reality that
you can, working toward constructing an accurate version of what
actually happened.

After waking up (sort of), I would meet a staffer around 6:00 or 6:30 at the "horseshoe" outside our building. I also did not have a car in Washington, and anyone who has used the rattletraps that pass for taxi-cabs in the city avoids them at all costs, so I generally tried to hitch a ride with the lucky staffer who drew the short straw to attend the meeting with me, typically my press secretary (a job so grueling that it was filled by five separate individuals in my eight years in Congress). We would then drive to an interview location in time to make an appearance sometime during the 7:00 hour on shows ranging from the *Today Show* to *Good Morning America* to cable news programs or even news programs for local markets around America. This often meant sitting in a cramped studio under harsh lights and getting grilled by a journalist; not exactly how I would prefer to start my day, but if that is what it took to get the word out, then I was willing.

After morning interviews, I would spend the rest of a "normal" twelve-hour workday meeting with constituents, attending hearings, reading legislation, talking with other members, and voting. If time allowed, I would also try to work in calls to talk radio programs around America. We literally did hundreds of such interviews during the two-year impeachment drive, and the ability of conservative talk radio shows to get their local listeners active on a particular issue was of enormous benefit. Talk radio played a large part in putting Republicans in office in 1994, and it played a similarly influential role in almost getting President Clinton out of office in 1999.

When the day started to wind to a close for most people, I would pile back into a car and drive to one of Washington's many television studios to discuss the same issues I had discussed earlier in the morning (along with whatever new twists had developed during the day). These programs started airing around 6:00 PM and didn't stop until midnight. Many of them actually broadcast from the same building—at 400 North Capitol Street—because the offices on one side of that building happened to feature the coveted perfect shot of the United States Capitol building so sought after by every television producer covering Washington. Consequently, C-SPAN, FOX, MSNBC, CNBC, NBC, and several smaller television stations had facilities there. CNN also had its offices nearby, and the other two networks would often make arrangements to broadcast from the area as well. This often meant we'd spend hours in the same building doing interviews, riding an elevator to a new floor, doing more interviews, and waiting around for more. On many nights, this left no time for eating, so my staff and I would scrounge around for food in the "green rooms" where guests waited for their turn in front of the cameras. FOX never had food, but they occasionally had soft drinks and fruit juice in a small fridge if anyone had remembered to restock it. About 25 percent of the time, NBC would have stale breakfast pastries, while CNN had a massive mechanical coffee dispenser that produced frighteningly large volumes of a funny-tasting brownish liquid.

During impeachment, each network was originating a large portion of its coverage from Washington, so the studios were a madhouse of guests shuffling in and out of chairs. Each suite of studios also had a makeup room, where your face would quickly be coated with enough cosmetics to make Tammy Faye Baker green with envy. After a few months of this, I started carrying my own box of wipes around just to get all of the crap off my face as soon as each interview ended. I also started to notice that they were shuffling guests through so fast that the earpiece you insert into your ear in order to hear the people you're talking to was often still warm from the guest before me. The producers assured me this was totally sanitary, but it was a less than agreeable sensation, so I also started carrying my own set of broadcast earpieces as well.

The day would typically end around midnight, and if I was lucky, I could talk one of my staff into driving me to Starbuck's Coffee at DuPont Circle, where I would chug down a cup of coffee with two shots of espresso before heading back to the office to work for a few more hours on all the paperwork that awaited me there. This was hard work, but I was used to it. For four years I had worked my way through Georgetown Law School at night while serving as a CIA analyst during the day, and I had not really slowed down since then, so long days were something I was used to and actively enjoyed.

Looking back, all of our work to get the public involved in the impeachment debate had, I believe, a profound effect on the outcome. Before we began our campaign, no one was even willing to say the "I-word." It was like trying to train new army recruits to run *toward* the sound of gunfire rather than away from it. The trick was to expose them to the sights and sounds of combat gradually so they wouldn't be so shocked and scared that they ran away and cowered in terror at the first crack of a rifle. From my perspective, the idea was to make sure every one of the 435 House members, 100 senators, and the various talking heads who held sway in our capital city heard the "I-word" as many times as possible from numerous different sources. If you're going to boil a frog, the saying goes, you have to turn the heat up gradually or he'll jump out of the pan.

Bob Barr consults with Chief of Staff Jonathan Blyth during House impeachment hearings.

Our work to turn up the heat gradually on impeachment played a critical part on two fronts. First, it ensured that a deal—such as censure—was less likely when the Starr report finally ignited the process. We had talked about impeachment so much that the debate was not so much over impeachment versus censure as it was over impeachment versus nothing. Without our efforts to prepare the ground, I strongly believe that a censure motion would have been the ultimate outcome of the process in the House, a step the skittish Senate would have come running to embrace with open arms.

Secondly, our work tipped the process in the House in favor of passage of the Articles of Impeachment. There were numerous moderate Republicans—as well as some conservative Democrats—who would never have even imagined supporting impeachment back in 1997. By getting their electoral base agitated about the issue, we sent them a clear message: if they did not vote in favor of the articles, there would be a price to pay. This put many Republicans from difficult districts in a bad situation, but I don't feel guilty about it. Being a congressman should not be easy; we should be forced to make hard choices, and the extent to which most choices have become easy is a reflection on how meaningless much of the legislative process has become.

6

Success in the House

Our campaign to soften up the ground was paying off. In 1998, the Judiciary Committee began the process of preparing for the impeachment debate we expected would occur at some point during the year. Early in the year, Henry Hyde had clearly realized that between the pressure our campaign was creating and the potential arrival of a report from Starr, impeachment was a distinct possibility. At this point, Hyde made one of the wisest decisions throughout the impeachment process, namely hiring David Schippers as the chief investigative counsel for the Judiciary Committee. The move was announced at the time as an addition of staff to conduct routine oversight of the Department of Justice. Of course, this did not fool anyone. Schippers and his team were brought in to prepare for impeachment, and pretty much anyone close to the process knew this was the case.

Schippers himself was one of those people you do not often encounter in Washington. A deeply moral man, he graduated from seminary and considered becoming a priest but opted for law school instead. Like me, he had put himself through a top law school by taking classes at night, so I knew he had an excellent work ethic. He was also a tough as nails prosecutor, used to trying difficult criminal cases in Chicago, one of America's roughest cities. Before that, he helped lead Bobby Kennedy's campaign against organized crime at the Department of Justice in the 1960s. This was a guy who had taken on organized crime at the peak of its power in America, but taking on official Washington, consumed as it was with maintaining the status quo, was a different story.

When Schippers arrived, he did what any competent prosecutor who wanted to get to the truth would do. He brought his own team with him. This started a subtle conflict that was not visible to the public but that would lead directly to President Clinton wiggling off the hook. Like all committees in Congress, the Judiciary Committee relies heavily on staff to get anything done. Members come and go with elections, but staff is always there, and they possess the institutional knowledge it takes to get much of anything done in the Byzantine world of Washington politics. This was even truer on Judiciary in many ways because the legal expertise required on that committee further limited the number of Hill staff capable of servicing effectively there to those with sometimes very specific kinds of legal backgrounds. During the House impeachment inquiry, most of the critical decisions were made by a handful of staffers and then presented to those of us on the committee as fait accompli, which we could accept or reject (though most were unlikely to do so).

During—and for that matter before—the impeachment inquiry, there were two kinds of Republican staff on the Judiciary Committee. The first were people like Staff Director Tom Mooney and Press Secretary Sam Stratman, who were fiercely loyal to Chairman Hyde. The second were committee lawyers such as Paul McNulty, who had come to the committee from the Department of Justice and wanted badly to return there as soon as a Republican took over the White House. Neither of these groups was particularly interested in expanding the impeachment inquiry. The first category, Hyde loyalists, were fiercely protective of their boss's reputation as a gentleman and were just as skittish as he was about expanding things beyond whatever Starr sent over. The second group, Department of Justice loyalists, were intent on maintaining and building their relationships with the official Washington legal establishment, many of whom were professional employees at Main Justice. Consequently, they were not going to push too hard to get the attorney general, the FBI director, or any other DOJ personnel to cough up information on issues outside the Starr report. Overlaid on all of this, of course, were the sometimes hidden, but always present hands of the Republican leadership.

Schippers collided with this brick wall when he arrived in Washington. Dave was not the kind of guy who would take "no" for an answer, so he continually pressed the professional staff on the committee to get out of his way and let him follow all the leads he had on the table (as any good prosecutor would do). Those of us who wanted a wider inquiry were keenly aware that the clock never stopped ticking. This was our window to direct the focus on issues that really mattered, and I am sure no one took this matter any more seriously than Schippers and his team. However, every time he tried to do the right thing—as he recounts in his best-selling book *Sellout*—career people on the committee would start stonewalling him, refusing to follow his orders and not even sharing information with him in many cases. This illustrates, yet again, that our own team—even at times with the best of intentions—posed one of the most significant obstacles to success.

On September 9, 1998, Kenneth Starr and his team of prosecutors delivered their long-awaited and much-discussed report to Congress. I remember this day well, because for several days leading up to it Washington was unable to focus on much of anything else other than speculation about its contents. Starr's reputation as a high-caliber jurist, Clinton's appearance before a grand jury, and a host of smaller events and facts combined to set a high bar for what official Washington expected from this report. Most expected it to be the beginning of Bill Clinton's Watergate, a tidal wave of facts that would quickly engulf the stonewall tactics that had become a hallmark of his scandal management team.

So when my chief of staff walked into my office and told me he had gotten a tip that the Starr report was on its way over in a couple of vans, I decided to walk down to the East Front of the Capitol building to watch its arrival. It was a beautiful fall day, one of those rare days when even Washington's muggy weather and concrete surfaces seem almost pleasant. The crush of people, most of them reporters from dozens of media outlets around the world, sent a clear message that something substantial was about to happen here.

Those of us who believed the Clinton White House was systematically abusing the public trust had high hopes that the Starr report would document such a *pattern* of abuse. What we got was one of the most airtight legal cases imaginable. Unfortunately, that case was based entirely on perjury and obstruction about the intimate details of a sordid affair conducted inside the White House. We were left with a strong legal case but one too narrowly focused to be anything but a difficult sell in the court of public opinion. This was a problem of enormous proportions because impeachment is as much a political process as it is a legal one.

Initially, our plan was to use the Starr report only as one part of the impeachment inquiry, focusing a significant amount of time and effort on issues we believed were far more serious, such as threats to national security. Unfortunately, the length of time Starr's team had taken to build this case meant that it was airtight but also that it arrived close to the 1998 mid-term elections. This, of course, ensured that even the smallest steps we took would be amplified tenfold in the context of a national battle for control of Congress. Furthermore, if we extended the inquiry long enough to achieve a full investigation, it would run into the next Congress, forcing us to obtain new authority and funding from a body with new members in order to continue our work—clearly an unlikely scenario. Here again, the independent counsel statute had focused so exclusively on the law that the political side of impeachment—the more operative side—was essentially ignored.

Bill Clinton followed the arrival of the Starr report with a meeting of his cabinet, in which he begged them all not to resign.

Predictably, they marched in lockstep to defend their patron, exhibiting the low level of honor and independent thinking America had come to expect from them. Reportedly, the worst Bill Clinton received from his own team during that meeting was a schoolmarm scolding from Health and Human Services head Donna Shalala. I am sure he was quaking in his boots as he listened to her. A few days later, Clinton held a news conference, sloughing off any possibility that he might take the honorable course and resign from office. At this point, it became even clearer that the Clinton White House would fight until the last man rather than give up its hold on power. Clinton was giving his cabinet, Congress, and the American people the high hat, and it was up to us to decide how to respond.

Two days later, the full House voted to make the Starr report available in its entirety to the public. In retrospect, this was clearly a mistake. The substance of the full report provided lurid details on which the media invariably seized to the exclusion of focusing on the much more important legal issues covered in the report. We ultimately made a similar mistake in the Judiciary Committee, releasing more information publicly than was advisable. While there may have been a better way to handle this, the simple fact of the matter is that we were faced with a lose-lose proposition. Either we released all the material, including the rather repugnant personal elements, or we risked being painted as selectively releasing materials to harm the president. Although I supported releasing all of the material at the time, if I had it to do over again, I would take a different position.

After wading through the Starr report and redacting limited portions of it, the Judiciary Committee voted on October 5—along strict party lines—to send a bill to the House floor authorizing an impeachment inquiry. On October 8, 1998, the full House voted to authorize an impeachment inquiry by the House Judiciary Committee. However, with less than a month to go until the November elections, there would not be an opportunity to do much investigating before the American people rendered something like a public verdict on our progress so far. Our plans were therefore significantly altered by one of the most important events in the impeachment debate—which occurred before it officially began—namely the midterm elections of 1998.

Following the House vote, Clinton went into hiding at a posh resort on the Chesapeake Bay near Washington, where he began conducting Middle East peace negotiations. These negotiations turned out to be a pointless charade, but that didn't really surprise anyone. They were little more than another excuse for Clinton to manipulate U.S. foreign policy in order to look presidential at an opportune moment. His departure was delayed only by his momentary pause to conclude a budget deal that basically gave him every funding item he wanted. The idea that Republicans caved on budget negotiations with a president we had just moved to impeach showed, if nothing else, how rudderless the party was at the time. Clinton's post-impeachment victory tour was marred only by an October 20th hearing at the Eight Circuit Court of Appeals where it appeared likely that Paula Jones's original sexual harassment lawsuit might be reinstated.

In 1998, our party reelection effort—led by Georgia congressman John Linder, who was serving a two-year term as chair of the National Republican Congressional Committee (NRCC)—lost seats in the House, bucking a historical trend in which the president's party is almost always the one losing ground. In fact, many pre-election polls indicated the GOP might lose control of the House, causing the normally cautious Republican leadership to be even less sure of itself.

The night of the November election, our campaign hosted its victory party at the Atlanta Waverly hotel, the same location where Speaker Newt Gingrich was holding court. As events took a decidedly negative turn for Republicans around the country, Newt remained cloistered in a hotel room with his advisors. As the national press corps waited for a glum Newt to comment on the results, they started asking me about impeachment, with the common presumption being, "Well, this election now means impeachment is dead, doesn't it?" All I could accurately tell them was that the results—whatever they were—would not alter my course.

Not surprisingly, the media assumed the 1998 election results were reason alone for the Republican Party to drop the impeachment issue. However, this was not going to happen for several reasons. First of all, we had not done *that* badly in the election. Most importantly, we had held on to the majority. In reality, the biggest mistake Linder and other party leaders made was dramatically raising expectations that the GOP would achieve significant gains. As late as the day before the election, Republican leaders were stubbornly sticking to their public façade that our party would gain, not lose, several seats. Consequently, even though we retained the majority, our rather average performance—the Democrats had only gained five seats and we still had our majority—was still interpreted as a huge defeat.

To the extent that the impeachment debate played a role in the election outcome, the most significant mistake our party made was acting inconsistently. Prior to the November election, party leaders ordered Henry Hyde to stand down the Judiciary Committee investigation until after Election Day. The idea was to avoid saying anything controversial that might upset the rosy outlook for Republican candidates. Then our leaders completely reversed course and did things like making political ads prominently featuring the Clinton scandals. One moment Newt would vow to hammer Clinton relentlessly for his illegal activities, and the next he would say things like his comment to the *Washington Post* in October 1998 that "the worst thing Republicans could do would be to narrowly focus on this scandal. That would be the most counterproductive thing to do."[1]

The message to the public from these contradictory actions was that Republicans were swaying in the breeze—acting for political reasons rather than principled ones. The only House leader who stood firm and unwavering on principle throughout the critical days leading up to the election was then-House Majority Whip Tom DeLay. Gingrich's top staff complained about DeLay's consistent message that Bill Clinton had committed crimes, abused power, and deserved punishment. However, they fortunately did not succeed in shutting him up. The wisdom of Tom's behavior in this and so many other areas is shown in the fact that most of the other leadership figures in office at the time are no longer around, while he is arguably the most powerful member of the House of Representatives. Even moderate Republicans respect Tom and follow his direction because—even though they do not always agree with him—they know he is working firmly from deeply held beliefs about the Constitution and the proper role of government. Standing consistently on principle may not always have short-term rewards, but it almost always pays off in the long run.

While I do not think impeachment was a decisive issue in the 1998 elections, including my own, I have no doubt it played a role in determining the choices of many swing voters who ultimately ended up in the Democrat column. Furthermore, many Republicans—myself among them—believed our lackluster performance was tied much more directly to the massive pork-laden spending bill we passed immediately prior to the election than to impeachment. This bill clearly disgusted many fiscal conservatives, the most consistent and strong base of our party's support around the nation. As a result, the Republican base did not turn out in force, while Democratic partisans were motivated by impeachment to vote in greater than normal numbers. With the Democrat base so energized, the last thing Republicans could afford to do was turn off our political base even further by dropping impeachment. We and our allies had done such a good job getting the base fired up about impeachment that setting it aside would spell disaster for the party, as even a neophyte political strategist would understand. Republican leaders were therefore in a political conundrum.

The facts aside, however, most Republican leaders appeared to blame the impeachment inquiry for the election losses our party suffered. Making the situation worse, Newt held a post-election

Bob Barr with House Majority Whip Tom DeLay

conference call with GOP House members in which he seemed disoriented and unsure of exactly why we had performed below expectations. Newt's team immediately deserted him, with such notable backstabbing comments as Linder's remark that "I remember when Newt Gingrich's wife left a press conference in tears when he blamed her. So I do not think he has any compunction about blaming me."[2] Powerful Louisiana congressman Bob Livingston organized a challenge to Newt for the Speakership, and Newt announced his resignation shortly after the election.

Given these events, an impact on our impeachment inquiry was inevitable. After the election, a clear message came down to us: "Get this thing over with as quickly as possible."[3] We were told in no uncertain terms by the House leadership that if we attempted to fund any kind of investigation once the next Congress began, our request would be denied. We would not be able to buy a box of paperclips if they would be used to hold impeachment papers together, much less pay the salaries of a team of lawyers and investigators. This left us with such a small window of time (less than a month) that any real in-depth investigation was essentially shut down.

This meant our initial efforts to expand the inquiry into more serious issues than affairs with interns would be DOA. Exactly one month after the election, the committee announced that no issues relating to campaign finance and national security would be part of the impeachment inquiry. Soon, Starr would personally announce that the numerous issues he had investigated—from Filegate to Whitewater—had not generated evidence of impeachable offenses. This stroke effectively cut the legs off any dwindling prospects we may have had after the election of investigating anything other than the Lewinsky matter. The vast majority of our effort would therefore have to go into presenting charges contained in the Starr report, or we risked suffering damage from factual errors resulting from the suddenly rushed timetable. We were betting all of our chips on one horse, and it was far from the best horse in the race.

Starr was, by himself, one of the most credible parts of the case he presented. The man was systematically attacked and belittled by the news media to the point that most people probably figured he had horns, forked toes, and a tail. It began when Clinton confidante James Carville set up a White House-backed slush fund with the mission of attacking Starr and obstructing his investigation. This occurred in late 1996, and as soon as Carville announced it I requested he be investigated for federal obstruction of justice charges, which unequivocally applied to what he was up to. His lawyers must have told him the same thing because he quietly ratcheted down his efforts almost as soon as he began them.

However, the Carville episode started a veritable media orgy of Starr-bashing that continued throughout the investigation, impeachment, and trial. The general thrust of the attacks was that Ken was a puritanical, religious fundamentalist obsessed with rummaging around Bill Clinton's private life. For example, many reporters made no end of the fact that he was rumored to sing hymns while jogging, which in the valueless culture of our nation's

Ken Starr reading from the U.S. Constitution.

capital apparently made him a religious fanatic on the order of Ayatollah Khomeini.

Of course, the real Ken Starr is nothing like the picture the media painted. He is, in fact, both one of the kindest and most decent human beings I have ever known, as well as a man possessing a phenomenally sharp legal mind. Ken already had a great legal track record, serving at the highest levels of the legal profession. As an independent counsel, he had already achieved substantial success, netting numerous convictions already in his investigation. In reality, his courageous decision to undertake this inquiry—as he well knew—foreclosed any chance he would ever have of being appointed to the Supreme Court, where he would have made an excellent addition to the bench.

Unfortunately, the independent counsel statute was structured in such a way that it deprived Starr of any real means of self-defense in the court of public opinion. If he revealed any details of his case prior to his report to Congress, he would surely be accused of illegal or unethical leaks of information and pilloried by the news media and Clinton's defenders (which happened anyway). As a matter of fact, one of the tools frequently used by the White House to attack Starr concerned such leaks. In short, the White House would cynically leak information on the grand jury testimony of witnesses from its side to the news media and then blame Starr for its own behavior. This was, of course, a calculated and dishonest scheme to discredit the office of the independent counsel, but it was not without success.

Consequently, Ken's first real shot at a public defense would be his presentation to the Judiciary Committee. This was the first time the nation would hear him speak directly, unfettered by his critics, detractors, and enemies. When he finished, there was little doubt that he was a force to be reckoned with. The Judiciary Committee would hear other witnesses, but none of them would have anything like Starr's impact.

To the committee and the American public, Starr presented an airtight summary of the case against the president. It clearly showed that Clinton had perjured himself and obstructed justice. Starr's presentation was carried on live television across the nation and indeed the world. But the public already knew about the case. What they were tuning in to see was the man who was presenting it. What they saw was not a vindictive partisan obsessed with getting the president at all costs but a humble, erudite, almost scholarly lawyer who came across as a straight shooter. When Starr finished a grueling presentation including extensive and brutal cross-examination, the entire room (except Clinton's lawyers and the Democratic committee members) erupted in spontaneous applause. In hundreds of hours of hearings, I had never seen anything like it.

Despite being maliciously battered during and before the hearing, Judge Starr's presentation brought an entire room—many of whom were hardened Washington insiders who likely disagreed with him on the issue—to its feet. With Starr's testimony, the charges instantly became much more believable to the public.

Unfortunately, Congress had lost so much of its deliberative character that, while Judge Starr's testimony made an enormous impact on the public, it scarcely budged the partisan battle lines on the Judiciary Committee. On that fateful day, I focused my remarks on this issue:

> Today's hearing may not change a single mind on this committee. We will spend the day asking Ken Starr questions, some of us motivated by a desire to learn, others motivated by a desire to score political points, and others driven by having a few minutes in the ever-shifting national limelight. When it's all over, those of us who think the president has committed impeachable conduct will continue to say so. Those of us who believe the president was the innocent victim of a vast conspiracy will continue to oppose impeachment.
>
> In many ways, this hearing is a paradigm for the illness ailing our democracy. In the days of Thomas Jefferson, Alexander Hamilton, Henry Clay, and Daniel Webster, television cameras were absent. However, the words that soared in these chambers made their absence scarcely noticeable. These men were not forced to reach a distracted and disinterested public in the instantly vanishing banalities we call television sound bites. Their words were based on principles that sprang from their hearts, grew in their minds, and gained acceptance in the forge of debates that shaped an infant nation. Unlike the speeches many offer these days, the words of our predecessors had the power to persuade because they were based on true ideas, and on an understanding of government and governing that is all but lost in most of what happens in the Congress of this last decade of the twentieth century. Debates mattered, and they actually swayed votes. Speeches enacted ideas.

What has happened to us? Where has our capacity to think rationally gone? The report we have read, and that we will discuss today, remains un-rebutted. Think about that. No one is questioning the facts.

What do the facts in this case prove? They prove the president lied to the American people and perjured himself before a federal court and before a grand jury. They also prove he engaged in an effort to obstruct justice and tamper with witnesses. These un-rebutted facts conclusively prove that, as we begin this debate, a prosecutable felon sits in our nation's highest office.

Additionally, I introduce into the record today a memo written by Jerry Zeifman, concluding the president has engaged in bribery. Mr. Zeifman, who served as counsel for Chairman Rodino in the Watergate hearings, is from a different political party than I am. We probably disagree on more than 90 percent of the major political questions. However, we share a reverence for the rule of law and a desire to vindicate it.

Sadly, I fear Jerry Zeifman may belong to another— vanishing—generation of political leaders; a generation willing to put partisanship aside in order to preserve the Constitution. Another leader of years gone by put it this way: Americans are free to disagree with the law but not to disobey it. For a government of laws and not of men, no man, however prominent and powerful, and no mob, however unruly or boisterous, is entitled to defy a court of law. If this country should ever reach the point where any man or group of men, by force or threat of force, could long defy the commands of our courts and our Constitution, then no law would stand free from doubt, no judge would be sure of his writ, and no citizen would be safe from his neighbors.

These words were delivered to the nation by President Kennedy on Sept. 30, 1962. The president made these remarks regarding one of the greatest moral questions we ever faced as a nation. That question was whether an American's skin color should void his ability to obtain equal justice under law. Fortunately for us, we answered that question the right way, beginning a successful fight for justice that forged the opinions of many in this room today.

We face the same question today. President Kennedy's words are no less applicable now than they were then. Bill Clinton may not agree with sexual harassment laws, but he must follow them. Bill Clinton may be a prominent person, but that does not give him license to lie in court.

We have a huge responsibility as a nation. We can close our eyes. But when we open them, the problem will still be there, looming before us with a brooding darkness. We can answer this question the wrong way. And allow the president to hold his office with the knowledge that he has committed multiple felonies. Or we can answer this question the right way. The only right answer to the question is to respond to presidential felonies with impeachment. Regardless of whether the president is ultimately removed by the Senate, we must take this step in the House, as directed by our Constitution, in order to establish a precedent that will prevent future presidents from engaging in similar conduct.

It was also at this hearing that I made one more attempt to remind the world that we were not limited to the material contained in Starr's original report. To get this issue firmly on the record, I put the question to Ken directly, and he responded that he "had a statutory duty, but you have a constitutional duty." With that succinct but precisely accurate statement, Judge Starr had confirmed that, as independent counsel, his role was only—legally speaking—a small part of the impeachment process as it was designed to work in the Constitution. This response further underscored the problem the Republican leadership had created by pushing the independent counsel into the starring role, at the cost of not allowing Congress to do its job as the Constitution required and the Founders clearly intended.

In the days following Starr's testimony, Judiciary Republicans made one of the greatest strategic missteps we took by deciding not to call factual witnesses on the charges themselves. The problem is that we made an inaccurate assumption that the Senate would definitely want to hear factual witnesses before voting on removal. Consequently, we decided to postpone what we presumed would be a repetitive process. Instead, we listened to legal experts and other individuals who had been convicted of perjury discuss the charges. Unfortunately, we completely misjudged how the Senate would handle this matter. Not only would it refuse to hear factual witnesses, but it would twist our actions against us, using the fact that we had not called witnesses as "evidence" that we did not really think they were important.

Perhaps the most significant result of the Judiciary hearings on impeachment was that they galvanized public opinion in support of impeachment. During this time, strangers constantly came up to me and thanked me for the work we were doing. Pilots, flight attendants, and fellow passengers would pass me notes on airline flights thanking me for standing up for what was right.

One small victory we were able to achieve was getting into the record a detailed report compiled by Larry Klayman's Judicial Watch, one of the outside legal firms that did much of the investigative work on Clinton scandals. The only reason I was able to do so is that I waited until late in a long day of hearings and asked for unanimous consent to add the report to the record. At this point, the Democrats were so tired that they sort of yawned and said, "Sure, Barr," which I have no doubt they regretted later. This report outlined much of the group's findings, and while neither the committee nor the House would pay it any heed, including it in the historical record would help ensure that at least future generations knew the facts on these issues.

In a final effort to attempt to expand the inquiry, I had arranged for a meeting with Larry Klayman and Dave Schippers. Dave agreed to the meeting, and I think he was impressed with the work Judicial Watch had done on evidence of bribery and privacy violations, among other things. However, the odds of getting the inquiry expanded were so low by then that the meeting was largely in vain.

Our work in Judiciary was also boosted by the chairmanship of Henry Hyde. Although Henry and I disagreed on several decisions he made during the process, he was—without fail—a truly decent and patriotic man who believed deeply in the Constitution. Even the Democrats seemed to be shocked out of their partisanship by the obvious depth of feeling Chairman Hyde showed on these issues. Our hearings could easily have degenerated into a partisan food fight, and the fact that they proceeded in as orderly a fashion as they did was due largely to Henry's occupancy of the chair.

Finally, after months of arguing about the issue, it came time to put up or shut up. The committee was ready to vote on the Articles of Impeachment. In the December 11th hearing prior to the vote on the articles, I argued that:

> When Ms. Jones tried to walk into a courtroom, that governor, now the president of the United States of America, slammed the door in her face, and it very nearly remained locked tight. In a society based on justice under law, such an egregious wrong cannot be ignored. We in this Congress on this committee absolutely cannot ignore it. Even more troubling is the evidence that this administration has used its power to do exactly the same thing to others. Need we remind America of the 900-plus FBI files brazenly and illegally misused by the White House? Anyone not possessing an infinite capacity for self-delusion knows, whether they're willing to say it or not, that the president perjured himself on multiple occasions and committed other acts of obstruction of justice. It is also glaringly evident he enlisted others, from cabinet officials to political operatives, in this endeavor, and that this endeavor continued into this very room.

Needless to say, the Democrats in the room were not happy with my pointed implication that they were also involved in helping President Clinton undermine the legal system. However, it did not matter what I said to them because they had made up their minds a long time ago. When the Judiciary Committee voted on the Articles of Impeachment, the outcome was a straight party-line vote, with one minor exception that occurred when one of the Republicans,

Lindsey Graham of South Carolina, voted against a single article but in favor of the other three. The Democrats marched in lockstep and voted against all the articles. They expressed extreme confidence in this vote, despite the fact that—according to the official logs kept in the committee document storage area at the Ford Building—several of them had not even bothered to spend a moment of their time even entering to view the evidence on the case. In fact, the Judiciary Democrats were so loyal to Clinton that they voted unanimously against holding an impeachment inquiry in the first place. Like so many of the participants in the trial, they had their minds made up and shut tight before the process began.

After passage by the Judiciary Committee, the Articles of Impeachment were on a fast track to the House floor. The legislative tactics Clinton's House defenders adopted to block the House vote actually were creative in their own right. One of the more notable examples was that of Florida Congressman Alcee Hastings, who had himself been impeached and removed from a federal judgeship prior to his election to Congress. Alcee actually argued that the House should impeach Kenneth Starr instead of Bill Clinton. After attracting some chuckles, his efforts went nowhere, but they showed how desperate Clinton's hardcore defenders had become.

During the House debate over impeachment, things started to take on surreal overtones. One of the oddest moments occurred when I walked into the Speaker's lobby adjacent to the House chamber, after making an argument in favor of impeachment in which I quoted John F. Kennedy. In the lobby, I spoke with a group of reporters who asked various impeachment-related questions. At the time, one of the many lesser Kennedys who populate Washington—in this case young Patrick, nephew of the former president—was hanging around the room. Patrick was one of those pompous characters you encounter frequently in Washington who completely personifies the phrase "snot-nosed rich kid." An admitted cocaine user, he made at least one trip to rehab before his family bought him a congressional seat in Rhode Island by spending a phenomenal amount of cash in this small state.

Patrick—outraged that I had dared to quote his uncle in support of impeachment—came running across the room, yelling that I was a "racist" who "lied" and was therefore not allowed to quote JFK. I reminded Patrick that House rules forbade this kind of behavior and—in a moment of self-indulgence—called him a "young man."

"I am a duly elected Representative who can say what he wants," the young Kennedy shot back.

"I am duly impressed," I responded before he stalked away.

I suppose this incident should not surprise me, since I am not the first American to be assaulted by a Kennedy. What was even stranger is that Patrick—apparently not content to let matters rest—went on to start another heated verbal exchange on the same day, this time with a member of my staff. This particular staffer grew up in downtown New York City, so he was certainly no stranger to heated verbal exchanges, and I am sure the two of them had quite a time shouting at one another.

During the debate on the Articles of Impeachment, things got so strange that it was difficult to maintain any sense of perspective. At the time, Clinton was attacking Iraq in an attempt to create a distraction, so there was a real possibility that his actions could ignite a full-scale war with Iraq or another nation. The aborted Livingston speakership—and Larry Flynt's role in that drama—also lent an air of warped crisis to the debate.

Despite the surreal nature of the events in those few days, the moment that the House passed two of the four Articles of Impeachment was one in which I admit taking a substantial amount of personal pride. Justice certainly does not win every struggle in Washington, and her victories are getting more and more infrequent as time goes on. To stand on the House floor and see a guilty president become the first person elected to that high office impeached, made all of the sacrifices I had endured during the past two years seem worthwhile. The personal attacks still raged, in fact increased, even after the impeachment vote in December of 1998.

Bob Livingston was by no means the only official targeted by the Clinton smear team. One thing I wrestled with when I considered taking a lead role in pushing toward impeachment was whether I really wanted to deal with the smears, lies, and scorched earth politics that would inevitably follow a successful attempt to hold a deeply corrupted and politicized president to account. This would be no easy battle, and there was no doubt it would take a personal toll. The question was whether the end result was important enough to make the price worth paying. I know Ken Starr and his family went through a similar wrenching process.

I first started to consider this problem as my wife Jeri and I sat side by side on an Amtrak train coming home from a bipartisan congressional retreat in Hershey, Pennsylvania. It was early 1997, and I had my nose buried in a stack of books detailing the legal and congressional precedents for impeachment.

Jeri turned to me with a concerned look and asked, "Are you serious about doing this?" I told her that, yes, I was serious, to which she replied, "You know they're going to come after you with everything they have, don't you?" I thought about it for a second and said the issue was so important that I could not ignore it. We agreed to weather the storm just as we had weathered past attacks raised during political campaigns, such as when an opponent falsely accused me, in a televised ad, of refusing to pay child support. After all, I thought, I had prosecuted white supremacists and drug lords as a U.S. attorney, and for a time we were required to have armed security at our home. Nothing Clinton's smear team might try could possibly be that bad, could it?

By the end of impeachment, there was little Bill Clinton and his defenders had not thrown at me in an effort to discredit the charges I had raised. This was not an easy task for them because I had been through brutal political campaigns already, and any allegation that might possibly be damaging had been either used by my opponents or rejected as politically ineffective. Getting additional information would take someone with a high level of financial resources and absolutely no ethical standards. Fittingly, Bill Clinton's number one henchman on this front was Larry Flynt, the notorious pornographer. Flynt's tactics, like those of any bully, were brutally simple and strikingly straightforward. He offered a massive bag of cash to any individuals willing to cough up salacious personal details on the private lives of prominent Republicans. By his own estimates, Flynt ended up shelling out several million dollars in this campaign.

Larry Flynt may have been the public face of this campaign to destroy anyone who dared criticize Bill Clinton, but I have never believed he was operating entirely on his own. As the editor of one magazine with close ties to the Clinton White House reported in 1998—as the impeachment effort was rapidly gathering steam—a "close ally of the president" warned that "Republicans with skeletons in their closets must assume everything is known and will come out. So the question is: Do they really want to go there?"[4] In a rare moment of public candor, one of Bill Clinton's closest associates told a national television audience that "the president said he would never resign, and I think some around him are willing to take everybody down with him."[5]

In March 1998, the *Washington Times* reported that the White House had compiled "special files" with negative information on specific individuals designed to "offset stories produced by the media seen as hostile to the president."[6] The list of targets for such files included me and Senator Fred Thompson. The message here was clear: if you try to hold Bill Clinton accountable, we will go through your personal life and reveal every damaging detail we can come up with in the most public fashion possible. It would not be long before all Americans realized how far the White House and its allies would go in making good on this threat.

Two of the early targets of the White House smear machine were Dan Burton and Henry Hyde, the Republicans chairing House committees most directly involved in investigating Bill Clinton's misdeeds. In September 1998, *Salon.com* completed its "investigation" of Henry Hyde's personal life. *Salon*—like the *Geraldo Rivera Show*—was one of a handful of media outlets that were wholly owned subsidiaries of the Clinton White House during impeach-

Bob Barr with Fred Thompson.

ment. In fact, as Tom DeLay detailed in a letter to all House members, *Salon* was "bankrolled by left-wing activists who have contributed tens of thousands of dollars to President Clinton." As DeLay went on to add, "*Salon* is a tool of the White House. *Salon*'s backers have only one agenda—protecting their investment in President Clinton at any cost." When stories appeared in these venues, they may as well have been official statements by the White House press secretary from the briefing room at 1600 Pennsylvania Avenue.

Hyde was a difficult target for Clinton's defenders because he was such an extraordinarily upright and respected figure. There was not anything related to Henry's public service that could be used against him. But Clinton's team was desperate, and they would stop at nothing to get even the smallest nugget of information that might momentarily distract attention from the fact that they were trying to protect a felon sitting in the Oval Office. In Henry's case, this search took them to a seventy-six-year-old retiree in Florida who helped them piece together the story of an affair that allegedly occurred in the late 1960s. Henry was forthright in his response, acknowledging that he had made a mistake long ago that his marriage was strong enough to survive. He went on to add that "[t]he only purpose for this being dredged up now is an obvious attempt to intimidate me and it won't work. I intend to fulfill my constitutional duty and deal judiciously with the serious felony allegations presented to Congress in the Starr report."[7]

At the end of the Hyde matter, the White House had succeeded in reopening long-closed personal wounds of a grandfather and career public servant who has lived the kind of life to which most of us would be honored to aspire. This grandfather deeply loved his wife and had lost her to a heartbreaking battle with ovarian cancer in 1992 after forty-five years of marriage. Although Henry is not a vengeful man and has probably forgiven the people who did this, for my part, I can only say that I hope they will someday be held accountable for what they did to him.

Dan Burton was also high on the list of White House targets. At about the same time, *Vanity Fair* and *Salon* were both actively digging through the details of Dan's personal life in Indiana. The same kind of process was directed at Idaho congresswoman Helen Chenoweth, one of our original impeachment inquiry co-sponsors. Soon after impeachment, the same crowd would target Newt Gingrich, even though he was out of office and a private citizen. In each instance, the Clinton White House lurked gleefully in the shadows, cheering on its allies as they attacked Republicans in a systematic campaign to obstruct one of the most important processes in our Constitution.

There was only one case, however, where these tactics had any real success. Larry Flynt was able almost single-handedly to end Bob Livingston's congressional career by uncovering—without a great deal of effort—the commonly known (at least on Capitol Hill) fact that he had personal indiscretions in his private life. Bob decided to leave office rather than have his name publicly dragged through the mud in a manner that would embarrass him and do even more damage to his family. At the time, of course, Livingston had also recently secured his position as the next Speaker of the House following Newt Gingrich. So by threatening to trumpet personally embarrassing material from a national podium, Flynt had taken out the highest-ranking Republican in the House of Representatives. This made him, for a brief period of time, the most feared man in Washington, D.C.

It is important to remember that none of the charges had anything to do with the official conduct of their targets. They were purely personal in nature, and their only intent was to do enough damage to their targets that our work in Congress would be rendered less effective. Fundamentally, this was obstruction of justice in its purest form, and it was no different than a mob boss threatening the family of a district attorney or promising to reveal damaging information on jurors during a trial. In each case, Clinton's team would attempt to create a certain level of moral equivalence, arguing that these individuals had made mistakes in their personal lives, just as he had.

Of course, the issues were anything but equivalent. None of us are saints, and if someone looks hard enough, there is always something about each of our private lives we would rather not have become public knowledge. Members of Congress are certainly no different. Like all humans, we make mistakes, learn from them, and try to do better. The relevant question is how we had conducted ourselves in our public capacities. We had not damaged national security, attacked the integrity of the criminal justice system, abused the most powerful public office in the world, or violated the constitutional rights of large numbers of American citizens. Bill Clinton had done all of these things, and this was the reason he was being impeached, not because of the affair he had with Monica Lewinsky or the long list of affairs that preceded it.

Along with Livingston, I shared the unenviable position atop Flynt's target list, and I have little doubt this was the result of direction from the White House or those close to it. For example, Clinton friend and confidante James Carville appeared in Flynt's autobiographical movie, and the pornographer refers to him as a "friend."

Documents subpoenaed from Carville's office show that the White House counsel's office repeatedly shared information by fax with him on perceived enemies of the president, including a copy of divorce proceedings in at least one case. Many of Clinton's leading defenders gleefully cheered Flynt on, unbothered by the fact he was a major purveyor of pornography. Democrat Senator Frank Lautenberg characterized Flynt's work as a "pretty good mission." The list goes on, and what it shows is that Larry Flynt was nothing more than another spokesman for the Clinton smear team, working with the active encouragement of the White House and Democrat senators and representatives.

We first got wind Flynt was up to something sleazy about me when a friend at the local courthouse mentioned that a private investigator named Dan Moldea had been sniffing around looking for court records from my divorce more than a decade before. Those records were sealed, but Flynt was able to obtain access to them by paying a large sum of money to my ex-wife. The information he obtained was not particularly interesting. During the divorce proceedings, I had cited a Georgia law that allowed me to remain silent on several issues, which he interpreted—wrongly—as a case of perjury. Additionally, Flynt reported that my ex-wife alleged I had urged her to have an abortion.

Neither allegation was true. But the charges put me in a position that was both politically awkward and personally painful. If I ignored the attacks, they would get that much less attention but would be presumed true. However, if I addressed them, then they would be accorded a level of legitimacy they did not deserve. At the time, my two sons were both in high school, and the foremost thought in my mind was that I did not want to do anything that would make things more difficult for them, as well as my staff (who urged complete silence). Ultimately, I decided to issue a flat denial of the charges in writing and in person on *Larry King Live*—since they were untrue—and leave it at that.

Interestingly, though reporters camped outside my Capitol Hill office for hours on end with their cameras and microphones at the ready, the national media actually ignored most of Flynt's charges. In fact, the night he revealed them, a top anchor for one of the major networks called our office and asked whether we planned to respond. In his view, the allegations were purely personal and related in no way to any legal or political issue, which was true. He told us his network would treat the charges as news only if we chose to respond to them, an eminently fair standard. After we stood up to Flynt and the charges he had spent thousands of dollars developing fell flat, his campaign to save members personally came to a fairly abrupt halt. Flynt published a glossy "Flynt Report" that contained no new information and then went back to his customary business of producing pornography.

Perhaps the most amusing rant against me came from one of Clinton's defenders, U.S. Representative Cynthia McKinney, a Georgia Democrat who gained notoriety chiefly for representing the interests of Third World dictators and constantly railing against all things Republican in Congress. In announcing her vote against the impeachment inquiry, she exclaimed—in her typically hyperbolic manner—that "[w]hat is amazing to me is that Gingrich's hand-picked handmaiden Bob Barr can lick whipped cream off a woman's breast and stand there with a straight face."[8] Although this partic-ular flight of Cynthia's imagination had little to do with reality, it was presumably rooted in an urban legend that I had once attended an event where I ate whipped cream—or an entire ice cream sundae, depending on which version of the story one hears—from the chests of one or more people at a Leukemia Society fund-raiser a decade before. There was a persistent story making this allegation that took on a life of its own on the Internet during impeachment. While I could have disputed it—noting, for example, that I had raised money for the charity by, among other good-natured stunts by myself and other public officials, licking a teaspoon of whipped cream off the shoulder of a fully dressed participant—it fell into the category of one of those charges I was better off not dignifying with a response. Either way, it shows how strange the attacks from Clinton's most hardcore defenders were starting to get toward the end of the House process. Absolutely any allegations, even myths and half-truths, were employed as ammunition against Clinton's detractors.

The allegation swirling the nation's capital must have had some traction, though, because left-wing filmmaker Michael Moore went to great lengths to hide behind the old trees on the Capitol grounds and jump out with great fanfare to quiz me about it and other nonsense. This was not my first encounter with Moore, who would often troll the halls of our office building, looking for me and other members he did not like and then hiding behind corners to ambush us as we walked by. Amazingly enough, many Republicans lived in fear of this guy. In fact, the Judiciary Committee and Republican Conference would actually e-mail warnings to members when he was rumored to be in town, implying—presumably—that we should hide in our offices and quake in fear underneath our desks like school kids in an air raid drill.

However, I rather enjoyed tangling with Moore, primarily for the comic value of our encounters. As most Americans know by now, Moore is a "documentary" filmmaker who has made a nice living for himself making factually questionable films that pander to every pet left-wing cause in America. The guy is living proof that America is a place where even smirking, fat, whiny guys with bad haircuts, ball caps, and mediocre intellects can be successful. For example, he recently got himself attention by calling Iraqi terrorists the equivalent of American minutemen in the Revolutionary War. I like having Moore on the national scene because he's a walking argument against the proposition that liberals make more logical and credible arguments than conservatives.

One of the more formidable enemies I encountered in the impeachment debate was celebrity lawyer and Harvard professor Alan Dershowitz. Dershowitz was closely involved with the White House in planning the impeachment defense strategy, and he mysteriously learned of my unintended appearance at the Council of Conservative Citizens meeting in South Carolina (a group with bizarre racial views that tries to pass itself off as mainstream and had managed to snare Trent Lott and Dick Gephardt with similar innocuous invitations). There is little doubt Dershowitz was handed this information by the White House smear machine. He waited to use it until he was testifying before the House Judiciary Committee, and I had made a reference to "real America."

In classic liberal victimization fashion, Dershowitz argued that this phrase was racist and that I must obviously be a racist, since I had spoken at one meeting of this group in a year when I made hundreds of public appearances. This, of course, was a crock. I have always deeply opposed racism with a visceral, gut-level response that probably dates back to the time I spent growing up as a minority, an American living in foreign nations where my dad worked on engineering projects. However, Dershowitz pressed his case and was assisted by four or five reporters and columnists who had proven reliable shills for attacking anyone who criticized Clinton. Once again, the Clinton "opposition research" team had been able to dredge up an obscure piece of information that could be used to make "their man" look a bit better by comparison.

Hateful—and in many cases mentally troubled—wackos around America apparently learned a few things from President Clinton and his defenders because they also started directing venom my way, all on their own. For example, we started receiving anonymous faxes alleging that my wife had tested positive for a terminal disease and recommending treatment options, which was—of course—untrue. In several cases, we received telephoned death threats followed by hang-ups. There was even one man from Florida who would call our office every morning at a few minutes after 9 AM, announce that "Bob Barr is a jackass," giggle, and hang up. I do not think this fellow bothered my staff too much, since I am sure they muttered the same words under their breath from time to time. In fact, the young lady who staffed our front desk actually managed to make friends with "the jackass" as he was known, and the two of them would exchange pleasantries after his morning call. Either way, these troubled individuals were most likely harmless, but it was still concerning to have this many deranged people taking such a personal interest in my family and me. Unlike President Clinton, we had no Secret Service protection . . . just a great staff, the Capitol Hill police who were always responsive when needed, and at home a dog, a burglar alarm, and the Second Amendment.

Regardless of their credibility—or lack thereof—Clinton's apologists still actively circulate personal attacks directed at me. They remain obsessed with the idea of somehow vindicating his legacy. A key part of their vindication campaign rests on continuing to discredit anyone who questioned Clinton's conduct during his presidency. For example, David Brock, the former conservative turned self-loathing gay liberal, recently wrote a book relaying many of Larry Flynt's charges against me as facts. Brock gained fame for doing a hatchet job on Anita Hill during the Clarence Thomas hearings, so it is in some ways unsurprising to see him putting his skills to work for his new left-wing masters.

Although charges by Flynt and others were repeated fairly frequently by the most hardcore of Clinton's defenders, they did not gain much credence. In fact, the only people who seemed to take Flynt's efforts seriously, or at least seemed to be scared by them, were Republicans. During the entire process, not a single senior Republican member offered to lift a finger in my defense or even give their personal support. In fact, I did not even get so much as a phone call from one of them. The only acknowledgment I did receive was that Henry Hyde revoked my status as one of the four leading House prosecutors in the Senate trial and filled my seat with Bill McCollum. Although Flynt had nothing and the media largely ignored his charges, they were at least serious enough to provoke a reaction from our skittish party leaders.

Though the price for helping push the House toward impeachment was personally a high one, I took—and still take—a great deal of solace in knowing how effectively we succeeded. At the end of the debate, we convinced every single member of the Republican caucus and more than thirty Democrats in the House to support opening an impeachment inquiry. When I began the campaign, our work was largely dismissed as a partisan joke, but approximately one year later a majority of the House agreed to do exactly what I had suggested.

Democrats were also not immune to attacks from the White House smear machine when they dared to criticize Bill Clinton. Paul McHale, then a Democratic congressman from Pennsylvania, was an early voice of criticism against Clinton. A colonel in the Marine Corps Reserve—and now an assistant secretary of defense— McHale was retiring from Congress and had the guts to look directly at the evidence against the president. After concluding that Clinton had broken the law, he urged him to resign from office. The White House immediately lashed out against McHale.

The *Geraldo Rivera Show* was a favorite venue for the White House to use in leaking information that more credible programs would refuse to cover. Rivera would put things on the air that the White House would not be able to talk a public access cable show in Peoria into covering. So when a "source very close to the president" told him McHale had lied about the military decorations he earned, Rivera immediately aired the charge. Of course, the allegations turned out to be completely untrue, but the message to other potential McHales was clear: speak out against the president and we're going to comb through your past, looking for any damaging fact, even a concocted one, and put it out on the national airwaves. In this case, the member the White House targeted was a deeply patriotic man with a spotless record. But that description certainly does not apply to all—or even a majority—of House and Senate members. I have little doubt that the McHale case encouraged others to keep quiet.

As history looks back on the process, I have no doubt some of the greatest kudos will go to the moderate Republicans who ultimately supported the Articles of Impeachment. This was a difficult vote for these members because many of them represented districts won by Bill Clinton. They were under heavy White House pressure to vote "no." They knew the White House would target them for defeat from the moment they cast their vote. Yet they voted to impeach.

These men and women stood to pay a real personal price for their vote, and they stood up before America and voted for what was right. If the Senate had shown half their courage, the outcome there may have been different.

One thing I will say for the impeachment process, it certainly created national spotlight that attracted more than its share of strange people. There was the group of protestors who dressed in conductor's caps and railroad uniforms and carried large whistles, marching in a circle and shouting "all aboard the Impeachment Express" over and over again. No one paid attention to them until they decided to follow CNN's Bob Franken around and stand behind his live camera shots. At that point exactly one person noticed them, and that person was an angry middle-aged CNN correspondent named Bob who I thought was going to beat them senseless with their own whistles if they did not go away.

Then there was the nice homeless lady who showed up in our office with an entire set of luggage full of what she alleged were deeply incriminating documents on Bill Clinton. My staff told her we would be fine with a verbal summary of documents, but she insisted on leaving them all with our receptionist and walking away never to be seen again. Sadly, the documents turned out to be primarily pages of newspapers copied from public libraries with handwritten scrawls on them. The most notable items in the suitcase were the four or five cockroaches that came scurrying out when we opened it.

These two cases are a limited sample of the people drawn to the impeachment process like moths to a flame when the klieg lights of the media started to heat up. When an act of the impeachment drama began at a particular location, media hordes descended on the spot like locusts gobbling up a cornfield. With all of the lights, cables, cameras, satellite dishes, and other assorted gizmos they brought with them, it often looked as if a scene from an alien invasion movie was being acted out on the grounds of the nation's Capitol.

America being the most dynamic capitalist society the world has ever seen, it was no surprise to see the private sector getting in on the fun as well. The many commercial mementos of impeachment that arrived unsolicited in my office are a testament to the degree to which the national imagination was captured by impeachment. The list included numerous bumper stickers, cartoons, a pocket knife, figurines, baseball caps, pens, cigars, cans of "impeachment" peaches, impeachment-themed coffee blends, and a set of wooden Russian nesting dolls that included a miniature Bob Barr.

Even members of Congress were encouraged by all the media and public attention to behave in ways that were strange, even for them. During the Senate impeachment trial, for example, House Democrat Sheila Jackson-Lee would wander over to the Senate every day and hang around for the entire process, taking notes to herself. This was puzzling since Sheila was neither a manager nor a senator (or a page, reporter, or clerk for that matter). Even stranger, she insisted on holding her own sparsely attended, one-woman press conferences right next to any group of House managers or senators who were being interviewed. The Texas congresswoman had a reputation on the Hill for coming completely unglued so frequently that no one wanted to work in her office. In an incident

Russian nesting dolls: Kenneth Starr, Henry Hyde, Linda Tripp, Lucianne Goldberg, and Bob Barr.

recounted by one of her many former assistants to the *Houston Press*, the congresswoman was not provided with the special meal she requested on an airline flight. This must have represented a grave insult because she screamed at the top of her lungs for more than a minute on the flight, saying, "Don't you know who I am? I'm Congresswoman Sheila Jackson Lee. Where is my seafood meal? I know it was ordered."[9] This—and similar incidents—prompted the airline to quietly request that she seek other means of traveling home. As one might imagine, she was something of a ticking time bomb, so her presence at the trial always added an air of uncertainty about what kind of insanity might occur next.

Impeachment also brought some random encounters that were quite interesting. Washington is, at heart, a small town. It looks like a large city on the map, but for people who work in government, it's not a large place. There are a limited number of places to eat, shop, get your car serviced, and do the countless other things one has to do in order to function in daily life. This often means you end up running into people in the strangest places. For example, one night I decided to go to Union Station—the city's largest train depot—to grab a quick bite to eat at the food court that fills its lower level. As I was walking through the main part of the station, I literally collided with Betty Currie, Bill Clinton's personal secretary with whom he had conspired to destroy evidence. Ms. Currie had a White House handler with her at the time, and her escort quickly shuffled her away, but only after we—much to her chagrin—exchanged pleasant "hellos" and "how are yous."

A similar event occurred with John Podesta, Clinton's chief of staff, at the height of the impeachment fight. We were both booked as guests on NBC's *Meet the Press*. Consequently, we were sitting in a small "green room" at the studios prior to our appearance. NBC is kind enough to provide uniformed waiters to serve breakfast pastries, coffee, and fresh fruit to its guests before the program. Podesta and I sat across from each other and enjoyed breakfast prior to the show, both doing our best to act unimpressed with the other's presence.

These vignettes represent just small illustrations of the ways the impeachment turned the world of the congressman from Georgia's Seventh District, and truly the entire nation's capital, into the Twilight Zone. However, no matter how strange things got, one thing was certain. They were never going to get strange enough to wake up more than a few members of that august body known as the United States Senate.

7

Failure in the Senate

The House may be a nice place in which to work, but the Senate puts it to shame. For example, the House cloakroom is a crowded, almost threadbare antechamber where you spend time only if you have no other alternative between votes. In the Senate, the sitting room adjacent to the chamber is filled with some of the most comfortable La-Z-Boys I have ever plopped down in. In the House, we were used to getting our own water, but the Senators each had a personal glass that was studiously refilled on a regular basis by a bevy of blue-blazered pages. The only upside to this was that my chair was located so close to the desk of ultra-liberal California Senator Barbara Boxer that when I sat down, her water glass invariably shifted. On two occasions, the glass spilled, drenching her papers. While I did not do this on purpose, it was at least interesting to watch the Senate pages go into emergency response mode, assuming that the U.S. government would come to a screeching halt if that water was not immediately sopped up and all evidence of its presence erased.

Senate privilege also extends to unusual places. If you use the men's room reserved for senators—which we House impeachment managers were graciously allowed to sully with our presence—you do not have to risk dirtying your suit coat by brushing it against the floor. A full-time government employee stands waiting by the door to hold the coats of senators while they do their business in bathroom stalls. I am sure this particular government expense is most reassuring to overtaxed families in real America when they sit down each month to decide whether, for example, to take a vacation or save money for their kids' college. However, to senators, this is one more thing they deserve; the people of America—in their minds— *owe* it to them. The list of similar perks goes on, but I am sure you get my point: the Senate is a nice place to spend time, and once people get there, they will do virtually anything to avoid being forced to leave.

At the time of the trial, Senate Republican leaders faced a dilemma. They badly wanted impeachment to go away, but they knew that if they summarily dismissed it, they would pay a political price; their conservative base would view them as gutless and weak, and their liberal opposition would beat them up for the same reason. Therefore, there would be a trial with at least the appearance of legitimacy. It remained to be seen whether it would be a show trial or a serious effort to uncover the facts pertaining to the Clinton administration's abuse of power.

On January 7, 1999, the thirteen House impeachment managers, led by Henry Hyde, marched in procession across the Capitol from the House to the Senate. It was a short distance, but those steps were some of the heaviest I have ever taken. During my time in the House, I had never visited the Senate floor, even though we had privileges to do so (and vice versa). Walking into that chamber for the first time carrying such a heavy burden was an awesome moment. We were welcomed to the Senate by Strom Thurmond, who was ninety-six at the time. Throughout the trial, Thurmond was—paradoxically—one of the most alert senators, never failing to wish good morning or good afternoon to "my friend from Georgia" if we encountered each other on the Senate floor. Henry Hyde then spoke the words, "Mr. President, the managers on the part of the House of Representatives are here and present and ready to present the Articles of Impeachment which have been preferred by the House of Representatives against William Jefferson Clinton, President of the United States." From this point forward, like for Marlow in Joseph Conrad's *Heart of Darkness*, there was no turning back. After Henry read the Articles of Impeachment passed by the House, the lengthy process of swearing in the Senate as jurors—and Chief Justice Rehnquist as judge—began. At that moment, I was still wondering whether this would be a real trial, or, as I suspected, a meaningless set of debates with a foregone outcome.

Unfortunately for our nation's long-term interests, the extreme longing of the majority of the members of the U.S. Senate to be considered "nice" quickly reared its ugly head. In our early negotiations with the Senate, the typical pattern was that whenever a major decision was made, the Senate Democrats took a position, the House managers took a position, and the Republican senators took no position. It therefore came as no surprise that our "negotiations" were not negotiations at all but an exercise in seeing how quickly the Senate Republicans could give the Democrats whatever they wanted.

Still, I was dispirited to hear Trent Lott—who I knew generally to be a straight shooting conservative—announce at the start of the trial that the Senate would "have a bipartisan Senate conference so that we can talk to each other and listen to each other." That's right, there we were presenting a case supported by the majority of the membership of the U.S. House for removing the president from office, and all the Senate could think to do was get the guys together to hold hands and sing "Kumbayah." Maybe I am being too tough on the Senate, but I think that by the time someone gets elected to that august body, they should be capable of making up their minds on a matter this important without grandstanding in front of ninety-nine of their buddies. I was wrong, and hearing this kind of compromising language on the first day of the trial was definitely not a good sign.

My concerns were confirmed the next day when Democratic leader Tom Daschle announced following the bipartisan love-fest that "[t]he comity and the chemistry" were "evident from the very beginning." Translation: we screwed the House impeachment managers big time and then we blew sunshine at each other for a few hours. True to form, the Senate passed impeachment trial procedures by a 100-0 margin that streamlined the process into a fast-tracked show trial, with no guarantees that the House would be able to present even a single witness in support of our case. When he initially came to the other side of the Capitol to discuss the procedures in the Senate, Lott referred to our case right off the bat as "garbage." True to his initial statement, he and the Republican leadership in the Senate treated the case exactly like industrial-grade waste accidentally dumped on the Senate's pristine doorstep, which it only wanted to remove as quickly as possible (preferably without touching it).

This outcome was made possible by the fact that the Constitution is silent on the particulars of how an impeachment proceeding should be conducted. As in so many cases, the Founders had shown great wisdom by leaving this provision open to interpretation by future generations. Unfortunately, however, this also means that most impeachment procedures are merely precedents from earlier cases, often incorporated into the Rules of the Senate. Knowing this, it was almost heartbreaking to watch the Senate set precedents that would not only harm our case, but also make trying future impeachments that much more difficult. Make no mistake about it, as long as humans keep on being human, there is no doubt these provisions will be applied again in the future. If future impeachments are not conducted according to fair procedures, history can lay blame squarely with the Senate Democrats who insisted on protecting the president at all costs in the name of partisanship, and with the Republican leaders who bent the rules to allow them to do so in the name of bipartisanship.

On January 11, the managers and the White House released our dueling sets of documents about the charges. Ours was 105 pages long, the Clinton rebuttal was 13 pages, and neither document unveiled any new information or committed either side to act in a new way. Not to be outdone, the White House responded on January 13 with a 135-page rebuttal of the charges. Either way, this was classic pretrial maneuvering at its finest, and I doubt that anyone other than the lawyers for both sides and the poor journalists who had to report on them actually read the documents.

It was also on January 11 that I walked into a meeting of the House managers, which began with Henry Hyde bluntly announcing my removal from the team that would be cross-examining witnesses and my replacement by Bill McCollum of Florida. This was the single worst piece of news I received during the trial. It was absolutely crushing because the captain of my own team had thrown me overboard on an issue I cared deeply about and did not bother to offer an explanation for his decision. I was so disappointed at this decision that I vanished for the rest of the afternoon, walking the mall in front of the Capitol and visiting the National Gallery of Art, sending my staff into a panic. The upside about wandering the Smithsonian is that all the masterpieces there remind you of how much of the world's hopes for success are wrapped up in the "American experiment." If that experience does not stir patriotic sentiment in your heart, there isn't much hope for you. Also, while at the National Gallery, I was approached by several couples that recognized me and personally thanked me for leading the impeachment effort. In the end, I returned to finish what I had started in the Senate. Of all the insults I had taken in my career in public service, however, this one stung the worst.

In retrospect, Hyde's decision probably had a fair amount to do with an ill-advised—even if perhaps true—remark I had made about senators having an attention span much shorter that the average juror. No Democrat in the Senate was going to let me live that comment down, and they repeatedly trotted it out as a public reminder that the House managers had no respect for the traditions of the Senate. At an earlier period in American history, I have no doubt they would have called us "uppity" House members who had grown "far too large for our britches." Additionally, I am sure that

McCollum worked hard to get a greater share of the limelight, since he wanted badly to be a senator and assumed—wrongly, as it turned out—that the impeachment trial would enhance his credibility and electoral prospects in Florida. McCollum lost his first Senate campaign in Florida, helping hand the seat to a Democrat, and at the time of this printing he is well on his way to losing a second campaign.

Either way, this was how I found myself sitting in the United States Senate on January 14, 1999, at 1:05 PM listening to Henry Hyde begin the presentation of impeachment charges against William Jefferson Clinton. The Senate had outfitted a table for the managers team so we could all cluster together. Some of us faced the Democratic side of the Senate, where we could watch the senators react to presentations, while others faced the chief justice perched on the Senate dais and the podium for speakers in front of him. Our slightly curved table sat to the chief justice's right, while the president's defense team occupied a similar table to the left.

Sitting there, I was again struck by the coherence of the basic case we were presenting. Sure, we should have been talking about several things other than a salacious sex scandal. Yes, Bill Clinton had systematically attacked individual freedom and neglected his responsibility to secure our country. But lying under oath was still a serious matter for anyone and even more serious when the accused was a trained lawyer serving as president.

Following Hyde, Wisconsin congressman Jim Sensenbrenner began his presentation. One of the first things he pointed out was that three judges had been impeached in the 1980s for lying under oath. So much, I thought, for the argument that we were only discussing Clinton's personal life and not anything for which there was historical precedent for impeachment. Obstruction of justice was also a serious crime and one of the foremost reasons for President Nixon's troubles. President Clinton was clearly guilty of both crimes, and it gave me some comfort to know that the precedent on their relevance to impeachment was crystal clear and favored our case.

For the remainder of that day and the next, we continued to sum up our case against the president. On January 15, I took the floor with the charge of tying together the facts and the law, making our case that our version of the facts was correct and that removal from office was the appropriate legal remedy.

As I was concluding my presentation, Iowa senator Tom Harkin—one of the most liberal members of the U.S. Senate—rose to raise the first and only objection of the impeachment trial. His basic quibble was that I had stated the Senate was sitting like a "jury," a characterization he apparently felt was technically inaccurate. Chief Justice Rehnquist agreed with him, and we were instructed never to use the "J-word" again in what I can only imagine will go down as one of the more absurd footnotes of the trial. The Democrats in the Senate, of course, did not really care what we called them and used the objection as a way of scoring PR points. Standing at the ready after Harkin stepped into the spotlight were numerous Democrats ready to attack us for doing such an awful thing as calling the senators "jurors." Typical of the reaction was the junior senator from my home state, Max Cleland, who said our presentation was "demeaning" and he did not like being "lectured to."

The real, fundamental issue was that as "jurors," the senators would be bound by the facts and law, a prospect they found undesirable. As noted in Harkin's objection, the Senate viewed themselves in a class by themselves, above normal laws, not as mere "jurors," and therefore free to base their decisions on whatever political or personal grounds they desired. They would not be bound by the law and the facts (as would traditional "jurors"). Staking out this principle publicly and early on was part of their strategy. And, of course, the Republicans in the Senate sat silently, like sheep, and let them do it. Meanwhile, the chief justice, presiding over the Senate trial because the Constitution required him to, not because he wanted to, was more than happy to rule quickly and summarily in favor of Senator Harkin without allowing me or Henry Hyde (who had already risen from his seat at the impeachment managers' table

to join me at the lectern) to note for the record our objection to the
senator's ridiculous and self-serving objection.

On January 19, White House Counsel Charles Ruff began his
defense of the president. Ruff was one of the most skilled and
impressive law professors I encountered at Georgetown, and I knew
he would be a formidable adversary in the Senate. I was not disappointed. Ruff's chief responsibility was to rewrite the definition and
history of impeachment in a way that would allow his client to
wiggle off the hook.

On the same day, President Clinton visited the House to deliver
his State of the Union address. This was yet another example of the
degree to which Clinton seemed to feel no shame for his actions;
and he, much more than our side, recognized the power of symbols.
The year before, I had attended Clinton's speech and endured a fair
amount of media criticism by reporters who felt I did not smile and
clap enough. This year, I quietly stayed in my office and watched the
speech on television. I simply could not stand to sit there and listen
to Clinton show such callous disregard for the legitimacy of the
impeachment process and of the institution in which it was being
carried out.

While some of us urged the Speaker to postpone inviting
Clinton to deliver his message until after the impeachment (something clearly within his power to do), our leaders, now vying with
their Senate counterparts for "nice-guy" awards, would have none of
it. So in the middle of the Senate trial on impeachment charges, we
had Bill Clinton receiving standing ovations from those who had
already deemed him unfit to serve and by those currently listening
to evidence urging his conviction. It was no different than inviting
an indicted criminal out to a local restaurant to have dinner with
the members of the jury who would rule on guilt or innocence. It
was a disgraceful episode, and it was also politically moronic. The
last thing we needed to do at this point was give Clinton a chance to
look and act presidential, and there is no forum more suited to
looking and acting like a president than the State of the Union

address. I fully expect that I will go to my grave wondering why our leaders did this, unless their intent was to help Clinton "beat the rap" and remain in office.

After the State of the Union, the Senate trial shifted into high gear, both because our preliminary arguments were wrapped up and the Senate wanted the trial over *right now*. January 21 marked the conclusion of the presentation of President Clinton's case by his defense team. Batting cleanup was former Arkansas senator Dale Bumpers, a folksy and masterful speaker who played the country lawyer for the assembled senators. His rambling but highly effective speech essentially made the point that Clinton's failings were purely personal and that the real problem was with a judicial system run amuck. "I doubt that there are few people, maybe nobody in this body, who could withstand such scrutiny. And in this case those summoned were terrified not because of their guilt, but because they felt guilt or innocence was not really relevant. But after all of those years and $50 million of Whitewater, Travelgate, Filegate, you name it, nothing, nothing, the president was found guilty of nothing, official or personal."[1]

Of course, what Dale Bumpers conveniently left out of his speech is that Clinton had not been found guilty because he had not been prosecuted. If any other person had done what Bill Clinton had done, he not only would have been prosecuted, but convicted, sentenced, and put in jail. Obviously, no prosecutor in America was going to bring an indictment against a sitting president. But that is precisely the reason the Founders put the impeachment provision in the Constitution. The whole point of the trial was to determine his guilt or innocence. By arguing that Clinton had already been tried and cleared—when he had not—Bumpers conveniently gave the senators cover to vote against removal, even though presented with a clear factual case for doing so. Like any masterful attorney, he was giving the jury a plausible reason to do what it wanted to do, even though its desires ran contrary to the facts and the law. Put colloquially, the senators were chicken, and Bumpers was giving them a place to hide. In any event, Bumpers's speech to the Senate ended the initial maneuvering in the case, and we prepared to present the evidentiary portion.

The next day, the team of House managers was dealt a significant, though not unexpected, setback by the Senate. We had worked hard to whittle our list of witnesses to the lowest possible number, anticipating pressure from the Senate to end the trial quickly. That list included Lewinsky, Clinton, Vernon Jordan, Kathleen Willey, Dick Morris, Sid Blumenthal, and several other key players. I argued strongly in favor of keeping Willey on the list and dropping Jordan. I knew that his slick legal tactics and warm manner honed by years as a corporate attorney would have the Senate eating out of his hand in a few minutes. Presenting Kathleen Willey, on the other hand, would help show the Senate how far the president's allies were willing to go in criticizing the women he had attacked. This was also the day the senators were allowed to submit questions to the chief justice for the prosecution and defense to answer. Some Republicans—most notably Phil Gramm and Bob Smith—gave the White House a hard time for opposing witnesses, but their maverick efforts had no real impact on the outcome.

As we learned the very next day, much of this debate over witnesses was in vain. The Senate sent word that Republican leaders wanted the deposition stage ended that week. As usual, the messenger was Senator Rick Santorum. The Senate leadership apparently thought that—as a former House member and conservative—Santorum would be someone we would like. Rick is a nice guy, but he didn't seem to be calling too many shots in the Senate. His job was more or less to deliver bad news to us, let us chew him out for it, and then wander back to do something more productive. On more than one occasion, I almost felt bad for the guy; he suffered more than one shouted insult from the team of managers, including at least one "f___ you!" (not from me). However, my sympathy was quickly tempered by remembering that this was a member of the GOP leadership structure in the Senate who seemed to spend most of their waking hours finding new ways to cripple our case. Shooting the messenger was cold comfort, but it was all we could do at that point.

Santorum's message was clear. The Senate would allow only two witnesses. We might be able to squeeze in one or two additional witnesses by negotiating, but that would be it. At this moment, my flagging confidence in our ability to present our case fairly disappeared. It seemed the Senate Republican leadership would roll over and play dead if Ted Kennedy even looked at them askance. In retrospect, I'm amazed they demonstrated as much backbone as they did. The ridiculous thing is that our party held a solid majority in the Senate at the time. There was no reason we had to roll over time and time again. We could not force a vote on impeachment; that would depend on the facts of the case and public opinion. But we could at least ensure that a full presentation of the facts was made so that the Senate could say it did not hide the truth from the people or from its own members. In the end, what our constant compromises got us when the game was over was a bunch of Democrats voting in lockstep to keep Clinton in office. Neville Chamberlain would have been proud of these guys for taking appeasement to a new level!

To make a long story short, we ultimately ended up with three witnesses, who we could question not in the well of the Senate, but in a remote location. We graciously were allowed three witnesses, I'm sure, only because Ted Kennedy or Robert Byrd said it was okay. In any event, the witnesses we chose were Monica Lewinsky, Vernon Jordan, and Sidney Blumenthal. Clearly, Lewinsky was the most important witness in the case, and calling her to testify was largely a foregone conclusion. However, Jordan and Blumenthal were, I thought, less than desirable choices given the constraints we faced. I have already mentioned Blumenthal's background, and Jordan was one of the smoothest and most effective corporate attorneys in the nation. Both were skilled at dealing with public forums and legal proceedings, and I had no doubt that questioning them and getting anything useful would be an exceedingly difficult proposition, given the procedural straightjacket within which the depositions had to be conducted.

In my view, other witnesses would have been much more effective in building our case. For example, Kathleen Willey was such an obviously credible witness with a painful story to tell—of being sexually assaulted by the president in the Oval Office and systematically harassed afterward—that her testimony might have swayed even a few of the coldest and most calculating hearts in the Senate. Even if we had chosen Willey, however, it is unlikely the Senate would have permitted her to testify. In choosing our witnesses, we were also acknowledging the reality that the Senate would not allow anyone to appear if they were even remotely likely to change the outcome or make a vote against removal more difficult.

Contrary to normal legal proceedings, the depositions were run against a clock, so all an enterprising witness who wanted to avoid saying anything meaningful had to do was simply blather on and on about nothing of import. Essentially, this meant that we, the prosecutors, had lost control of the testimony and handed it to the witnesses. We either let them run out the clock or came across like jerks by constantly cutting them off. We were not going to win either way. The Senate knew this, and I have no doubt that they structured the taped depositions and the entire trial the way they did on purpose. The Senate's goal was to ensure the process did not change course substantially because of anything that occurred in that room. The fix was in, and the suckers were truth, justice, and the American people.

As Henry Hyde constantly reminded us, we could not control the cards we were dealt, so the best response was to make the best of what we had to work with, even though the odds of winning were— at this point—miniscule. So, on February 8, I began my closing remarks in the trial. At this point in the game, everyone on the managers team knew that—absent a miracle—President Clinton was going to take a walk on the charges against him. The Senate did not have the stomach to do much of anything with uncertain political consequences, and removing a president from office clearly fell into that category.

While we knew we would lose the battle at hand, we also knew there was a more important war to fight. Helping win that war meant firing an effective salvo in the controversy that would soon follow, about how history should define the Clinton legacy. With this goal in mind, I prepared my final remarks in the Senate trial of William Jefferson Clinton.

One of the odd things about the impeachment process was that you would go through intense periods of action, followed by lulls that were almost surreally calm. While I have never fought in combat, I imagine this kind of movement between extremes must be a common sensation experienced by soldiers in battle. One of those odd and extended periods of calm took place as I traveled back from the Republican retreat in Williamsburg, Virginia, to make my closing arguments in the Senate trial. The stretch of road from Williamsburg to Washington is mostly a lonely one, with trees crowding over the interstate on both sides in many areas. I was driving alone. As a member of Congress, you rarely do anything alone, so merely being by yourself often seems odd. On that drive, the most powerful feeling I experienced was one of intense loneliness. This was a surprisingly common sensation I experienced in the impeachment process, and it struck most powerfully in Washington.

At home, friends and family surrounded me, and they understood exactly what I was doing and why it was important that I do it. In Washington, I often spent time with people who were indifferent to what I was doing, who thought it was all a big joke, or who were actively opposed to impeachment. Making things even worse, as one of the non-millionaires serving in Congress, I could not afford to buy a home there in a decent neighborhood in addition to our house in Georgia. So when I was in Washington, I slept on the institutional couch on the other side of my office from the desk where I worked all day. For these reasons, the drive back to Washington from Williamsburg was one of the least enjoyable I have ever taken. It was also disconcerting to drive from one of the cradles of American democracy—Williamsburg—still preserved in something close to its original form, to Washington, where the republic was, well, not exactly in the shape the founders would have preferred.

Back in Washington, the impeachment trial was shifting into high gear. On February 8, the task fell to me to make the closing argument in the Senate impeachment trial that would tie together the facts and the law, making the case for removing Bill Clinton from office. Speaking from the Senate well, I said,

> Distinguished and worthy adversarial counsel for the president, including my good friend and former Georgetown law professor, Charles Ruff, gentlemen and ladies of the Senate, my name is Bob Barr. I represent the Seventh District of Georgia, but in a broader sense I represent the country because I have been directed, as every one of the other twelve managers of the House has been directed by the American people, by a majority vote of the House of Representatives, to urge you to review the evidence and issue a verdict of conviction on the two Articles of Impeachment passed by the House of Representatives.
>
> Two days ago, all of us celebrated the birthday of former President Ronald Reagan. During his first year in office on May 17, 1981, this president, known for giving voice to America's best and most decent instincts, spoke to the American people from Notre Dame University. Though spoken nearly eighteen years ago, and clearly not in contemplation of an impeachment, the former president's words provide guidance for you here today.
>
> It was that date that President Reagan spoke of a certain principle; and in so doing, he quoted another giant of the twentieth century, Winston Churchill. Specifically, President Reagan spoke of those who derided simple, straightforward answers to the problems confronting our country; those who decried clarity and certainty of principle, in favor of vagueness and relativism. He said, "They say the world has become too complex for simple answers. They are wrong. There are no easy answers, but there are simple answers. We must have the courage to do what is morally

right. Winston Churchill said that 'the destiny of man is not measured by material computation. When great forces are on the move in the world, we learn we are spirits—not animals.' And he said, 'there is something going on in time and space, and beyond time and space, which, whether we like it or not, spells duty.'"

Duty. A clear, simple concept. A foundational principle.

Your duty is clearly set forth in your oath; your oath to do impartial justice according to the Constitution and the law.

In the past month, you have heard much about the Constitution and about the law. Probably more than you'd prefer; in a dizzying recitation of the U.S. Criminal Code: 18 U.S.C. 1503. 18 U.S.C. 1505. 18 U.S.C. 1512. 18 U.S.C. 1621. 18 U.S.C. 1623. Tampering. Perjury. Obstruction. That is a lot to digest, but these are real laws and they are applicable to these proceedings and to this president. Evidence and law, you have seen it and you have heard it.

You've also seen and heard about straw men raised up by the White House lawyers and then stricken down mightily. You've heard them essentially describe the president alternately as victim or saint. You've heard even his staunchest allies describe his conduct as "reprehensible." Even some of you, on the president's side of the aisle, have concluded, "there's no question about his having given false testimony under oath and he did that more than once."

There has also been much smoke churned up by the defense

Men and women of the Senate, Monica Lewinsky is not on trial. Her conduct and her intentions are not at issue here. Vernon Jordan is not on trial and his conduct and his intentions are not at issue here. William Jefferson Clinton is on trial here. His behavior, his intentions, his actions—these and only these are the issues here. When the White House lawyers raise up as a straw man that Vernon Jordan may have had no improper motive in seeking a job for Ms. Lewinsky; or that there was no formal "conspiracy" proved between the president and Vernon Jordan; or that Ms. Lewinsky says she did not draw a direct link between the president's raising the issue of a false affidavit and the cover stories, keep in mind, these are irrelevant issues. When the White House lawyers strike these theories down, even if you were to conclude they did, they are striking down nothing more than irrelevant straw men.

What stands today, as it has throughout these proceedings, are facts—a false affidavit that benefits the president, the coaching of witnesses by the president, the secreting of subpoenaed evidence that would have harmed the president, lies under oath by the president. These reflect President Clinton's behavior; President Clinton's intentions; President Clinton's actions; and President Clinton's benefit. Not through the eyes of false theories, but by the evidence through the lens of common sense.

You've heard tapes and read volumes of evidence. Not pursuant to the process we as House managers would have preferred, but much evidence nonetheless, has been presented.

Many are saying, with a degree of certainty that usually comes only from ignorance, that there's nothing I or any of us can say to you today, on the eve of your deliberations, to sway your minds. I beg to differ with them. Moreover, we have been directed by the people of this country, by a majority vote of the House of Representatives, to fulfill and reaffirm a constitutional process and to present evidence to you and argue to you.

There is much, in urging a vote for conviction, that can be gained by turning to, and keeping in mind, President Reagan's words to America, to do duty: Duty unclouded by relativism, unmarred by artificiality. Duty that lives on after your vote—just as America will live on and prosper after a vote to convict. Duty untainted by polls. The country's fascination with polls has wormed its way even into these proceedings when, just a few days ago, we heard one of the White House lawyers cite polls as a reason not to release the videotapes.

Polls played no role in the great decisions, decisive decisions that make America a nation and kept it a free and strong nation. Polls likewise played no role in the great trials of our nation's history that opened schools equally to all of America's children, or that provided due process and equal protection of the laws for all Americans, regardless of economic might or political power.

Yet, it is in many respects polls that threaten to become the currency of political discourse and even of judicial process as we near to enter the twenty-first century.

Your duty, which I know you recognize today, is and must be based not on polls or politics, but on law and the Constitution. In other words, principle.

What you decide in this case, the case now before you, will tell America and the world what it is we have, as a foundation for our nation, not just today, but for ages to come. It will tell us and this nation whether these seats here today will continue to be filled by true statesmen. Whether these seats will continue to echo with the booming principles, eloquence, and sense of duty of Daniel Webster, John Calhound, Everett Dirksen, Robert Byrd. I would add to that list of statesmen my fellow Georgian and your former colleague, Sam Nunn, whose concern for duty and our nation's security caused him recently on CNN to raise grave concerns over our nation's security because of the reckless conduct of this president. Will the principles embodied in our Constitution and our laws be reaffirmed, wrested from the pallid hands of pollsters and pundits and from the swarm of theorists surrounding these proceedings? Will they be taken up by you and placed squarely and firmly back in the hands of Thomas Jefferson, Alexander Hamilton, James Madison, George Washington, Abraham Lincoln, Martin Luther King Jr., and so many other true statesmen of America's heritage? Principles that have stricken down bigotry, tyrants, and demagogues; principles that, through open and fair trials, have saved the innocent from the hangman's noose; and likewise have sent the guilty, clothed in due process, to the nether regions.

It is principle, found and nurtured in our Constitution and our laws, that you are now called on to both use and reaffirm.

Not only America is watching, the world is, too. And, for those who say people from foreign lands look down on this process and deride this process, I say, "not so."

Let me speak briefly of a man not born in this country, but a man who has made this his country. A man born not in Atlanta, Georgia, though Atlanta is now his home. A man born many thousands of miles away, in Eritrea. A man to whom President Reagan surely was in a sense speaking, both in 1981 when he spoke of America's eternal sense of duty and in January 1985 when he spoke of the "American sound" that echoes still through the ages and the continents.

The man whose words I quote is a man who watches this process through the eyes of an immigrant, Mr. Seyoum Tesfaye. I have never met Mr. Tesfaye, but I have read his works. He wrote, in the *Atlanta Journal and Constitution* just three days ago, on February 5th, that this impeachment process "is an example of America at its best . . . a core constitutional principle that profoundly distinguishes America from almost all other nations." He noted without hyperbole that this process, far from being the sorry spectacle that many of the president's defenders have tried to make it, truly "is a hallmark of representative democracy," reaffirming the principle that "no man is above the law—not even the president."

These are not the words of the House managers; though they echo ours.

These are not the words of a partisan.

These are the words of an immigrant. A man who came to America to study and has stayed to work and pay taxes just as millions of us do every day.

Men and women of the United States Senate, you must, by affirming your duty to render impartial justice based on the Constitution and the law, reaffirm those same laws and that very same Constitution, which drew Mr. Tesfaye and countless millions of other immigrants to our shores over the ages. This is not a comfortable task for any of us. But as Martin Luther King Jr. correctly noted, in words that hang on my office wall and perhaps on some of yours, it is not in "times of comfort and convenience" that we find the measure of a man's character, but in times of "conflict and controversy." This is such a defining time.

Obstruction of justice and perjury must not be allowed to stand. Perjury and obstruction cannot stand alongside the law and the Constitution. By your oath, you must, like it or not, choose one over the other, up or down, guilt or acquittal. I respectfully submit on behalf of the House of Representatives and on behalf of my constituents in the Seventh District of Georgia that the evidence clearly establishes guilt and that the Constitution and laws of this land demand it.

I will not claim these words were the soaring oratory of a Daniel Webster, a Henry Clay, a John C. Calhoun, or any of the legion of great Americans who had spoken on critical issues and critical times. However, I believe they encapsulated the question we faced and the course we should have taken. I have never spent more time reading, rereading, and editing a single speech, and doubt that I ever will again. If only it had been the case that we lived in a time when Congress actually deliberated, these words and those of my fellow impeachment managers might have made a difference.

Along these lines, I observed one of the most amazing cases of odd behavior by a senator during my closing presentation. Its source was Alaska senator Ted Stevens. Stevens chairs the Senate Appropriations Committee and consequently owns one of the most heavily kissed backsides in Washington, D.C. He is constantly besieged by a cornucopia of special interests, all seeking their own slice of taxpayer money from the budget pie. He is a guy who is used to having everyone around him act exactly as he wants them to. Early in the trial, he had emerged as one of the most strident opponents in the Republican conference to putting together a real trial. He wanted the spectacle of the impeachment trial to end as quickly as possible so the Senate could get on its real business—which as he saw it was doling out taxpayer monies.

Still, I expected Stevens at least to keep his opinion to himself during the actual trial. Needless to say, I was surprised to look up during my initial presentation and see him slowly moving his hand back and forth across his throat while staring me down. Either the guy was having serious thoughts of suicide, or he was giving me a sign to sit down and shut up. Here, I thought, was Senate arrogance at its best.

Looking back on the trial as it drew to a conclusion, it became increasingly evident that the style of arguments made by both sides could best be seen through the speeches of two individuals. Those men were Henry Hyde, who spoke in favor of removing Bill Clinton from office, and Dale Bumpers, who argued against removal. It was like watching the heavyweight title round of the legal profession. Bumpers, a former Senator, played the country lawyer, appealing to the Senate's institutional history and sense of decorum. Hyde, a Chicago attorney with a deep respect for the Constitution, made a more "legal" presentation, arguing from fundamental principles of American democracy. Both speakers repeated the same kind of substance we had covered in earlier arguments, but the style in which they made their cases was truly a sight to behold. Their arguments were emblematic of the entire process; Hyde focused on the Constitution while Bumpers focused on the kinds of skilled and clever arguments a top-shelf defense lawyer would make for a guilty client. It was senatorial tradition and the Washington Establishment on one side and the Constitution on the other. The Constitution won out in the House, but it never stood a chance in the Senate.

At high noon on February 12, 1999, the Senate began to vote on the Articles of Impeachment. The first article charged the president with lying to the grand jury in the Jones case. In my mind, this was the most obvious and straightforward article. It was obvious the man had lied to a grand jury. While we all found the substance he chose to lie over distasteful, there was no getting around this basic fact without all kinds of contortions, such as debating the meaning of the word "is." Although I knew by then that we would not achieve a 2/3 vote on either of the articles, I expected this one to draw something like a straight party line vote. Unfortunately, several Republicans defected and no Democrats crossed party lines, leaving the first article without even a majority of senators supporting it.

The second article focused on all the things Clinton did to obstruct the judicial process in an effort to cover up his affair with Lewinsky. This case was also clear, but it was somewhat more complicated than the crystal-clear charge of perjury. However, the second article drew an even split in the Senate, with only five liberal Republicans from the northeast (one of whom, Jim Jeffords, would soon leave the party altogether and cast his lot with the Democrats) breaking ranks to support Clinton.

The most annoying, yet weirdly honest vote against impeachment came from Robert Byrd, the West Virginia Democrat who is the undisputed master of pork-barrel spending in the Senate. If you look up "crusty" in the Senate dictionary, I have no doubt you will find Byrd's smiling face drawn in pencil beside the entry. Byrd would later gain further infamy by telling a national television audience that "I've seen a lot of white niggers in my time; I'm going to use that word." Of course, this is the same great American who described brave African American soldiers in World War II as "a throwback to the blackest specimen from the wilds."[2] For some reason, the Senate views this guy as one of its foremost constitutional experts and its "unofficial historian." This seems odd to me, but like I said, the Senate is a strange place.

Byrd's take on the situation—which set a standard for many other Democrats—is that Clinton was clearly and unequivocally guilty of obstruction of justice. As Byrd himself put it, "the evidence against Mr. Clinton shows that he willfully and knowingly and repeatedly gave false testimony under oath in judicial proceedings." He went on to add that when the president "breaks the law himself by lying under oath, he undermines the system of justice and law." It sounded like an open and shut case for removal to me, but not to the senior senator from West Virginia. Byrd acknowledged we had proven our case but simply refused to vote in favor of Clinton's impeachment. His reason was largely that it would tarnish the image of the Senate. What he meant was that he was not going to vote for impeachment because, like so many senators, he cared more for public opinion than principle, for appearance more than substance. To many senators, the meaning of "is" truly is a matter of constant debate.

The most absurd vote of all was the one cast by Arlen Specter. In their desperation to avoid taking any kind of concrete position on the matter, Specter and his staff combed through so many law books that they finally settled on a concept from ancient Scottish law. As he put it, "[u]nder Scottish law, there are three possible verdicts: guilty, not guilty, and not proved." I can only imagine the raise given to the lucky lawyer on Specter's staff who tracked down this little nugget.

Here was an escape hatch, which Specter was desperately seeking and more than willing to use to avoid voting yea or nay, a goal he achieved by casting a made-up vote of "unproved." In other words, he argued that the president may have been guilty or innocent, but that nothing shown during the trial proved the charge one way or the other. He could have just as easily and logically voted "purple" or "tree." This nonsense seemed in many respects to epitomize the whole Senate reaction to having to deal with the messiness of an impeachment trial in the first place. (Even the Senate chaplain, who began each day of the impeachment proceedings with a prayer, signaled his view of the House managers when, in his final prayer on the last day, he asked the Lord's blessing on everyone involved except, as I recall, the managers.)

One of the strangest things about the entire episode in the Senate is that all of the senators who stuck a knife in our backs every time we tried to present a full case to the American people were obsequious after the trial ended. Letters from individual senators started arriving in my office, many addressed to "Bob" and signed "your friend." Arlen Specter (the same guy who voted "unproved" on our case), wrote and thanked me for "an excellent job in case presentation." The Senate staff even took the old office chair I sat in during the trial, put a brass plaque on the back of it, and delivered it to my office so I would have something by which to remember them.

The disinterest of the Senate may have been the biggest reason Clinton was not removed from office, but the focus on which the impeachment was built ran a close second. Allegations of extramarital affairs dogged Clinton even before his election, beginning with the famous press conference Gennifer Flowers held on January 23, 1992, at an Arkansas hotel, where she famously discussed a long-term affair with then-governor Clinton. However, the strength of her allegations was noticeably diluted by the fact that she sold them to the *Star* tabloid. This set an important precedent for the Clinton administration: the allegations leveled against him were often so unbelievably sleazy that even his worst enemies found them revolting and would rather swallow crushed glass than discuss them publicly.

By arguing the case on issues stemming from unusually shame-less public conduct involving a young employee less than half the president's age, the House ensured many members of the public would view the charges as disgusting and politically motivated. While I thought they were based on sound principle, even I found the details of the charges so revolting that reading about them in committee documents was a chore, to say nothing of discussing them on national television where—for example—my mother might be listening to what I said.

One of the main reasons for the focus on Lewinsky was that Kenneth Starr was appointed as independent counsel. Ken is one of the most brilliant appellate lawyers in America. The problem is that he's an appellate lawyer and not a trial attorney, a "street prose-cutor" if you will. Good appellate lawyers are able to focus like a laser on a single case, seeing it from dozens of different angles and memorizing every fact that might possibly pertain to it. Great appellate lawyers like Ken are the elite attorneys of the legal profes-sion because they can do this better than anyone else (and believe me, it isn't easy). However, one thing you are not going to see a lawyer used to arguing (and in Ken's case judging) cases in appeals court is flexibility.

Criminal prosecutors handling trials are, on the other hand, able to juggle multiple charges and multiple areas at once, focusing alter-nately on one or the other, dropping the ones that do not pan out, and investigating new avenues as they appear or shift. A good prosecutor has a solid sense of what a jury will and will not buy, and they have a nose for those aspects of a case that will appeal to the people deciding it. In this case, the jury was the Senate and, in a larger sense, the American public. What our team should have realized early on is that while the Lewinsky allegations were the most legally clear-cut charges, their appeal to the jury we cared most about was almost nil. No one—in the Senate or outside it—wanted to be repeatedly embarrassed by listening to the gory personal details of Bill Clinton's liaisons with a young White House intern, no matter what he did to cover it up.

Paradoxically, Monica Lewinsky may well be the single biggest reason why Clinton was not removed from office. If the focus had turned to more serious issues, such as neglect of national security and systematic abuse of power, the outcome of the process would likely have been dramatically different. However, I and the dozen other House managers had no choice but to play the hand we were dealt by the leadership of the Republican Party, even though I had argued strenuously for a stronger hand. In the end, I believe we played it heroically considering the odds against us on both sides of the aisle, in both houses of Congress, and from the other end of Pennsylvania Avenue.

8

Liberalism, Conservatism, and Clintonism

Commentators often remark that Bill Clinton changed the Democratic Party forever, but he also left his mark on the Republican Party. His one-time top strategist, Dick Morris, guided him to the strategy of "triangulation," which essentially means beginning the political game with no hard and fast commitments and taking whatever position will most ensure one's own political success at the expense of one's opponents. It is often said in Washington that "you can get a lot done if you don't care who gets the credit." Clinton changed this maxim to "you can get a lot of credit if you don't care what you do," and it proved to be a successful strategy, at least in terms of political expediency.

I do not think the Clinton administration began its first term with the idea that principles did not matter. In fact, the early days of Clinton's presidency were marked by a series of political blunders that could only be explained as the actions of a true believer. For example, as top Clinton aide George Stephanopolous recounts in his memoir of those early days, the administration was committed to creating a "cabinet that looked like America."[1] Due to poor planning and prior commitments, this left Clinton in a position where he felt pressured, if not forced, to nominate a woman to serve as attorney general. In January 1993, Clinton, desperate to find even a remotely qualified candidate fitting his profile, nominated first Zoe Baird and then Kimba Wood, who were both quickly forced to withdraw their nominations in embarrassment following questions of past misjudgment and misconduct.

Of course, we all know how the attorney general fiasco finally ended. We got Janet Reno, who ran the department with such feckless mediocrity and fumbling incompetence that she often seemed to drive the Clinton White House nuts as much as she did Republicans. The only thing Reno was good at was holding on to her job, a task she pursued with the dedication of a career bureaucrat who knew she did not deserve to hold her current post and who would never again reach a professional pinnacle anywhere near as high. Everyone, including the career lawyers at the DOJ, knew who the real power was, and it was no one occupying the Department of Justice executive offices at 10th and Constitution. It was the couple residing a half-dozen blocks down the street at 1600 Pennsylvania Avenue.

At the same time he was busy ensconcing Janet Reno at Main Justice, Clinton attempted to create socialized medicine in America through a task force headed by his wife, Hillary. In an effort to pander to the gay vote, he attempted to force the military to accept openly homosexual soldiers. These attempts were also miserable failures, resulting in plummeting approval ratings and worldwide embarrassment for the new president. Our neophyte president seemed to screw up everything he touched, particularly when it involved a principle important to his core base of liberal support.

I will be the first to say that I think selecting an attorney general through affirmative action, bringing failed socialized medicine from European welfare states to America, and welcoming gays in our military all seem like colossally stupid ideas. I do not think these policies are good ideas, and I think most Americans agree with me. But one thing you cannot say is that they were not motivated by sincerity. Bill Clinton—warped as his views might have been— believed these things were right. However, the American people begged to differ. It seemed that the more he tried to stick with his principles, the more the voting public, as reflected first in the polls and later in the off-year elections of 1994, punished him for it.

So Bill Clinton absorbed an early lesson in his presidency: sticking with principle is not easy when you are the president. It is far simpler to go with the flow and act as if you have no core beliefs. If you are willing to do this—and Boy Clinton, to use Bob Tyrrell's most apropros moniker, was—you can achieve far more political security than dedication to principle will ever bring you. This was especially true for Clinton, since his agenda was so radical that there was no way the country would ever go along with it.

Clinton's decision to reject dedication to principle as a foundation of his presidency was reinforced when congressional Democrats suffered massive losses in the 1994 midterm elections following his first two years in office. While Clinton did not make all those members bounce checks from the House bank, he did set them up with vote after vote that sabotaged them in their home districts. In fact, he was one of the major reasons I won an election to the House against a popular eleven-year incumbent, Buddy Darden of Georgia. The aptly-named Buddy was everyone's friend, but he made the mistake of paying for a seat on the Appropriations Committee with his votes in support of Clinton's 1993 tax increase and his 1994 gun control legislation. He forgot, for one brief term in Congress, that there's one thing you do not raise in West Georgia—taxes—and one thing you do not take away from citizens—their guns. He capped these decisions by going for a morning jog with Bill Clinton and being shortsighted enough to have the press come take his picture.

Of course, we were more than happy to blow up the photograph to massive size and travel across the Seventh District with it in tow, reminding voters who their representative had been palling around with in D.C. lately. The reaction of conservative Georgia voters to these three things was instant, negative, and overwhelming. Other incumbents who supported Clinton's pro-tax, anti-gun policies suffered similar fates. Clinton was, if nothing else, observant. He noticed these results and he absorbed and applied the lesson they taught to every aspect of his presidency from then on.

After the elections and the events before and after them, Clinton apparently decided that sticking to his guns on principle was no way to govern. He began throwing his liberal allies overboard on issue after issue. He ignored gay supporters by signing the Defense of Marriage Act, which I drafted and Congress passed in 1996. He alienated urban minority support by signing Republican welfare reform legislation into law. He undercut his own government expansion program by signing the Balanced Budget Act of 1997. He quit trying to nominate true believers to top posts and settled for establishment moderates instead. He espoused dovish policies but then bombed foreign countries as a political distraction. He sold environmentalists down the river, failing to adopt tough policies on clean air and water, despite having the quintessential Mr. Green as his vice president.

The truly breathtaking thing about this sudden shift is that the left just sat there and took it. Jesse Jackson even quit his day job (I am still not certain what his day job is, but he allegedly has one) to become personal spiritual counselor to the First Family during the impeachment. To be sure, there were notable exceptions, liberals who actually figured out that Clinton was discarding their cherished principles like used sheets of toilet paper and who reacted in outrage. Most notable among them was the writer Christopher Hitchens, who is about as far to the left as anyone can get while still maintaining any level of credibility in the mainstream media. In *No One Left to Lie To*, his short and scathing critique of Clinton, Hitchens systematically eviscerates Clinton and his allies for betraying principle after principle for the sake of expediency. Hitchens and a handful of other liberals figured out what Clinton was doing to them but never managed to sell their case to the American left in a meaningful way. Consequently, they found themselves as unusual allies with conservative Republicans with whom they disagreed on almost every issue other than an extreme distaste

for Clintonism and all it espoused. They did the right thing ultimately—by supporting Clinton's impeachment—though for the
wrong reasons.

The message of the Clinton White House to liberals was clear.
"We don't care what you think, and your dedication to principles is
only going to drag us all down. You need to get with the program
and realize that you either support us or you'll get a Republican in
the White House." Interestingly, this message worked for a short
time (as its mirror image seems to be working for George W. Bush
and the conservatives), but it probably also had a lot to do with
Ralph Nader's successful efforts to whittle down Al Gore's left-wing
base in 2000. In politics, you can get away with selling out your close
friends once or twice because political friends will tolerate more
than real friends will. But you risk major problems if you do it too
often. Interestingly, though, Hillary Clinton appears to be heading
down the same path as she maneuvers for national office, with
antiwar activists, gay groups, environmental groups, and advocates
for the poor in New York starting to complain publicly that they are
getting a lot of talk and precious little action from their junior
senator on the issues they care about.

Bill Clinton is not the only one who learned this lesson. He taught it
to the Republican Party in the Kafkaesque "Great Government
Shutdown of 1995–1996." The federal government shutdown was
the GOP version of the National Health Plan. It was our party's self-
inflicted Waterloo, and after it happened our leaders apparently
resolved never again to stand on principle if it would cost them at
the polls. In fact, as Dick Morris—the inventor of triangulation—
told me on my radio show recently, Republicans have completely
learned how to emulate Clinton's behavior and are now more than
skilled enough to play in his league.

After we won the majority by sending fifty-two incumbent
Democratic House members packing in 1994, House Republicans—
particularly the freshman class—were dedicated to pursuing real
change in Washington in a way that will probably not be seen again

for decades. We met in "conference" meetings to plan strategy, and the environment in those meetings was absolutely electric. For the first time in years, good ideas made their way into law without languishing in committee rooms for months or years, or being quashed by senior members opposed to anything that might rock the boat. Newt Gingrich led the House exactly as one might expect a former college professor to do with his students, demanding the most carefully considered ideas and tactics from members and then acting on those suggestions when they reached the level of excellence he expected. With this kind of leadership and drive, we quickly accomplished everything promised in the Contract with America. We were poised to continue down the path, dramatically reshaping American government, significantly increasing individual freedom, and returning the nation to a path much closer to that envisioned in the Constitution than had been the case for much of the past century.

Like all good things, our progress—which had already suffered a body blow with our failure to follow up on our Contract with America success in spring 1995—came to a grinding halt in the winter of the same year. First, Tom Daschle developed the strategy that Democrats in the Senate are using still today to block any real progress on issues from nominating judges to balancing the budget. By manipulating the Senate rules, Bill Clinton's allies in the Senate were able to take a great deal of the positive legislation we passed in the House and suffocate it. Of course, the severe lack of backbone demonstrated by the Republican Senate majority did not help matters one bit.

The debate reached a head about a year after the Republican takeover, when Clinton systematically and repeatedly vetoed the appropriations bills we sent him. To give a brief civics lesson, these thirteen spending bills must be passed every year, and without them the federal government cannot legally spend money. They are created by Congress based on budget suggestions of the president and are normally perfunctorily signed into law. Nor do they typically encounter serious roadblocks in the House and Senate, mainly because they are generally stuffed full of expensive political goodies requested by individual members of both parties. In fact, the appropriations process is one of the most sickening spectacles one could imagine, with House and Senate members trading their votes in return for a bridge, a museum, a study of bovine flatulence (I am serious, this actually happened), or whatever other multimillion-dollar waste of taxpayer money suits their fancy. During my service in Congress, I was repeatedly promised such goodies in return for votes on everything from spending bills to trade agreements. I never did accept the Faustian bargains I was offered, although in many respects it would have been far easier to have done so.

In the House, with our historic majority beginning in 1995, we worked hard to buck the trend of Washington pork politics, passing appropriations bills that—while far from perfect—were some of the most fiscally responsible Washington had ever seen. We sent these bills to the White House hoping the president—who professed to be committed to a balanced budget—would see the wisdom of what we had done and sign them. Our basic line of thinking was based on the assumption that President Clinton had a core set of principles he was trying to enact, just as we did. We were more than willing to take both sets of principles to the nation and let the citizens decide which should govern public policy.

However, as our leaders began negotiating with the White House, it became clear that Clinton really did not care what was in the bills. We found ourselves negotiating with a president far cleverer than our negotiating team. Clinton decided early in the process that he did not want to make a deal because he was thinking several moves ahead while our team was only thinking about the next move. Bill Clinton wanted to shut down the federal government and blame Republicans, while we wanted to enact fiscally responsible bills. Clinton's ever-shifting requests and unwillingness to negotiate in good faith made any kind of compromise impossible, though our folks at the budget negotiating table did not realize this fact until we had already lost the battle. Our goal was policy and Clinton's was politics. With these dynamics at play, the federal government "shut-down" of 1995 was inevitable.

I say "government shutdown," but that is not really what happened. In point of fact, all essential government services remained up and running throughout the entire period. If anything, it was a shining example of how little the nation actually missed the services of most of the federal employees who briefly were not on the job. Since you could not tell any difference when they were gone, it was interesting to speculate as to what they were doing from their cushy taxpayer-funded perches in the first place. Soon, bureaucrats from obscure government agencies began to appear on the airwaves moaning and groaning about how American society would come to a screeching halt if they did not get back to work. As I drove into work each morning from my then basement apartment in the Washington suburbs, I listened to local radio stations delivering hourly updates on each day of the great "government shutdown," accompanied by somber funeral music that almost had me weeping for the plight of all those inactive bureaucrats.

As the process continued, Clinton and the congressional Democrats hammered Republicans day in and day out, successfully selling the public on the line that they were so dedicated to principle that they simply could not support our spending bills. Again, the disturbing reality is that Clinton's policy of triangulation only worked because his own teammates kept playing with him even as he stabbed them in the back. No matter what Clinton did to them, their response seemed to be "Thank you, sir! May I please have another?" So long as he did not touch sacred cows like abortion and affirmative action, Bill Clinton got away with systematically selling out the people who put him in office. At the same time, the Republican leadership simply assumed the public agreed with us (a year earlier they had elected us to a majority after all), and did next to nothing to make an effective case for our position. Soon, GOP poll numbers started sinking and Clinton's numbers started rising.

The more this happened, the more our leadership starting questioning our strategy. They fell directly into the trap set by Clinton and started basing their actions on overnight polling data and morning headlines. Instead of playing for long-term public approval, we quickly compromised in an effort to bring our numbers back up right away. Ironically, however, we shifted policies just as the polls apparently were beginning to reflect public understanding of—and appreciation for—what we were trying to do.

When Republicans finally waved the white flag of surrender and caved in to Clinton's budget demands, the approach taken by our leaders was particularly disturbing. Through late fall and early winter 1995 as the "crisis" played itself out, in meeting after meeting Newt had been urging us to hold tough. Newt repeatedly reminded us that principle had gotten us where we were and must always be our ultimate guide. In the end, however, Newt changed course suddenly and completely, telling us we were going to give Clinton what he wanted, and we had by-God better support it. He even told us—for the first time to my knowledge—that he was going to keep a list of every member who did not vote to cave on the Clinton spending package and that the list would later be used to punish us.

One of the things that always set Newt apart from his Democrat predecessors was that he had—prior to that point—always urged us to vote our consciences and our districts. I knew something major had broken inside our party leadership during the shutdown, and I doubted things would ever be the same again. I was not wrong. For the first time in my congressional service, I found myself questioning my presence in Washington. If I was merely going to be asked to be a rubber stamp for this kind of nonsense, I was not sure I wanted any part of the system.

Since I worked for the citizens of the Seventh District, not Newt Gingrich, I was among only a handful of Republicans who voted against the bill. This appeared to make many Republicans unhappy. Typical of the reaction was the comment from Georgia Republican Mac Collins—an older, often incomprehensible and always surly former trucker who imagined himself the dean of our state delegation—that you have to play on a team in Washington, and I just could not keep going off and making my own rules. Being a hard-headed kind of guy, I figured that if an establishment Republican like Mac was getting upset, I must be doing something right, and I resolved to continue working in the same manner.

The lesson top Republican officials drew from this experience was that principle is bad policy. The more we stuck to our guns, the less likely we were to win elections. We became transfixed with winning the news cycle, and we gave the public no reason to believe we were sincere about what we were doing. The predictable result was that the American people assumed we were not truly committed to fiscal responsibility in the first place but had been playing politics the whole time. This became a self-fulfilling prophecy for the party, with leaders figuring that if we were going to get blamed for playing political games, we might as well get the benefits from actually doing it. For example, by the time 1998 rolled around the Republican leadership had given up all pretense of passing lean appropriations bills and passed a bloated, pre-election omnibus bill that was virtually indistinguishable from what the Democrats might have passed when they controlled Congress.

From this point forward, the Republican Party came to believe that triangulation was unbeatable as a political principle. By simply doing whatever was popular with at least 50.1 percent of the public on a given day, they figured we could maintain our majority indefinitely. Of course, this also meant there would be little ideological consistency to our party platform. Sometimes we would be budget hawks, and other times we would be free spenders. One day we would support making entitlement programs more fiscally sound, the next day we would enact new, big government promises that would make LBJ feel right at home. The list goes on, but the basic argument that the Republican Party also responded to Clinton by forsaking any consistent devotion to principle is a difficult one to dispute.

During the impeachment process, it became clearly evident how deeply the political tactics developed and refined by Bill Clinton had been adopted by the Republican Party. It is unquestionably the case that any truly principled Republican would have actively worked to remove Bill Clinton from office (as would any principled Democrat confronted with the true breadth of what Clinton had done to abuse his office). However, our party's leaders felt differently. Sure, they wanted to attack Clinton enough to keep his approval ratings down and make sure the GOP base remained activated. But the last thing most of them wanted to do was actually remove Bill Clinton from office.

When I talk about this group called Republican leaders, I am referring to all the folks—self-appointed or otherwise—who really pull the strings of the Republican Party. These people are the ones who determine which bills make it to the floor, whether they pass, who gets to amend them, how federal agencies implement them, which candidates run for office, which campaigns get the funds it takes to win, and myriad other decisions that make up the total policy output of the Republican Party.

You may expect, as I did early in my career, that these leaders are duly elected from among the ranks of representatives who are duly elected by the people. This is certainly how democracy should work. There's no doubt that people like the Speaker of the House, top cabinet officials, and national party chairs exercise substantial influence within both parties. However, their influence—in the majority of cases—is more than matched by the power of Washington insiders who have never been elected to anything. These are the people who serve as chiefs of staff in top congressional offices and the White House, shifting offices as elected officials come and go. Others on the list include lobbyists controlling millions in election funding, and the handful of pollsters, strategists, and admen who consult for most successful campaigns. A reasonable number of these people also work in the news media, writing columns, hosting television shows, and determining which viewpoints the public gets to hear. For both parties, these—more than anyone else—are the folks influencing major political decisions. So when I say the words "Republican leaders," I mean not only the people holding top offices, but also the regiments of unelected powerbrokers calling the shots behind the scenes.

There are at least three reasons why Republican leaders felt they should keep Clinton in office. First, many Republican pollsters and political consultants felt that the most expedient thing the party could do would be to allow Clinton to stay in office, slowly twisting in the wind, and end his term as a crippled president. They wanted the media to dog him until his last day in office, making him—and Al Gore, the likely Democrat nominee to succeed him—look terrible until the next inauguration. After all, they reasoned, Clinton had such a propensity for creating scandals that we were sure to benefit from a daily stream of them as long as we kept him in office. While this strategy may have made political sense, it is deeply and irreparably unpatriotic. The point these political hacks failed to grasp with their "death by a thousand cuts" strategy is that there is a reason we try to win elections. The people who supported our party did so because they wanted us to lead, to make America better, and yes, to hold accountalbe those who broke the law. By pretending to hold Clinton accountable but not actually doing so, we were giving a corrupt president a free pass to continue ripping away at the fabric of our nation as well as lying to all of the grassroots activists who were working to keep our party in office.

Secondly, many Republicans had grown accustomed to dealing with Bill Clinton. They felt that they understood him and could work with him. It was as if they had the same kind of "arrangement" a cheating husband might have with his wife. They knew they were being taken advantage of, but they were afraid of what would happen if they ended this relationship to which they had become accustomed and replaced it with the unknown. At least they knew what they could count on from Bill Clinton, and there was no telling what would happen to their roles in the party if Al Gore became president and all the pieces on the Washington chessboard shifted around. Plus, Clinton sometimes doled out policy rewards to GOP leaders, such as ultimately signing the Republican-sponsored Balanced Budget Act and welfare reform. Republican leaders felt that if a weakened Clinton stayed in office, they might get even more. There is no force in Washington more powerful than inertia, and Bill Clinton clearly took advantage of this force. Better the devil we know . . . .

Finally, most of our own leadership was simply scared. Tom DeLay had the guts to go after Clinton, but he had no counterpart in the Senate and often fought a lonely battle in the House. Cutting away all of the tangential arguments related to the process, impeachment was an uncertain road. Like nervous corporate CEOs, the leadership structure of the Republican Party and it corporate patrons preferred predictable consistency above all else. They felt they could deal with any reality as long as that reality was stable. Furthermore, none of them wanted to be the first to stick their heads out of the trench and lead a charge. By the time impeachment rolled around, their political will had been largely broken, and when the 1998 elections did not culminate in a GOP landslide, they collectively tucked their tails and ran. Consequently, as the impeachment case left the House and went to the Senate, the backbone our leaders were still occasionally demonstrating had turned to jelly.

The end result of all these factors was a policy of attacking Clinton when seen as necessary while making certain he remained in office—to strike wounding but not fatal blows to the president. To those of us who were actually conducting investigations and working to move the impeachment process forward, this meant the only thing we could consistently expect from our leadership was inconsistency. On one day, they would cheer us on, giving us the resources we needed to do our work and promising to back us. The next day, they would become scared we were getting too close to doing real damage to Clinton, and they would reign us back in. When we tried to do major things, such as pass contempt of Congress resolutions against Janet Reno or get live witnesses in the Senate, our leaders were nowhere to be found. I do not believe this kind of behavior was due to coincidence or even incompetence. Our leaders may not have behaved in a consistent fashion, but they were nothing if not intelligent. They knew exactly what they were doing, and their plan—which they succeeded in implementing—was to damage Bill Clinton as much as possible while still keeping him safely parked at 1600 Pennsylvania Avenue until George W. Bush could run.

By the end of the Clinton administration, the Republican Party—with a handful of exceptions—was just as unprincipled as Bill Clinton. We had absorbed his political tactics so completely that we did not even seem to remember a time when we had acted any differently. If Diogenes had wandered the streets of Washington circa 1999 looking for a principled man, his search would have been no less successful than his attempt to find an honest man in Athens in ancient Greece. They existed, but their number was so few that the poor philosopher would have had to wander for years to expect a chance encounter with one. And, when he did succeed, as likely as not it would be because he found a hardworking person from real America who was walking down the street in search of a gift for their grandkids after visiting the Smithsonian.

In sum, the people who were most dismayed by the Clinton presidency were not liberals or conservatives, but anyone with principles, whether on the right or the left. The biggest open question this situation has left us is whether Congress still has any capacity for deliberation. Does party membership amount to little more than the kind of choice a college freshman makes in choosing a fraternity or a young criminal makes in choosing a neighborhood street gang in which to participate? If parties are merely labels, rather than representations of deeply shared principles, then the answer is "yes."

If all members care about is getting re-elected, we may as well save the public the expense of having Congress meet in person in Washington, and just let all the members vote from home without listening to each other speak or sitting through comments by witnesses on pending legislation at committee hearings. Of course, this would be consistent with what most modern presidential administrations want—a Congress that is either impotent or subservient. Requests from the executive branch to pass its legislative proposals without hearings are becoming more, rather than less, common, even as the complexity and importance of that legislation makes it imperative that the Congress conduct searching and substantive—if time-consuming—hearings (as was *not* done with the USA PATRIOT Act in 2001).

Fortunately, there are a handful of individuals dedicated to principle serving in Congress. Just as the impeachment process renewed American history's stock of villains, it also provided heroes. They are people like the brilliant and quiet appellate lawyer who took on a president at great personal cost and the gruff, street-brawling Chicago Democrat who helped impeach a president for whom he had voted. They are people like Kathleen Willey and Linda Tripp who cared more about seeing justice done than their personal careers or reputations. Their number includes respected journalists who risked ridicule to expose presidential wrongdoing and House members who suffered defeat for casting politically unpopular but deeply principled votes. Then there are the hundreds of thousands of American citizens who took time away from making a living and worrying about their families to advocate doing the right thing for our nation. These people are true heroes of American history. We can only hope their number increases as the American people respond to the excesses of a House and Senate full of incumbents caring nothing about principle and hiding behind empty party labels.

9

Righting History:
The Clinton Legacy

More than anything else, the impeachment and trial of William Jefferson Clinton was about history. For anyone involved in the debate, we lived intensely in the present, but never forgetting that the stakes in the race were historical. History would be our toughest critic and our strictest judge. On Clinton's side, he knew that—from a public policy standpoint—his administration was all but over. He did not have much time left on the clock as it was, and he had called in so many favors during the impeachment process that his political capital on the Hill was nil. With Republicans controlling both houses of Congress for the remainder of his term, the impeached president would not benefit from a rubber stamp Democratic majority in either house. Clinton and his handlers had to know that he would spend the remainder of his time in office in largely a custodial role. Sure, he could—and would—stage lucrative photo ops, take hugely expensive presidential boondoggles, help out a few friends, sign treaties, and maybe even bomb a Third World country or two, but he clearly was not going to be sending any major legislation on issues like health care or gun control over to the Hill with the expectation that it would be anything other than dead on arrival.

On our side, we had spent the past several months immersed in the constitutional history of the United States. The Founders had left the impeachment standard of "high crimes and misdemeanors" open to interpretation by future generations. Therefore, we spent a great deal of time studying those fateful days in 1787 when the Constitution was drafted and the ratification debate followed. In fact, both sides quoted liberally from the *Federalist Papers* throughout their arguments. We also looked at the seventeen past cases in which Congress had moved to impeach, and we heard a parade of legal scholars and historians give us their various inter-pretations of constitutional history. If nothing else, the impeachment process forced many Americans to remember that the country did not spring into existence thirty seconds before they were born.

All of this study of history made it crystal clear that making, or perhaps preserving, history is what the impeachment and Senate trial were really all about. To be sure, everyone did not share the opinion that we had any influence over the course history would take. Appearing on PBS after the impeachment, Clinton's poet laureate Robert Pinsky said, "Such speculation may be futile; what will be recalled and what will vanish like a dent in dough? Who knows?" Pinsky's "dent in dough" analogy is clever, but it is simply untrue.

Clinton opened the battle over his legacy in his remarks from the same Rose Garden where he and I first met almost three years earlier. First, he argued that "the Senate has fulfilled its constitu-tional responsibility bringing this process to a conclusion." The clear implication of this statement is that the Senate had a constitutional responsibility to acquit the president. Then, in classic Clinton fashion, he skipped through a brief apology and asked for a "time of reconciliation and renewal for America." One thing I have done in my life is listen to a lot of political speeches. I have gotten pretty good at translating them into real English. With that in mind, here is a simpler version of what Bill Clinton was really saying in the trite statement he read from the Rose Garden on that February day in 1999:

> I got away with it. That's right. I abused power in dozens of different ways, politicizing the presidency to a degree never seen before and endangering American national security. But the Republicans tied themselves in knots by going after me for a sleazy affair with one of my interns. So, I'll apologize for that affair, but that doesn't mean I'm going to stop doing it. Hell, Hillary doesn't even care what I do, so why should I even try to exercise any kind of self-control? Anyway, I know you're as sick of hearing about my dalliances in the Oval Office as I am of having to defend or deny them. The only way you're going to stop hearing about cigars and dresses and Communist Chinese fund-raisers and FBI files and perjury and obstruction is if you let me start talking about health care, education, and the environment. And you'd better let me do it. Otherwise, the next thing I do will make this whole episode seem like a mild embarrassment.

Clinton summed up how he felt about the entire matter in an interview with Dan Rather after impeachment. As a fawning Rather tossed softball after softball to Clinton, the truth about the president's attitude toward impeachment showed through. Clinton actually told Rather he was honored to have been impeached because it gave him the chance "to defend the Constitution."[1] If that is not arrogance carried to delusional extremes, I do not know what is—or what "is" is.

In his remarks following the trial, Judiciary Chairman Henry Hyde said we had accepted a role as "stewards of the oath." By this, he meant we had taken up the mantle of defending the idea that witnesses should tell the truth in judicial proceedings and that when they lied, they would be held to account. While the Senate failed to take seriously Clinton's obligation to tell the truth, our nation's courts—and the legal profession—certainly did not. In his first post-impeachment plea deal, Clinton had his law license suspended in Arkansas for five years (thanks to an action brought by the Atlanta-based Southeastern Legal Foundation, which I once headed) and was forced to pay a $25,000 fine for his actions. In 2001, Clinton was forced to resign in disgrace from the Supreme Court bar after he was suspended and threatened with permanent disbarment from the Court. When the Court entered its first order "In the Matter of the Discipline of Bill Clinton," his ever-present legal alter ego David Kendall initially pledged to fight back. He quickly changed directions and resigned instead. Although the U.S. Senate bought his argument for relativistic morality and "contextual truthfulness" and took a pass on disciplining Clinton, it turns out that at least some judges and prosecutors still get pretty upset when attorneys lie under oath.

There are clearly other elements of the Clinton legacy that are being furiously spun by his defenders as great successes. The Balanced Budget Act of 1997, which Clinton finally signed, represented not his but the Republican Congress's blueprint for turning our deficit-based economy around. Also regarding the economy, Clinton's economic "success" amounts to little more than the same kind of shortsighted policy cowardice he exhibited in every other aspect of governing following the first two years of his presidency. Although I am not an economist, it is clearly evident that much of the economic growth in the 1990s was built on the false promise that the Internet would instantaneously revolutionize virtually every aspect of American life. The reality of the Internet has been marked by a slower, evolutionary process, and many of the changes it has brought have not led to dramatic economic gains.

Undoubtedly, President Clinton's economic team realized the stock market had risen to unsupported highs in this Internet bubble. However, they were not willing to expend any short-term capital to reduce its size, despite the long-term economic benefits of doing so. In fact, the Clinton administration engaged in a credit-claiming orgy over the Internet bubble, promoting it at every opportunity and even encouraging Vice President Al Gore's hilarious claim that he invented the Internet. The thankless task of letting air out of the bubble ultimately fell to some of Boy Clinton's adult supervisors, most notably Alan Greenspan. When the bubble finally did burst, the damage was greater than it would have been if it had deflated earlier. Of course, this was fine with Clinton because—true to form—the real impacts of the Internet economy deflation fell primarily on George W. Bush.

Even before the Internet bubble got going, Clinton had failed to offer any kind of concrete economic plan. *National Review* editor Rich Lowry has conducted a detailed analysis of Clinton's economic record. In his view, the Clinton economic plan was no plan at all. He wrote that "Clinton almost exactly duplicated the Bush economic program from 1990. Both Bush's 1990 plan and the Clinton plan in 1993 featured modest increases in the top income-tax rate, more Medicare payroll taxes on top earners, an expansion of the Earned Income Tax Credit for low-income workers, a gas-tax increase, and an increase in the alternative minimum tax."[2]

That's right. The same Bill Clinton who ran against the Bush economic plan adopted it as his own, a now-familiar pattern of triangulation also practiced adroitly by Britain's Tony Blair. At the end of the day, the economic plan Bill Clinton offered America at the point in his administration when he actually had a popular mandate to lead was an exercise in mediocrity amounting to little more than "tax-and-spend lite." Bill Clinton's focus in 1992 on the economy was nothing more than a campaign slogan, and the argument that he was in any way responsible for economic growth in the 1990s is yet another fiction invented by his defenders.

Bill Clinton's presidency was one missed opportunity after another. America elected a president who was brilliant, but could still relate to the common person. He had grand plans for solving many of the greatest problems facing America, the threat of terrorism, the plight of millions who work hard and can't make ends meet, the lack of an effective system of paying for health care, crumbling moral foundations—the list goes on. He was presented with a golden opportunity

for leading the nation in a search for real solutions to these problems. America was at peace and the dominant world power both
militarily and diplomatically. Our economy was roaring and our
supremacy was unquestioned. Yet Bill Clinton accomplished strikingly little in his presidency.

In my view, Bill Clinton will go down in history as a failed president because he had the intelligence and opportunity required for
greatness but suffered from fundamental character flaws. By the end
of his eight years in the White House, the American people understood this fact. They had expected so much from him and he had
failed to deliver on so many fronts, a failure made worse by the fact
that his promises had been so grandiose. There is no core to Bill
Clinton, no principle he will not sell out, no lie he will not tell, no
rule he will not break if he believes doing so will best serve his
immediate interests.

The one thing Bill Clinton did—and I presume still does—
believe is that government can be used to solve most of the
problems facing Americans. In this sense, he has an almost childlike
naïve belief in the effectiveness of power to change behavior. The
problem is that in his drive to obtain power, he sold out so many
principles that when he finally achieved it, he could think of
nothing to do with it. He was a man who sold out so many times
that he completely lost sight of whatever moral compass nature
might have blessed him with (if he ever even had one).

Young Bill described this path himself in a conscience-stricken
letter to an ROTC official he had deceived in order to avoid the draft
long enough to get into law school. In that letter, he wrote that he
"decided to accept the draft in spite of my beliefs for one reason: to
maintain my political viability within the system." At an early point
in his life, Bill Clinton was faced with a war he deeply believed was
wrong. He admired the courage of his friends who at least had the
guts to refuse to fight and accept the consequences for doing so. Yet,
because he wanted a career in politics so badly, he was willing to
take what he knew to be an immoral course of action in order to
achieve the power he craved. The only difference between this

young Bill Clinton in college and the one we elected to the presidency is that by the time he reached middle age, Clinton had suppressed his conscience so frequently that it was largely silent, if not dead. A complete and total lack of moral conviction and character enabled Bill Clinton to be one of the best politicians America has ever seen and one of the most craven, corrupt, and ineffectual figures ever to occupy the Oval Office.

Principled liberals and conservatives alike—at least those still paying attention—may understand exactly how much damage Clinton did during his eight years in office. However, there's at least one group of people that thinks his formula was a roaring success. That group is the latest pack of win-at-all-costs office seekers running on the Democrat side of the aisle. As the *New York Times* recently reported, Clinton, "the youngest ex-president in modern times, is still the go-to guy in Democratic politics."[3] Every serious Democratic contender for the presidential nomination in 2004 sought out his advice on both tactics and policy, looking for guidance on how to win the nomination. Among candidates, the perception is that the Clinton formula worked. The basic perception is that Clinton was good on policy and politics and bad at keeping his pants zipped. This is not true, but unless the historical record is corrected again and again, we will likely relive the Clinton presidency again and again, until an even more spectacular failure occurs.

The challenge we face is further complicated by the degree to which the individuals who will write much of the history of the Clinton administration are completely devoid of objectivity on the question. Remember that pompous history professor you swore would never impact your life again after your first year in college? Well, he is back, along with a bunch of his pals. These individuals are the self-styled "intellectual giants" who occupy posh distinguished chairs in academic ivory towers around the country. One of the most well-known such historians is Arthur Schlesinger Jr., whose remark that Ken Starr was "America's No. 1 pornographer" caused the *Washington Post*'s David Broder to dub him "James

Carville in cap and gown." During impeachment, a bunch of these intellectual giants got together to write up a statement telling Congress we were wrong to pursue impeachment. All told, more than four hundred of America's most prominent historians signed their names to what Broder—considered the most respected dean of Washington journalists—called "a tenured trashing of Congress for meeting its responsibility" that "says more about the state of the history profession than about the law of the land."[4]

I would be impressed if anyone who signed that statement also agreed not to pretend to do serious, unbiased historical work on the Clinton presidency. Clearly, that is not going to happen. These four hundred historians—and many of their compatriots—are dedicated to using their platforms as distinguished scholars for partisan political purposes. Looking at a sample of the faculty who signed the document reveals that many of them have as much professional expertise on the presidency as, say, a teenage clerk at a local fast food restaurant. The specialties of these folks include every obscure historical topic under the sun, ranging from radical religious movements to the history of cinema. Yet they felt obligated to pretend to be experts qualified to tell Congress how to handle one of the most important constitutional questions to arise in the history of republic. The ringleader of the bunch—Schlesinger—was even rewarded for his loyalty, in classic Clinton fashion, with a coveted Humanities Medal for "lifetime achievement." This is not a group of people the American people can trust to accurately portray what occurred in Bill Clinton's presidency. However, if we do not seek out and repeat the truth about the Clinton administration, these are the people who will take over the field in our absence.

When Bill Clinton left office, he left in his wake a trail of moral relativism, diminished respect for the law, economic mismanagement, lost freedoms, damaged institutions, ruined lives, and weakened national security. On every indicator that matters, Bill Clinton left America worse off after he was elected than we were when he took office. One of the most important legacies we can leave to our children and grandchildren is an accurate portrayal of what Bill Clinton really meant to America. As I learned in a college philosophy class, "truth is that which is the case." It *does* matter what "is" is. But the truth matters more.

Notes

Preface to 9/11: Clinton and National Security

[1] Louis Freeh, memo to the attorney general, 24 November 1997.

[2] Don Fowler, memo to Janet Reno, 31 December 1995.

[3] Louis Freeh, memo to the attorney general, 24 November 1997.

[4] Charles Labella, *Interim Report*, http://www.worldnetdaily.com/news/article.asp?ARTICLE_ID=17528.

[5] Bob Woodward, "FBI Had Overlooked Key Files in Probe of Chinese Influence," *Washington Post*, 14 November 1997.

[6] U.S. House of Representatives, report 105-851.

[7] Personal interview, April 2004.

[8] Bill Gertz, *Betrayal: How the Clinton Administration Undermined American Security* (Washington, D.C.: Regnery, 1999), 33-34.

[9] U.S. House of Representatives, report 105-851.

[10] Michael Hedges, "Criminals Get Citizenship in Rush to Sign Up Voters," *The Plain Dealer*, 5 September 1996.

[11] William Branigin, "INS Accused of Giving in to Politics; White House Pressure Tied to Citizen Push," *Washington Post*, 4 March 1997.

[12] David Schippers, *Sellout: The Inside Story of President Clinton's Impeachment* (Washington, D.C.: Regnery, 2000), 37.

[13] *Meet the Press*, NBC, 23 August 1998.

[14] *Associated Press*, 13 May 2004.

Pimping Out the Presidency: Clinton and the White House

[1] Gary Aldrich, *Unlimited Access* (Washington, D.C.: Regnery, 1998).

[2] These laws are changing rapidly due to so-called "campaign finance reform." However, the legal regime I describe is the one that applied during the 1996 presidential election.

[3] Dick Morris, *Behind the Oval Office* (New York: Random House, 1996).

[4] Information on this and other Judicial Watch lawsuits is available online at <www.judicialwatch.org>.

[5] George Stephanopoulos, *All Too Human (A Political Education)* (Boston: Little, Brown, 1999), 248.

[6] Gary Aldrich, *Unlimited Access* (Washington, D.C.: Regnery, 1998).

[7] Joseph Curl, "Air Force One items put on sale over Web; Appear on EBay after reported thefts," *Washington Times,* 27 January 2001.

[8] Barbara Olson, *The Final Days: The Last Desperate Abuses of Power by the Clinton White House* (Washington, D.C.: Regnery, 2001), ch.6.

[9] "Pardongate: Play-by-Play," *Time Magazine Online,* <http://www.time.com/time/nation/article/0,8599,100795,00.html.>

[10] Remarks by Sen. Zell Miller, 11 February 2004.

Ripping Away at Our Rights: Clinton and the Constitution

[1] James Bovard, *Feeling Your Pain: The Explosion and Abuse of Government Power in the Clinton-Gore Years* (New York: St. Martin's, 2000).

[2] Interview with Bill Clinton, *Rolling Stone,* November 1993.

[3] John Heilemann, "Big Brother Hill," *Wired Magazine,* October 1996.

[4] James Benet, "True to Form, Clinton Shifts Energies Back to U.S. Forces," *The New York Times,* 5 July 1998.

[5] David Cay Johnston, "Clinton Proposes Hiking IRS Budget to Find Tax Cheats," *New York Times,* 27 February 2000.

[6] David Stout, "From a Modest Start to a Threat to the Presidency," *The New York Times,* 15 November 1998.

[7] Stuart Taylor, Jr., "Her Case Against Clinton," *The American Lawyer,* November 1996.

[8] Bill Press, "Mr. President: Come Clean," *The Atlanta Journal-Constitution,* 18 March 1998 (originally published in *The L.A. Times*).

[9] Lois Romano and Peter Baker, "'Jane Doe No. 5' Goes Public with Allegation; Clinton Controversy Lingers Over Nursing Home Owner's Disputed 1978 Story," *The Washington Post,* 20 March 1999.

[10] Libertarian Party News Release, August 1998.

Investigating Clinton: What Went Wrong?

[1] Louis Freeh, memo to the attorney general, 24 November 1997.

[2] Joseph Story, *Commentaries on the Constitution of the United States*, 3 vols. (Boston, 1833).

[3] "Constitutional Grounds for Presidential Impeachment," report by the staff of the impeachment inquiry, Committee on the Judiciary, House of Representatives, Ninety-third Congress, second session.

On the Road to Impeachment

[1] "Barr Impeaches His Own Reputation," *Atlanta Journal-Constitution*, 19 March 1997.

[2] "Rightist Illusions in Print: One Man's Imaginative Clinton Impeachment," *Cleveland Plain Dealer*, 9 December 1997.

[3] Mazlan Nordin, "The Tummler Among American Politics," *New Straits Times-Press* (Malaysia), 21 November 1997.

[4] Laura Ingraham, "Impeachment Chic: Invoking the I-word Only Hurts Republicans," *Washington Post*, 26 October 1997.

[5] *Larry King Live*, CNN, 10 June 2003.

[6] Later, in June 1998, Helprin penned another magnificent essay that helped galvanize public opinion in support of removing Clinton from office—"Statesmanship and Its Betrayal" (Imprimis, 1998).

[7] "The Reliable Source," *Washington Post*, 14 January 1999.

[8] Jerome Zeifman, "'Cancer on Presidency' Cited in Vote Switch to GOP," *Knoxville News-Sentinel*, 29 October 1996.

[9] Mark Sherman, "Gingrich Talks Tough on Scandal; Funding Tied to Cooperation," *Atlanta Journal-Constitution*, 30 April 1998.

[10] Richard L. Berke, "Political Memo; In Iowa, G.O.P. Hopefuls Laud Family," *The New York Times*, 14 June 1998.

[11] Jill Lawrence, "In Iowa, Republicans Come Out of the 'Values' Closet, Hopefuls Get Chance to Slam Clinton While Playing Up to Christian Right," *USA Today*, 15 June 1998.

[12] Richard Fenno, *Homestyle: House Members in their Districts* (New York: Harper Collins, 1978), 18.

Success in the House

[1] Dan Balz, "Ready, or Not? New Gingrich and the Republican Party See the Prospect of a Historical Shift in Power. But They're Still Struggling to Make the Whole Exceed the Sum of Its Parts," *The Washington Post*, 25 October 1998.

[2] Mark Sherman, "Gingrich Power Play Riles Linder; Blame Game Puts Georgia Allies at Odds," *The Atlanta Journal-Constitution*, 6 November, 1998.

[3] For some reason, our leaders did not like to call impeachment by name.

[4] *Salon.com*, <http://archive.salon.com/news/1998/08/05news.html.>

[5] George Stephanopolous, *This Week*, ABC News, 8 February 1998.

[6] Paul Bedard, "White House Uses the Media to Sully Its Foes," *The Washington Times*, 30 March 1998.

[7] Reported by *Salon.com*, <http://www.salon.com/news/1998/09/cov_16newsb.html.>

[8] Mark Sherman and Rebecca Carr, "McKinney, Lewis Stand Out on Vote; Georgians Were Among Five Democrats Voting Against Any Impeachment Inquiry at All," *The Atlanta Journal-Constitution*, 11 October 1998.

[9] Tim Fleck, "Flying Miss Sheila," *The Houston Press*, 14 May 1998.

Failure in the Senate

[1] Former Senator Dale Bumpers, "Remarks to U.S. Senate," 21 January 1999.

[2] Roger Franklin, "Lott Debacle Sidesteps Ugly Face of US Racism," *The New Zealand Herald*, 23 December 2002.

Liberalism, Conservatism, and Clintonism

[1] George Stephanopolous, *All Too Human (A Political Education)* (Boston: Little, Brown, 1999).

Righting History: The Clinton Legacy

[1] *60 Minutes II*, 31 March 1999.

[2] Rich Lowry, "Naked Ambition: The Clinton Legacy Laid Bare," *National Review*, 27 October 2003.

[3] Katherine Q. Seelye, "Clinton Enjoys Role as Adviser in Chief," *The New York Times*, 4 January 2004.

[4] David S. Broder, "The Historians' Complaint," *The Washington Post*, 1 November 1998.

Index